A Constructive Critique of Religion

Also available from Bloomsbury

Postsecular Feminisms, edited by Nandini Deo
Religious Pluralism and the City, edited by Helmuth Berking, Silke Steets and Jochen Schwenk
Secular Assemblages, Marek Sullivan

A Constructive Critique of Religion

Encounters between Christianity, Islam, and Non-religion in Secular Societies

Edited by
Mia Lövheim and Mikael Stenmark

BLOOMSBURY ACADEMIC
LONDON • NEW YORK • OXFORD • NEW DELHI • SYDNEY

BLOOMSBURY ACADEMIC
Bloomsbury Publishing Plc
50 Bedford Square, London, WC1B 3DP, UK
1385 Broadway, New York, NY 10018, USA
29 Earlsfort Terrace, Dublin 2, Ireland

BLOOMSBURY, BLOOMSBURY ACADEMIC and the Diana logo
are trademarks of Bloomsbury Publishing Plc

First published in Great Britain 2020
Paperback edition first published 2021

Copyright © Mia Lövheim, Mikael Stenmark and Contributors, 2020

Mia Lövheim and Mikael Stenmark have asserted their right under the Copyright, Designs and Patents Act, 1988, to be identified as Editors of this work.

For legal purposes the Acknowledgements on p. viii constitute an extension of this copyright page.

All rights reserved. No part of this publication may be reproduced or transmitted in any form or by any means, electronic or mechanical, including photocopying, recording, or any information storage or retrieval system, without prior permission in writing from the publishers.

Bloomsbury Publishing Plc does not have any control over, or responsibility for, any third-party websites referred to or in this book. All internet addresses given in this book were correct at the time of going to press. The author and publisher regret any inconvenience caused if addresses have changed or sites have ceased to exist, but can accept no responsibility for any such changes.

A catalogue record for this book is available from the British Library.

A catalog record for this book is available from the Library of Congress.

ISBN: HB: 978-1-3501-1309-1
PB: 978-1-3502-7784-7
ePDF: 978-1-3501-1310-7
eBook: 978-1-3501-1311-4

Typeset by Deanta Global Publishing Services, Chennai, India

To find out more about our authors and books visit www.bloomsbury.com and sign up for our newsletters.

Contents

List of Contributors — vii
Acknowledgments — viii

Introduction: Constructive Criticism in Secular and Religiously Diverse Society *Mia Lövheim and Mikael Stenmark* — 1

Part One Philosophical and Theological Perspectives

1 Criticizing Religion in a Secular Democratic Society *Mikael Stenmark* — 17
2 Secular Criticism of Religion *Stephen LeDrew* — 32
3 Academic Feminism as Immanent Critique: Three Feminist Theological Critiques of Patriarchy *Ulf Zackariasson* — 44
4 Internal Critique in Muslim Context *Mohammad Fazlhashemi* — 58
5 Criticism and Christianity *Charles Taliaferro* — 73

Part Two Law, Politics, and Education

6 Courts as Critics: Nuancing the Insider/Outsider Binary *Effie Fokas* — 87
7 Framing Religious Criticism in a Secular Cultural and Legal Order: Subsidies to Muslim Youth Organizations *Pia Karlsson Minganti* — 99
8 Critique of Religion in Public Commissions on Cultural and Religious Diversity *Lori G. Beaman and Solange Lefebvre* — 112
9 The Crocodile and the Gardener: Swedish Radical Nationalism and Critique of Religion *Per-Erik Nilsson* — 124
10 Tolerance and Criticism within Religious Education *Malin Löfstedt and Anders Sjöborg* — 135

Part Three Civil Society, Media, and Family

11 Illusive Religion in the Public Sphere: The Debate on Confessional Independent Schools in Sweden *Johan von Essen* — 151
    Appendix: Debate articles in 2017 on confessional independent schools — 163

12 Criticizing Religion in Mediatized Debates *Linnea Jensdotter and Mia Lövheim* 164

13 Parenting Choices, Religious Faith, and Critical Engagement *Martha Middlemiss Lé Mon and Ninna Edgardh* 177

14 Postscript: Toward Constructive Criticism of Religion *Mia Lövheim and Mikael Stenmark* 190

Notes 199
Bibliography 205
Index 230

Contributors

Lori G. Beaman is Research Chair in Religious Diversity and Social Change, Department of Classics and Religious Studies, University of Ottawa, Canada.

Ninna Edgardh is Professor in Ecclesiology, Uppsala University, Sweden.

Mohammad Fazlhashemi is Professor in Islamic Theology and Philosophy, Uppsala University, Sweden.

Effie Fokas is Senior Research Fellow at the Hellenic Foundation for European and Foreign Policy (ELIAMEP), Greece and Research Associate of the London School of Economics Hellenic Observatory. She is also a participant in the Henry Luce/Leadership 100 project on Orthodoxy and Human Rights (Orthodox Christian Studies Center, Fordham University).

Linnea Jensdotter is a PhD student in Sociology of Religion, Uppsala University, Sweden.

Stephen LeDrew is Assistant Professor in Sociology at the Department of Sociology, Memorial University of Newfoundland, Canada.

Solange Lefebvre is Chair for the Management of Cultural and Religious Diversity, Université de Montreal, Canada.

Malin Löfstedt is Associate Professor in Didactics of Religion, Uppsala University, Sweden.

Mia Lövheim is Professor in Sociology of Religion, Uppsala University, Sweden.

Martha Middlemiss Lé Mon is Director of the Uppsala Religion and Society Research Center and PhD in Sociology of Religion, Uppsala University, Sweden.

Pia Karlsson Minganti is Associate Professor in Ethnology, Stockholm University, Sweden.

Per-Erik Nilsson is Director of the Centre for Multidisciplinary Studies on Racism (CEMFOR) and Associate Professor in Sociology of Religion, Uppsala University, Sweden.

Anders Sjöborg is Associate Professor in Sociology of Religion, Uppsala University, Sweden.

Mikael Stenmark is Professor in Philosophy of Religion, Uppsala University, Sweden.

Charles Taliaferro is Professor in Philosophy at St. Olaf College, Minnesota, USA.

Johan von Essen is Professor in Worldview and Civil Society Studies, Ersta Sköndal Bräcke University College, Stockholm, Sweden.

Ulf Zackariasson is Associate Professor in Philosophy of Religion, Uppsala University, Sweden.

Acknowledgments

The present volume emanates from a series of workshops and roundtable discussions on religion and criticism made possible by the interdisciplinary center of excellence and research program *The Impact of Religion: Challenges for Society, Law and Democracy*, established at Uppsala University for the period 2009–2019 and hosted by the Uppsala Religion and Society Research Centre (CRS). Scholars with different disciplinary backgrounds and areas of expertise were invited to explore this topic with a future publication in mind. International scholars working with similar issues were brought in to further enhance the scope and quality of the discussion. The *Impact of Religion* program, furthermore, provided financial support for the planning and editing of the volume through funding from The Swedish Research Council. For more information about the program, visit www.crs.uu.se.

The editors want to thank the authors for fruitful discussions and for their contributions. We are also grateful to Lalle Pursglove and Camilla Erskine at Bloomsbury for their support in making this volume possible.

Introduction: Constructive Criticism in Secular and Religiously Diverse Society

Mia Lövheim and Mikael Stenmark

During the past decades, debates about the public presence of religion in secular, democratic societies have grown ever more pronounced in the spheres of politics, law, and media throughout Europe and North America. At the heart of these debates is the question of how societies characterized by secular principles concerning the division of power between religion and state, often set against the background of a dominant Christian heritage, should accommodate differences in lifestyles and motivations based on a broader range of religious worldviews, most notably Islam (Weller 2016). For secular-liberal societies that embrace freedom of religion and rational political deliberation based in freedom of expression as core principles, these debates raise fundamental and difficult questions pertaining to the rights of citizens, political representation, the sovereignty of the state, and relations between minority and majority groups in a given population.

Political debates and media reports throughout Europe and North America tend to focus on alarmist issues such as religious violence, terrorism, or clashes of values within for example workplaces, family law, and education (Furseth 2018; Hjelm 2015). In addition, these debates are often characterized by polarized arguments concerning a diversity of religious versus secular worldviews as a problem for the functioning of a democratic society. The critique of religion embedded in the latter debates runs parallel and is often connected to a tradition of critique of religion which originates from European Enlightenment philosophy and focuses on the irrationality of religious belief and on the dangers of religion as illusion and/or oppressive ideology (see Beaman and Lefebvre, this volume; Drees 2010; Asad et al. 2013).

A growing number of international publications have addressed this situation, focusing on varieties of state and political governance of religious diversity (see, for example, Dawson 2016; Giordan and Pace 2011; Lefebre and Brodeur 2017), contestations of religion in the media (Lundby 2018; Abdel-Fadil and Årsheim 2019), the relation between religion and secularism in political discourse (Habermas 2006; Butler et al. 2011; Calhoun, Juergensmeyer and VanAntwerpen 2011; La Borde 2017), or the critique of religion in theological and philosophical debate (Larson and Ruse 2017; Fergusson 2009; Khalil 2018; Grey 2018). This book departs from this wealth of previous research and introduces a different focus through the concept of *constructive criticism of religion*.

Much of the critique of religion expressed in current as well as long-standing debates has tended to increase hostility and conflict between people of religious and secular worldviews rather than encourage mutual revision of belief, values, and patterns of behavior. In this context, therefore, there is an urgent need to engage in discussions of how the current situation can be developed toward constructive interaction and critique across diverse religious and secular commitments. In order for such a constructive and critical interaction to take place, two related investigations seem necessary. The first concerns a thorough analysis of critique expressed in actually occurring debates around religion in particular institutional settings, with the purpose of revealing when and how more constructive forms of criticism become expressed. The second process concerns exploring what a constructive criticism that is able to overcome the problems of increased polarization and standstill might look like.

The aim of the book is, thus, to analyze when and how constructive and successful forms of criticism emerge in debates and dialogue between people who embrace different faith or worldview commitments living in secular democratic societies. But it is also to study how particular social or institutional contexts such as media, jurisprudence, legislatures, education, and civil society enable and constrain such forms of critique and their content. In other words, the book provides an analysis of what role critique of religion could or should play in public life and discusses how various social institutions enable and constrain the shape and content of that critique within the broader framework of a secular democratic society.

This twofold objective—to disentangle differences between various forms of critique of religion and to analyze how these are shaped by institutional contexts—implies that we bring together philosophical and theological analyses of arguments in critique of religion with more sociologically oriented analyses of how particular social institutions shape communication and interaction between individuals and groups with different backgrounds, resources, and motivations. Furthermore, our focus on revealing and exploring more constructive forms of criticism is directed to religious worldviews as well as secular worldviews, although our emphasis is on the former. A key argument running through the book is that in order to develop constructive forms of critique, a more thorough and systematic investigation of resources for criticism located within religious worldviews themselves is needed. Such an approach enables, we believe, an innovative way of addressing the question of why some strategies for critique of religion seem to be more beneficial for constructive engagement, whereas others rather increase intolerance, polarization, and conflict.

This book approaches criticism of religion from a broad range of worldviews and outlooks (atheist, Christian, Muslim, right-wing, and liberal political) and from different academic perspectives (history of ideas, philosophy, theology, sociology, media studies, law, education). Such an interdisciplinary approach is necessary, we argue, because our aim is to understand the interplay between (1) different forms of criticism of religion and their grounds of justification, (2) how criticism is received and conceptualized within particular religious frameworks, and (3) how particular contexts of social interaction shape the content and form of this criticism, all in order to assess to what extent criticism can be constructive and successful in revising beliefs, values, or behavior that hinder enhanced understanding and transformative learning.

The model we propose for this task, which is further discussed in Chapter 1, focuses on the following interrelated aspects:

a) The actors offering the critique: Are the critics—as individuals, groups, or institutions—situated inside or outside of the religion whose beliefs, values, or practices are the target of criticism?
b) The critics and the form of critique: What kinds of reasons or arguments are used by the critics and is the goal of the critical engagement positive or negative? Is it reformistic, revolutionary, or debunking?
c) The actors receiving the critique and their religious context: How is the criticism conceptualized and responded to by the target group, and what kinds of reason-giving or arguments have epistemic and moral authority within that framework?
d) The institutional context in which the critique is expressed: What are the implicit and explicit values and rules that enable, limit, and structure patterns of speech and social interaction?
e) The interplay between the critics and the receivers of the critique in terms of relations of power: Who is permitted to offer criticism and respond to it? What position is silenced or ignored? How do dominant discourses and access to resources and influence, for example, between majorities and minorities in society, affect the possibilities of speech and action among the actors involved?
f) The impact in terms of the various outcomes of the critique: Is the criticism leading to increased hostility, polarization, and radicalization or to acknowledgment, self-criticism, enhanced understanding, and transformative learning?

This interdisciplinary ambition is not without difficulties. Researchers taking part in such discussions have to be prepared to cross over entrenched disciplinary boundaries. The experience of writing this book has made it clear that a spirit of mutual interest, generosity, and courage is necessary. Furthermore, a crucial precondition for the interdisciplinary work undertaken in this volume is to clarify and, if not agree on at least comprehend, central theoretical concepts and methodological premises used by other researchers.

Key Concepts: Critique, Religion, and Institution

A common starting point for our inquiry is the very basic idea that *critique is an expression of disapproval of something or someone*. Thus, religion is criticized when someone expresses disapproval of a particular target, either one religion or many religions ("the something") or the participants themselves, the religious believers ("the someone"). It is most of the time more accurate, however, to say that the target of the critique is not really the individuals, but rather what they say, believe, value, or do, the institutions they have created, or the communities to which they belong and their separate and sometimes overlapping traditions.

Thus, by "critique of religion" we mean an assessment or evaluation that is directed by someone, for instance an individual, a group, or an institution, against religion as such (all religions), against a particular religion as a whole (say Christianity or Islam), or against a part of it (a specific tradition or community within that particular religion), in order to reject it, to question it, or to point out that something needs to be changed in it.

Moreover, *constructive* are such forms of critique which, rather than undermining or debunking a (religious) worldview, aim at modifying or reforming it in order to handle a particular problem, objection, or challenge that affects the parts involved in the situation. *Successful* critique is that which leads to changes in the direction the critics intended in some of the beliefs, values, or practices of the target group. However, if criticism is understood as a part of what Jürgen Habermas has termed "complementary learning processes" (Habermas 2006), the expected outcome could be that the critics' perspective is transformed so that they in their critical engagement gain a deeper understanding of the target group's worldview and realize that the criticism was (more or less) misguided, unjustified, or insufficient. It might even de-center their own perspective and call into question their own worldview and self-understanding. In a broader sense, we could then say that critique is constructive and successful if it promotes self-criticism, humility, enhanced understanding, and transformative learning, rather than increasing arrogance, polarization, and radicalization. As will be discussed further in Chapter 1, forms of *immanent criticism* might provide a successful means to unlock polarized understandings of other worldviews (Stout 2004), especially in cases where the target is, for example, a form of religion that diverts substantially from the dominant discourse within particular sectors of secular societies. Immanent criticism might, moreover, be an effective way of showing respect for fellow citizens who hold differing points of view. Arguably, real respect for others takes seriously the distinctive point of view which the other person holds.

Following from this approach to critique, we consider the meaning of religion as *constituted and contested rather than given*. As several of the chapters in the present volume demonstrate, different and competing understandings of what religion is or should be lie at the heart of the critical arguments we analyze. Religions as forms of belief and knowledge construction are situated in and shaped by processes of social interaction and by social structures in the form of norms, rules, and institutions (Berger and Luckmann 1966; Hjelm 2014a: 4). In a situation of heightened diversity and contestation, the meaning of religion is constituted in the interaction between various actors with different and sometimes opposing interests (Lövheim and Lied 2018). The meaning of religion is thus subject to change through social interaction in a particular situation. However, the possibilities of ascribing meaning to religious symbols, beliefs, and practices is also conditioned by established traditions and institutional structures in, for example, a national context, where these traditions and structures function as "authoritative guides" in contestations of religion (Beckford 2003). By "institutional structures," we refer to assumptions, values, beliefs, and formal and informal norms that over time develop within a particular domain of social life. These patterns provide meaning to social existence, organize social interaction, and shape the functions and the allocation of resources for action that are available within this domain (Engelstad et al. 2017).

This also applies to various forms of criticism of religion. Different social institutions provide different conditions for the realization of constructive criticism that enhances reorientation, understanding, or transformative learning. The cognitive, social, and material resources made available by particular institutions enable as well as limit and structure what forms of communication, action, and subjectivity, and what patterns of social interaction, become more dominant than others over time (see Hjarvard 2014: 131).

What Is at Stake? Debating Religion in Secular Society

It is often argued that the attack on the Twin Towers in New York on September 11, 2001 became the starting point of a new discourse on the "return of religion" as a public and political issue in secular, Western societies. As pointed out above, contemporary critique of religion has formed a central part of this discourse. Meanwhile, within academia, a growing body of research has developed during the past two decades targeting various dimensions of the discourse on the "return of religion." As argued by Grace Davie (2015), this situation is both beneficial and problematic with regard to the production of knowledge about the place of religion in a late modern, secular, and diverse society. In this introduction, we will limit ourselves to a number of themes that are particularly significant in setting the scene for the chapters in this book.

The conceptualization of religion as a problem is often set against certain values that implicitly or explicitly become constructed as essential for modern, democratic societies. Critique of religion often represents a core element of this problem-centered approach, and previous research in, for example, political science, sociology, law, critical religion, and media studies has thoroughly mapped out several of the main tenets of such discourses. One of the central arguments of the present volume is, however, that a critical discussion of *varieties within this critique* has often been missing—variety in terms of both its aims and its impacts, potential or real.

Religious Pluralism—Religious Diversity

The idea that contemporary society is characterized by a larger plurality or diversity of religious beliefs as well as of secular worldviews has often been presented as a given in previous research. Religious and cultural diversity is seen as an epitome of modern, in contrast to premodern, societies. Religious diversity is, furthermore, often depicted as a challenge for the functioning of democratic societies in representing an explicit or implicit cause of tensions between individuals and groups with different interests and motivations (see, for example, European Commission calls for research funding). As such, this challenge needs to be addressed through regulations, negotiations, accommodation, and dialogue. Religious diversity is therefore a descriptive as well as normative concept. A clear distinction between different dimensions of the concept is necessary for understanding the empirical characteristics of the situation as well as for a more nuanced discussion about various forms of critique of religion and how these take shape in contemporary society.

Sociologist James A. Beckford argues (2011) that the term "religious pluralism" can be applied in four different ways, which are often conflated in the debate: (a) a plurality of expressions of religion in society; (b) normative or ideological views about the positive values of this plurality; (c) frameworks of public policy, law, and social practices that accommodate, regulate, and facilitate religious plurality; and (d) relational contexts of everyday interactions between individuals and groups identified as religious. The first aspect of empirically discernible changes and varieties between and within religious groups will to some extent be addressed in the first section of the book, within the chapters presenting varieties of critique of religion within Christianity, Islam, and atheism. The chapters in the following section will address aspects of religious diversity that concern normative and ideological views about religious diversity, as expressed as critique of certain forms of religion, and critical opinions about religious diversity within the various social institutions that are the focus of case studies. Some chapters will also discuss criticism of religion within the context of handling everyday experiences of life in a religiously diverse society, for example, in school, in civil society, and through parenting.

Secularity and Post-Secularity

The aim and scope of this book are also set against the background of critical debates concerning the concept of secularity and the secular society. These debates concern the meaning of the secular, as well as a critical discussion about its limitations for understanding a religiously diverse society as a social and political reality (Lind, Lövheim and Zackariasson 2016; Calhoun, Juergensmeyer and VanAntwerpen 2011; Mendieta and VanAntwerpen 2011). Scholars such as José Casanova (2011) and Talal Asad (2003) have argued for the need to clarify the historical and colonial roots of the concept "secular," and to distinguish between various modes of secularism. This book takes as its starting point the attempts to formulate a distinction between the social and historical process of secularization, the secular as a condition, and secularism as a political ideology that was introduced through these debates (see Calhoun, Juergensmeyer and VanAntwerpen 2011). It also engages with Asad's argument that "religious" and "secular" are mutually constituted rather than dichotomous concepts.

Jürgen Habermas' seminal article "Religion in the Public Sphere" (2006) entails another significant starting point for the discussion of constructive criticism in this book. Habermas' argument rests on the idea that a "post-secular society," a notion with which we engage critically below, needs to find a way to accommodate the continuing global vitality of religion and to include religious perspectives as a key resource in the forming of democratic societies. From this perspective, neither what he terms "militant secularism" nor "radical multiculturalism" as a contemporary political discourse is a plausible option (Habermas 2008). In Habermas's understanding, both of these discourses lack the potential to find a balance between shared citizenship and cultural difference. The "militant secularism" discourse approaches religion with a polemic stance that is no longer valid in a post-secular situation, while the "radical multiculturalism" approach suffers from a relativism that disregards any universalistic claims and thereby loses a valuable basis of critique of discrimination against minorities.

Jürgen Habermas' arguments inaugurated a discussion within sociological studies of religion concerning the relation between the "awareness that one is living in a post-secular society" (Habermas 2006: 4) and the social fact of a "return" or new visibility of religion. This debate has its roots further back in the discussions about de-privatization and public religion, initiated by José Casanova with the publication of *Public Religions in the Modern World* in 1994. The lack of empirical studies about the increased visibility of religion and post-secular awareness in Western societies caused a debate about whether this phenomenon was primarily empirical or discursive—meaning a shift in scholarly discourse on religion (Davie 2015: 28–29). Hjelm (2015: 8) points to the risks of confusing visibility and debate over religion—as portrayed in, for example, the media—with an increasing importance of religion among individuals or of religious organizations in society. While some research has argued for new possibilities of religious organizations acting in society as, for example, welfare providers (Bäckström et al. 2011), later studies point out that the arguments and practices of religious minority organizations in particular have often fallen outside of the scope of state policies, thereby inadvertently contributing more to exclusion than an engagement with, and understanding of, their needs and rights (Ferrari and Pastorelli 2012; Shah, Foblets and Rohe 2014).

From this point of view, the present situation can be read as a "return of secularism" (cf. Hjelm 2014b; Beckford 2012). This trend, which arguably has become stronger in the last decade, is expressed in a more polarized and harsh critique of religion. In Europe, critique of religion, in particular Islam, has increased radically as a theme in political discussions and the media following the arrival of large number of refugees from civil wars in Syria, Iraq, etc., in 2015 and changes in the political landscape (Brubaker 2017). In particular, this trend means that certain issues come to dominate the debate, such as religious clothing, the rights of women and LGBTQ people, or religiously motivated violence. The way religion becomes visible in contemporary secular society is thus conditioned to certain forms and expressions of religion. Religion becomes handled in a way that focuses on its presumed value or problem for secular society, not on the particular beliefs of a given religion and how these might contribute to the common good of society (Hjelm 2014b, 2015).

Philosophical Approaches to Critique of Religion

Within the field of philosophy, the shortcomings of strong secularist arguments of the kind exemplified by, for instance, Richard Dawkins' *The God Delusion* (2006) and Christopher Hitchens' *God Is Not Great* (2006) have been discussed. Philosophers that in general accept the worldview commitments which underline the kind of atheism which Dawkins and Hitchens embrace have nevertheless responded by suggesting that what needs to be developed is a more "humane" or "enlightened" form of atheism than the "militant" or "aggressive" atheism of which these so-called New Atheists are spokespersons. In criticizing religion, one should instead, as Philip Kitcher argues, recognize and affirm the positive moral and existential roles that religious conviction plays, in terms of how beliefs may "play a critical role in making [believers'] lives bearable" and provide answers to the question of "why their lives matter" (2008: 14; 2014). It is the metaphysics and epistemologies of religion that should be criticized, dropped, and replaced with naturalism and the deliverances of science (see also Levine 2011; Pigliucci 2013). But religious people are hardly likely to be persuaded to abandon their beliefs unless the enlightened secularist or atheist can offer viable alternatives to them. Others secular philosophers like Thomas Nagel find the metaphysics quite plausible and agree with Dawkins, Hitchens, and the like that blind faith and the authority of dogma are dangerous to a democratic society, but emphasis that "the [religious] view that we can make ultimate sense of the world only by understanding it as the expression of mind or purpose is not. It is unreasonable to think that one must refute the second in order to resist the first" (2010: 26). The strong secularist arguments have also been criticized by philosophers and intellectuals more inclined to accept theism or a religious outlook on life, for being question-begging and ill-informed about what religion is all about, or for increasing hostility and even religious radicalization (Ganssle 2009; Plantinga 2011; Khalil 2018).

Alternative argumentation strategies, to replace strong or aggressive secularism, have also been proposed by for example Butler et al. (2011) and Nussbaum (2012). Lastly, one important forerunner to this book, *Is Critique Secular?* (Asad et al. 2013), is worth mentioning. This book focuses on the "Danish cartoon controversy" in 2006 and raises the question whether critique belongs exclusively to forms of liberal democracy that define themselves in opposition to religion.

Constructive Criticism, Accommodation, and Dialogue

Finally, something should be said about the relation between the concept of constructive criticism and arguments in previous research concerning accommodation and dialogue as a way of handling divergent, conflicting opinions about religion in contemporary society.

The focus of this volume differs in at least two ways from the aim of the studies of religious dialogue that can be found in theology and interreligious studies (Cornille 2013). Interreligious dialogue is an attempt to promote interaction between religious traditions to achieve a better understanding of the beliefs and practices that are central to other traditions. It promotes a conversation between religious traditions so that people can appreciate commonalities and differences within them. The first difference between this approach and interreligious dialogue has to do with the individuals or groups that participate in the activity. In religious dialogue, religious people from different traditions engage with each other in order to understand the other traditions better. In criticism of religion, on the contrary, a significant partner is secular people or people who do not consider themselves to be religious but rather self-identify as atheists, secular humanists, skeptics, or agnostics. The second difference between the approaches concerns the goal of the activities. The aim of religious dialogue is to achieve better understanding of the other, whereas the aim of criticism of religion is rather to express one's concern that something is wrong or needs to be changed. Perhaps we could say that whereas interreligious dialogue is an attempt to promote interaction between religious traditions to achieve a better understanding of each other, constructive criticism of religion is an attempt to promote forms of public debate in which people encounter and engage one another in critical but respectful and nonhostile ways. The task undertaken by the constructive criticism scholar is to explore the conditions for civil disagreement among individuals and groups with different and conflicting convictions about what constitutes a good life and about religion's role (or lack thereof) in that venture.

In this regard, the present volume resonates with Lori Beaman's argument against the pervasive and shared discourse of accommodation and tolerance that has come to resonate across countries such as Canada, the UK, Germany, and the Nordic countries. Beaman argues that this discourse effectively preserves, rather than revises, a hegemony of religious and cultural majorities (2017: 1). She therefore proposes a shift of focus in the discussion to equality, or more precisely "deep equality." This concept aims to capture a process in which religious difference is confronted, lived with, and negotiated in everyday life and which is characterized by agonistic respect and recognition of similarity rather than hostility and polarization. In order for this ideal to be realized, she argues, scholars as well as politicians on various levels have to lean into, rather than disregard, the way people of different worldviews interact in various settings of day-to-day life.

Outline and Contribution of the Book

This book starts out from the debates in previous research but aims to take these one step further by combining an analysis of various forms of criticism of religion in secular society and an exploration of how more productive ways of critically engaging with differences in worldview commitments can be cultivated. Through analyzing the interplay between arguments in criticism of religion and how contexts of social interaction shape the content and form of this criticism, the authors of the chapters address the question of when constructive criticism can reach intended goals, as well as why such efforts may fail. For this purpose, the book combines theoretical discussions and empirical case studies of different reasoning strategies used by Muslims, Christians, and secular-minded citizens in political debate, media, civil society, jurisdiction, education, family life, and the academic community.

The chapters in the volume are written by scholars with research experience from Sweden, Canada, the United States, France, and Greece. Thus, it addresses criticism of religion in countries with various historical and societal conditions with regard to the interaction between religious actors, the private life of citizens, and public institutions. Several chapters analyze cases from a Swedish context. Along with the other Scandinavian countries, Swedish society has a long history of a strong, secular state that provides public services to citizens such as extensive welfare benefits, free education, and public service media. Support for egalitarian values and practices and the level of trust between people has traditionally been high. International conflicts followed by increased migration during the latest decades, along with a political-economic crisis in Europe, have brought new challenges to this traditional model, and new political divisions are articulated (Lundby and Repstad 2018; Furseth 2018). Thus, Sweden is an interesting case for analyzing if and how constructive criticism of religion can be developed in a society characterized by a secular tradition and a new religious and cultural diversity.

The authors in this volume, furthermore, represent a range of different scholarly disciplines that take a more descriptive approach, such as history of ideas, sociology, media studies, and those with a more normative stance, such as philosophy, theology, law, and educational studies. Our aim is neither more nor less than to *suggest* ways in which an inquiry into various forms of critique of religion can be undertaken and the kinds of results it could generate. Nevertheless, we believe that an interdisciplinary attempt to identify issues, and points of agreement and of tension between various disciplines, represents a necessary and fruitful way of working toward more comprehensive answers to the questions raised in this introduction.

The volume is structured in three parts, where the first, "Philosophical and Theological Perspectives," focuses on philosophical and theological perspectives. In the opening chapter "Criticizing Religion in a Secular Democratic Society," Mikael Stenmark, who works in philosophy of religion, distinguishes between four overarching critical engagement strategies (the secularist, the restrictionist, the open, and the internal) one could use or merely assume when one criticizes religion. He argues, in line with the open strategy, that we need to investigate much more thoroughly what resources for criticism can be found within religious communities themselves and to what extent these could be used also by people *outside* these communities as a ground for criticism (so-called immanent criticism). His suggestion is that the most constructive and successful forms of criticism might be those that employ these internal reasons and particularly so when the target is a religion or a specific form that religion takes that diverts substantially from the religious or secular worldviews we have ourselves.

In the next chapter, "Secular Criticism of Religion," Stephen LeDrew, who works in sociology, explores two different strands of secular criticism of religion: scientific atheism (including New Atheism) and humanistic or anthropological atheism. The first group of secular people stresses scientific authority and religion as an enemy of science, whereas the other group opposes religion more for its perceived harmful social and political influence and works to promote social justice more so than science. LeDrew argues that the second form of secular criticism is more constructive, since it emphasizes positive social changes rather than aggressive attacks on the irrationality of religious belief. It offers a prescription for the good society that could accommodate many different kinds of belief, provided that they do not conflict with the basic humanistic values of freedom and equality.

In the subsequent chapter, "Academic Feminism as Immanent Critique: Three Feminist Theological Critiques of Patriarchy," Ulf Zackariasson, who works in philosophy of religion, analyzes immanent critique as a form of constructive criticism of religion via a study of the critiques of Islam, Judaism, and Christianity, respectively, offered by the feminist academics Asma Barlas, Rachel Adler, and Kwok Pui-Lan. He highlights that all of them stress the egalitarian element of tradition that they believe is an inherent feature of monotheism. This, in turn, gives them leverage to criticize past and current hierarchies and power structures as religious shortcomings. The stress on the egalitarian element helps each theologian, in different ways, to launch an immanent critique of their own religious tradition. So Barlas, Kwok, and Adler all aim to use resources from within the tradition itself to bring about change. Zackariasson argues that such undertaking requires that the critics are perceived as trustworthy—as competent and reliable insiders. Thus, the price the immanent critics must pay is that not merely their arguments but also their competence, commitments, and motives might become part of the debate.

Mohammad Fazlhashemi, who works in Islamic theology and philosophy, stresses in "Internal Critique in Muslim Context" that religious traditions have always brought forward many critics within their own ranks, and that Islam is not an exception to this rule. Moreover, he points out that the immanent or internal critique has focused on different targets. It contains criticism of Muslim authorities, criticism aimed at Sharia laws and Islamic jurisprudence, and also anticlerical criticism. Another category of internal critique has concerned the interpretation of justice and its basic idea of considering Sharia law as eternal and unchangeable. He also stresses that the responses to the criticisms have been of different nature. One of the main reasons behind the differences has been the dissimilarities between different schools of law concerning the extent to which they allow the use of reason and critical thinking. The more of the latter, the greater the desire for a critical review of established thoughts and perceptions of the Muslim authorities.

The task that Charles Taliaferro, who works in philosophy, undertakes in the chapter "Criticism and Christianity" is to develop a philosophy of criticism from a broadly Christian point of view. He argues that such a model of criticism is based on at least six principles: (1) the primacy of loving the good, which would naturally and positively lead to a purification of one's motives behind the practice of criticism; (2) the importance of self-criticism prior to the criticism of others; (3) the golden rule: that is, only criticizing others the way one would wish to be criticized oneself (if the roles were reversed); (4) the avoidance of schism and persecution; (5) openness to criticism from non-Christian sources; and (6) the Good Samaritan virtue of intervening to protect a person who has been unfairly and cruelly criticized by others.

In the second part, "Law, Politics, and Education," Effie Fokas, who researches the intersections of religion, politics, and law, discusses how religious actors receive what may be considered as critique by courts. Her chapter "Courts as Critics: Nuancing the Insider/Outsider Binary" draws on research about the impact of European Court of Human Rights engagements with religion-related issues. The case in question, *Papageorgiou and Others v. Greece*, concerns implications of a reform of the Religious Education curriculum in Greece and was pending before the court in the spring of 2018. By exploring the dynamic of critique of religion issued by the European Court, the reception of such critique by representatives from the Greek Orthodox Church, and the role of third-party interventions, this chapter offers a further elaboration of the conceptions of insider versus outsider critique set out in the introduction to the volume.

Critique of religion in the context of increasing judicialization of religion is further addressed in the next chapter, "Framing Religious Criticism in a Swedish Secular Cultural and Legal Order: Subsidies to Muslim Youth Organizations." Pia Karlsson Minganti, who works in ethnology, discusses how external criticism of religion may (dis)enable constructive criticism and dialogue through an analysis of a legal process in the Swedish court system, where the Swedish Agency for Youth and Civil Society in 2016 decided to deny governmental funding to the national umbrella organization Sweden's Young Muslims. She argues that this case shows a change in the Swedish model for relations between state and civil society organizations, in which state support has been a way of acknowledging religious freedom as a cornerstone for democracy. This poses the question of whether and how courts can become sites for a constructive criticism of religion rather than enhancing antagonism and mistrust between the actors involved.

In the next chapter, "Critique of Religion in Public Commissions on Cultural and Religious Diversity," Lori G. Beaman and Solange Lefebvre, both of whom work in the area of religious diversity and social change, continue the exploration of the legal and political context through a discussion of critique as expressed by public commissions on cultural and religious diversity in Quebec (Canada), France, and Belgium. They examine how the public commission provides a structured format for critique of religion, but also how this critique is linked to the social and cultural contexts of these commissions. By identifying four drivers of critique that informed these contexts, they show how critique of religion from within and without are interconnected rather than strictly separated phenomena, and how this interplay shapes possibilities for the development of constructive criticism of religion.

Per-Erik Nilsson's chapter, "The Crocodile and the Gardener: Swedish Radical Nationalism and Critique of Religion," analyzes anti-Muslim statements in radio broadcasts produced by Swedish nationalist activists. Nilsson, who works from a critical religion perspective, focuses on how these statements are related to anti-Jewish sentiments and to conspiratorial racialization in the broader European radical nationalist milieu. While concluding that this type of critique cannot be classified as constructive, Nilsson argues that an analytical sensitivity to the contingency of categories of religion and race, as used in this discourse, is needed to understand the implications of critique of religion in European radical nationalism and populism.

In their chapter "Tolerance and Criticism within Religious Education," Malin Löfstedt and Anders Sjöborg, who work in the area of education and religion, investigate critique of religion in the context of non-confessional religious education in Sweden. Their focus is on teachers' reflections and didactical strategies for handling critique of religion as expressed in the classrooms, and with regard to steering documents that emphasize, on the one hand, the stimulation of critical skills, and on the other hand, increased understanding of and tolerance for different kinds of worldviews. Using the concept of "critical religious literacy," they conclude that when teachers succeed in finding strategies that increase the pupils' ability to reflect on and communicate about religion in ways that include critical reflection about their own values and worldviews, religious education is more likely to contribute to a constructive criticism of religion.

The third part of the volume, "Civil Society, Media, and Family," opens with a chapter on criticism of religion in debates regarding confessional independent schools in Sweden: "Illusive Religion in the Public Sphere: The Debate on Confessional Independent Schools in Sweden." Here, Johan von Essen, working in the intersection of civil society research and theology, explores criticism of religion in the public sphere as mediated in debate articles published in Swedish daily newspapers regarding one particular issue. Von Essen concludes that the public sphere constituted by debate articles in this case did not promote a constructive criticism of religion, since the participants did not engage in a dialogue or conflict over religion but rather in a discussion about the legal status of confessional independent schools. This, he argues, shows how public spheres will not promote a constructive criticism of religion when used to influence institutionalized politics instead of for internal interactions among actors in civil society.

The structuring influence of the media on debates and criticism of religion is the focus of the subsequent chapter, "Criticizing Religion in Mediatized Debates," by Linnea Jensdotter and Mia Lövheim, both of whom work in the field of sociology of religion. They focus on how critique of religion was expressed in a Swedish debate concerning Muslim politicians in two different forms of media (editorials in the daily press and comments to news articles posted on Facebook) and discuss how the affordances of these forms enable a constructive critique of religion. They conclude that even though the mediatized debates generated a great deal of polarization, they also enabled participants to articulate ideological convictions and formulate rational and critical arguments, which in turn can enable mutual learning processes and alliances across entrenched positions. In such cases, mediatized debates may initiate a process of more constructive critique of religion.

In the final chapter, "Religious Faith, Parenting Choices, and Critical Engagement," Martha Middlemiss Lé Mon and Ninna Edgardh combine perspectives from sociology of religion and ecclesiology in an analysis of how actively religious Christian parents in Sweden negotiate decisions in everyday life based on religious beliefs and the strategies they develop when presenting such choices in meetings with others from outside their religious group. The parents' strategies for critical engagement with secular society is discussed through Lori Beaman's concept of "deep equality," with the aim of assessing whether this concept can be useful for analyzing forms of engagement with critique that involve a suspension of criticism or retreat to a "faith bubble."

In "Postscript: Toward Constructive Criticism of Religion," Mia Lövheim and Mikael Stenmark summarize some of the insights of the different contributions to this volume and identify where some of the challenges for future research might be located. One of the insights is that even if forms of immanent critique might be more constructive than more external forms of critique, several of the chapters reveal a dialectic movement where criticism is offered from an insider perspective in some respects and an outsider perspective in other respects. This shows that the categories of "insiders" or "outsiders" with regard to the religion whose beliefs, values, or practices become the target of criticism should not be conceived as a simple either-or alternative. Finally, several chapters show how willingness to examine different arguments and to critically reflect on one's own motivations, along with access to spaces where mutual disclosure and respect is encouraged, seems to be crucial in order to enable more constructive criticism of religion.

Part One

Philosophical and Theological Perspectives

1

Criticizing Religion in a Secular Democratic Society

Mikael Stenmark

Due to the increased plurality or diversity which characterizes contemporary society, there is now a veritable market in different worldviews, moralities, and lifestyles. On a nearly daily basis we encounter directly or indirectly (through social media) people with different—sometimes radically different—beliefs, values, and identities than our own, and the liberal democratic state has to find means to protect and respect its citizens without establishing or endorsing any of these competing worldviews or ways of life. At the same time, it must be legitimate for us, in the public life of a sound democracy, to criticize the religious or secular worldviews which our fellow citizens embrace. But how could and should this be done? If we want to live in a pluralistic society that is sustainable also in the long run, we need to address these difficult issues. We need to explore and learn how to cultivate ways to critically engage with one another on issues that concern the worldview commitments that set us apart.

Important questions to address, therefore, are the following: what options do we have when it comes to criticizing religions (and for that matter their secular counterparts such as secular humanism or naturalism)? How are we able to reach the others so that they take what we say into account? What is critique of religion (or of worldviews),[1] more precisely, and is it possible to develop constructive or successful forms of such criticism in secular democratic societies? And which ways of critical engagement have proven to be more or less dead ends in that they increase violence, conflict, and resistance rather than fostering peaceful coexistence, critical dialogue, revision of belief and practice, and exchange of ideas? Some of these questions are beyond my competence as a philosopher to address, but what I shall provide is an account of different forms of critique and also point out some of their strengths and weaknesses.

Within the academic community, as well as in the public intellectual discourse, a number of critical engagement strategies have indeed been proposed or used in dealing with these issues. In what follows, I will identify and rationally reconstruct some of these, try to evaluate them, and in the end argue that we should develop and embrace what I call the open strategy. Before exploring these questions, however, some things need to be said about what critique of religion could or should be within the context of a Western secular democratic society.

Critique of Religion

As indicated in the introductory chapter, by *critique of religion* we mean an assessment or evaluation that is directed by someone (for instance an individual, a group, or an institution) against religion as such, against a religion as a whole, or against a part of it in order to reject it, question it, or to point out that something needs to be changed in it. The first thing to pay attention to is that the goal of criticism is not the same as the goal of understanding, even if the first should include elements of the second activity. (It is hard to develop justified forms of critique if one does not really understand what one aims to critically assess.) When I criticize what someone believes, values, or does, I think that something is wrong, lacking, or unjustified; I am not expressing a desire to grasp or comprehend why or what it means to believe, value, or do these things. We could perhaps say that the logic of criticism differs from the logic of understanding. *Critique is an expression of disproval of someone or something*; the quest for understanding carries no such connotations. The target of the critique could be, as I have already hinted at, religion as such, that is, all religions, or a particular religion (say Christianity), or a certain denomination or form of that particular religion (say, Christian fundamentalism), or a specific belief, value, or activity of that particular religion (say, the belief in the inerrancy of the Bible or the convictions that abortion and same-sex marriage are morally wrong), or of a specific belief, value, or activity of more than one religion (say, that God exists, that the world is God's creation, that humans are unique, or that life has an ultimate meaning) but perhaps not all religions. So, one could question the prohibition of blasphemy, which could be found in both Christianity and Islam but not in Buddhism. Moreover, the critic or critics could be an individual, a particular group, or an institutional entity of some kind.

Let us spell out some of these aspects by taking criticism against science as a parallel case. Hence, I will assume that there is nothing special about critique that is directed at religion; it is merely an instance of a broader category. The target could, for instance, be religion, science, politics, education, media, secularism, socialism, or capitalism, either as ideas, institutions, or practices. Normally, we tend to think that critique comes from people outside of the practice in question (criticism from without), but it could just as well come from people who are engaged in the practice, from the religious or scientific practitioners themselves (criticism from within). This means that critique could be internal or external in relation to *whom* it is who offers or expresses the critique against the phenomenon in question. No clear-cut line could of course be drawn because people will disagree on who's in and who's out, who is a (true) religious believer or say a (true) Muslim or who is a (good) scientist or (genuine) representative of science and who is not. Moreover, the distinction is context-sensitive, so in certain debates I may be an insider, in others I may be an outsider, and sometimes it will be hard to tell what I am. Either way, many of us have no problems identifying, say, the atheist Richard Dawkins as an outsider in his critique of Christianity and Islam.

We must also take into account that critique of religion or critique of science could be external or internal in a different way. In that case, it does not have to do with who the critic is but with the *grounds* on which the critique is based. What kinds of reasons are presented against the object of criticism? Is it scientific reasons that provide the basis for the critique against scientific practice, or is it rather based on religious, moral, philosophical, or legal reasons? Some people are deeply worried about the destructive tendencies of modern science as these express themselves in for instance genetic engineering and biotechnology. They maintain that science in the end will undermine both human dignity and Mother Earth herself. Thus, essentially moral or ethical reasons provide the basis for this kind of critique of science. Or take as an example the critique that aims at those Jews, Christians, and Muslims who believe that the earth was created by God roughly 10–15,000 years ago and that God directly created each of the major species found on earth: it is a criticism to say that young earth creationism contradicts some of the findings and theories of science. Here we have external, more specifically scientific reasons which are used against the theology of creation embraced by these groups of religious practitioners. But the criticism could just as well have been from within their own ranks. Other Jews, Christians, or Muslims have argued that young earth creationism cannot find support in the Hebrew Bible, the Christian Bible, or the Quran, since such interpretation of Scripture goes against established traditional hermeneutical principles. Here we find an internal critique of the theology of creation that young earth creationists advocate.

To simplify, let us call reasons that are religiously grounded *religious* or *religion-based* reasons. One example of such a reason is when Christians claim that we should believe that all people have equal worth because we are all created in the image of God. It could be aimed at other Christians who deny that we all have equal value, and then it functions as an internal reason. Or it could be directed at people who reject or question that belief, like for instance some utilitarians or Darwinians do, and then constitute an external reason. Consequently, whether reasons given for or against a belief, value, or pattern of behavior are external depends on who or what the object of criticism is. There exists of course no clear-cut line between these different types of reasons, but we could without too much trouble give paradigmatic examples of each kind. Whether any of the reasons or arguments given above are (what philosophers call) good reasons or valid and sound arguments is, of course, a different matter. Here we find plenty of space for disagreement too.

There is also a third question we need to keep in mind, besides "*Who* offers the criticism?" and "On what *ground* is the criticism based?"; this third question is "What is the *aim* of the criticism?" In raising this question, we are interested in knowing what the one who is issuing the critique hopes to achieve with his or her critical assessment: what is its purpose? First, one could engage in a *negative* form of criticism. One can try to show that a way of reasoning, a belief, a value, an argument, or a theory is not convincing because there are good reasons to reject it, or that even if the premises of the argument are reasonable, perhaps even true, the conclusion does not follow. The previous example of critique against creationism is purely negative; it says what Jews, Christians, and Muslims should *not* believe about creation. If the goal of negative forms of critique is to show deficiencies or find faults or even to completely undermine the position criticized, the objective of *constructive* forms of critique is to investigate possible ways of improvement. With constructive negative criticism, then, the critic tries to show how a particular line of reasoning, an argument, or a point of view could become more coherent, justified, or convincing, if certain changes are made.

Many, including myself, have maintained that if theists (roughly, people who believe that there is a God, that the world is God's creation, that life has an ultimate meaning, and that humans are created in the image of God) take seriously that God neither had to create a world nor create it in a particular way—God could have done things differently—then it is a purely empirical question how the world came into existence and how life developed. Given our present state of scientific knowledge it is, therefore, reasonable for theists to believe that God has started, directed, and influenced the process of evolution; that is, God has used natural laws, the primitive soup of matter, and guided natural selection and mutations to create and develop life. Moreover, it is because God created us human beings in God's image that we are able to apprehend and know the world and this contingent fact about it. This philosophically and theologically grounded form of constructive critique implies that those Jews, Christians, and Muslims who are theists should accept evolutionary theory but reject a naturalistic interpretation of it (roughly, that there is no God or all-encompassing mind but that the world, at bottom, is wholly impersonal and that matter lies at the root of everything, that life merely is a product of chance, and that there is no purpose to be found behind how cosmic and evolutionary history unfolds). That is to say, they should reject creationism and instead accept theistic evolution. And of course you do not need to be a theist yourself to offer constructive critique of this sort.

After this overview and rough distinction between negative and constructive critique, we could perhaps say that *constructive critique of religion* signifies such forms of critique which, rather than undermining or debunking a religious worldview (including beliefs, values, and behavior), aims at modifying, reforming, or improving it in relation to a particular problem, objection, or challenge that has appeared. We also need, in one way or another, to consider the reactions of those that receive this criticism. It is presumably not merely the intentions or aims of the critic that determine whether or not a critical remark should be understood as constructive, but also how it is perceived by the target of criticism, the "critique-receiver." So, a critique against, say, Islamic veiling or punishment for blasphemy which is not meant to undermine Islam as a religion but is rather driven by a yearning to improve this way of life, but which nevertheless completely ignores the reasons that Muslims themselves give for these practices, cannot straightforwardly be conceived as a case of constructive critique.

Let me add a few more questions we need to consider besides:[2] (1) Who offers the criticism? (2) On what grounds is the criticism based? What kind of reasons are used in the argument? And (3) What is the aim of the criticism? Is its goal positive or negative, reformistic or debunking? These questions are: (4) Who is permitted to offer criticism and respond to it and who is silent, silenced, or ignored? (5) In what social or professional role is the criticism delivered by the critic and in which social setting or arena is it located? And (6) How successful is the criticism? What is its impact on people in general and on the target group in particular?

Whereas question (1) focuses merely on who is inside vs. outside of the religion or worldview which is the target of the critique, question (4) addresses issues of legitimacy, representation, and power when it comes to identifying the critic, the critique-receiver, and the "critique-responder," that is, he or she who actually responds to the criticism. (Notice that although we typically assume, I believe, that the critique-responder is someone within the religion or worldview that is the target of the critique, it could still be someone outside it.) Question (5) is often intimately related to (4), but analytically distinct. It has to do with the fact that what we can say and do is constrained or made possible in different ways by different contexts. The kind of critique of religion I could "afford" to give, to take merely one example, is enabled and constrained by whether I express it as a private person, a professor, or a prime minister and whether I do it in an academic setting, a popular science book, a daily newspaper, on Facebook, or at a private dinner party.

Question (6) focuses instead on impact and successfulness. Where question (4) requires of scholars of religion to perform a *power analysis*, and question (5) an *affordance analysis*, question (6) demands an *impact analysis*. This latter question is especially challenging in the context of critical engagement with groups of violent religious extremists and their tacit supporters. They could be, say, advocates of militant Islamism supporting ISIS or Christians who are prepared to burn down abortion clinics and kill doctors and nurses working there. How could critics reach such groups of people with their arguments and critique? This is an important issue, because what I am really interested in is whether we can offer or develop a model for a constructive critique of religion which has at least the potential to be *successful* in the sense that it actually changes the beliefs, values, or behavior of the target group. (A response, on the other hand, is successful if the critic realizes that the criticism is unfair or unjustified.) When can critique help rather than hinder revision of religious commitments? How could we criticize religions or worldviews that differ, sometimes radically, from our own, in a constructive and successful way? Notice, however, that I measure success here in terms of how the target group of the critique responds, and not in terms of how other people in society respond to it. (We can, of course, measure both kinds of responses.) So, for instance, an argument against ISIS showing that their actions violate human rights might be an argument that many people in secular democratic societies in the West find completely compelling, but it might lack evidential force against the target group and their supporters because their basic beliefs and ethical norms are not the same as those espoused by many in secular democratic societies.

Sometimes convincing a third party, located closer or further away from the target of the critique, is actually what we aim at with our critical engagement. A criticism of Islam in this regard might, therefore, not be intended to change what a group of Muslims think on these issues, but to convince the general public that the critique is not merely justified but that we (say, in Europe) ought to severely limit the number of immigrants from certain parts of the world. We can call such arguments "third-party target-arguments." However, those critics want to convince with their arguments might be much more closely related to or associated with the target group. In arguing against militant Islamism, critics might not think that they realistically could convince these extremists themselves, so their objective is primarily to formulate a critique of ISIS or similar groups of Muslims that has a real possibility of reaching Muslims living in the European Union, for example, young people who are exposed to the danger of being recruited by such extremist groups.

A Secular and Pluralistic Society

What also is essential is that we situate critique of religion within a social context, in a broader sense than question (5) does. What I am particularly interested in is the following: How could and should (constructive) critique of religion be formulated or stated *within a secular and pluralistic society*? How could we, those of us who live in such a society, critically engage with one another when it comes to the worldview differences that set us apart? So, I am talking about a liberal democratic society which is "secular" and "pluralistic." Let me try to be a bit more specific about what I have in mind when I use these notions. When I say that our society is *pluralistic*, I simply mean that what characterizes it is the coexistence and social interaction of people with very different beliefs, values, and lifestyles. Within contemporary Western society, there is now a veritable market in worldviews and moralities. It is in this sense a pluralistic society.

I will use the notion of "secular" in this chapter to describe a certain outcome of certain changes in this plurality or diversity. But notice first that there is another way one could talk about being secular, and that is by relating it to the so-called the secular state. The notion of "secular" is then used to express an idea about a particular relation between the state and religion(s): roughly, the idea that a state should not take a stand on religious issues. A state should not favor, say, Christianity over Islam or vice versa. It is people not states who believe in God or go to churches or mosques. It is understandable that this way of talking about the state as secular is widespread, because in the original case the views between which the state must be neutral were all religious. But this is not the case anymore, and that is an important point. Today, there is a great variety of alternative nonreligious outlooks on human life as well, and there are many nonreligious people. The core idea of liberal democracy is, however, that the state should protect people in their belonging to *whatever* outlook or worldview they chose, and treat them equally whatever their choice. For this reason, I agree with Charles Taylor that we need a radical redefinition of secularism: "We think that secularism (or *laïcité*) has to do with the relation of the state and religion; whereas in fact it has to do with the (correct) response of the democratic state to diversity" (2011: 36). In other words, we should resist talking about the secular state and instead talk about state neutrality. As he furthermore remarks, "The state can be neither Christian nor Muslim nor Jewish, but, by the same token, it should also be neither Marxist, nor Kantian, nor utilitarian" (2011: 50). The state should, to the extent that it is possible, be neutral in respect to the different worldviews, conceptions of the good, or substantive ways of life that its citizens embrace.

Rather than using the notion of "secular" in this way, I suggest that we use it to refer to a particular change in Western society. What I have in mind is that there is a growing number of people (more so in some European countries than others) who do not consider themselves to be religious, or hesitate to call themselves "religious," or use the qualifier "I am not religious, but . . ." when self-identifying, or describe themselves as agnostics, or simply say that they are atheists (Thiessen and Wilkins-Laflamme 2017: 64). Europe is increasingly populated by what sociologists call "religious nones." Now, I think we should also resist the terminology of religious nones, at least if it is taken as synonym for nonbelievers, because it is not like these people totally lack life-orienting beliefs or values. It is rather that they hold other things as true than religious people do in their lives. They embrace secular worldviews or are—consciously or unconsciously—searching for secular alternatives to traditional religions, or as Taylor phrases it, they try to develop immanent construals of human flourishing (2007: 9). Such a conceptualization is certainly plausible if we define a *worldview*, roughly, as the constellation of attitudes, beliefs, and values that people, whether consciously or unconsciously, hold and which constitute their understanding of who they are, what the world is like, what their place in it is, what they should do to live a satisfying or good life, and what they can say, know, and rationally believe about these things. I thus suggest that we call them "secular people" and we thereby have a suitable contrast to "religious people" (not denying that there are many borderline cases). Moreover, we could call reasons or arguments that are based on the acceptance of a particular secular worldview, say naturalism, "secular reasons." A secular critique of religion, then, would be a critical assessment based on those reasons that secular people gather from within or derive from their own substantive worldview commitments. "Public reasons" would be those reasons that people on either side of a critical assessment of religion can accept, independent of their own particular worldview or way of life—although they might disagree about their strength or relevance.

We should also avoid calling secular construals or outlooks on life "secularism." This because secular people could embrace secularism but they need not do so; that is, they are not necessarily "secularists" in the sense of having an anti-religion stance. *Secularism* comes in many forms, but I would say that all of them aim at minimizing the influence of religion on society (or on all aspects of life) and hope that religion will one day cease to be a live option for people. The core idea is that we should actively strive to minimize the influence of religion first on politics and eventually on society as a whole; this is essential to the defense of science, democracy, and human flourishing. Society is better off without religion because it is not only false or at the very least irrational, but also dangerous to human well-being and a democratic society. We should therefore actively push history forward toward the goal of a nonreligious world. However, secular people could and many of them do reject this vision of a future society without religion (I will come back to this issue in the second half of this chapter). They could be individuals who feel bound to give religion up, even though they mourn its loss. Or they might, like the secular philosopher Jürgen Habermas, believe that secular Western society needs access to religious beliefs, values, and practices, if it is not to cut itself off from key resources for the creation of meaning and identity (2006: 10). So, secularists are a subgroup within the larger group of secular people.

Hence, the issue I think we need to address is as follows: what could and should (constructive) critique of religion be in a society in which (a) many, sometimes even the majority of people, are secular, and (b) the objective of the state is to remain as neutral as possible in respect to the different worldviews or ways of life that their citizens embrace? Note though that it is not self-evident that (a) and (b) coincide: a state can, like the United States or Brazil, be aiming at worldview neutrality though the great majority of its population is religious.

But there is one more important aspect of the context of criticism that we need to take into account as well, especially if we would like to critically engage and overcome certain forms of religious violence. It is that the plurality or diversity we find in contemporary Western (especially European) societies has changed in yet another significant way, namely, by means of the growing number of Muslim immigrants. This emerging form of religious plurality challenges some deeply held European assumptions. One of them is that religious faith is more or less a private matter and could therefore be proscribed from public life. Many Muslim immigrants have a very different understanding. They want to live out their Islamic life incorporating Islamic beliefs and values in an all-compassing manner which includes civil society and the public square of their new countries. Moreover, the worldview neutrality of liberal democratic societies might go directly against the idea many Muslim immigrants take for granted, that the state should be governed by God and God's laws and that religious leaders should have a significant impact on legal and political matters (Geaves 2010: 124–39). They might also tend (mistakenly, if my analysis above is correct) to identify liberal democracy with secularism, as Shabbir Akthar does, when he maintains that "many Jews and Christians, unlike virtually all Muslims, live conscientiously and comfortably within the arrangements of the liberal secular humanist state. Islam is now unique in its existential decision . . . to confront rather than accommodate the secularist worldview" (2008: 7). Moreover, many Muslim immigrants would be inclined, initially at least, to find atheists or secular people not merely believing what is self-evidently false but also morally offensive (Akthar 2008: 91).

There are of course many exceptions—and we might have to take into account that the initial stances of immigrants might differ from the ones they develop in the years to come; my point is merely that "we," understood as the majority group, who live in a secular Western society here face a situation in which "we," in our critique of religion, actually try to bring together traditions that in certain respects share relatively little by way of common background, and thus the challenge is profound if "we" want these persons to take our critique into account and actually change some of their beliefs, values, or practices (that is to say, if "we" want our criticism to be successful and perceived as constructive). Hence, as scholars we should add a condition (c) to specify the social setting I am particularly interested in a bit further. If so, the key issue we face would be something along these lines: What could and should (constructive) critique of religion be in a society in which

(a) many, perhaps even the majority of people, are secular, and in which
(b) the objective of the state is to remain as neutral as possible in respect to the different worldviews or ways of life that their citizens embrace, and in which
(c) a large number of Muslim immigrants are becoming citizens—people with a quite different understanding of what the role of religion should be in society relative to those (typically) held by the majority population?

We do now have an understanding of what critique of religion is in a secular and pluralistic society, some of its presuppositions and obstacles, as well as an idea about what it would mean for a critique to be constructive and successful. Let us now take a closer look at different critical reasoning strategies or models of criticism. I will present them as ideal types so the people, in this case scholars, scientists, or public intellectuals that exemplify them, cannot be expected to completely fit the models. There are, in other words, more possibilities open within and between the secularist strategy, the restrictionist strategy, the internal strategy, and the open strategy than I can fully do justice to in this context.

The Secularist Strategy

I will call the first strategy of critical engagement on religious issues the *secularist strategy*. The old version of it was a quite passive strategy, saying implicitly that we don't really have to reason with religious people; we could do it if we like but it is not strictly necessary, because the modernization of a society results in the decline and eventually the disappearance of religion. The new secularists realize that this does not seem to naturally happen, so they try actively to push history forward to this goal of a nonreligious world.

Secularists' answer to the question of how to overcome religious opposition and violence is simply that we must try to create a world without religion. We must save our children from having a religious upbringing and religious education. It is religion itself that is the problem and we should not accept or defend religion in any form. As the perhaps most influential atheist of our time, Richard Dawkins, phrases it: "I am not attacking any particular version of God or gods. I am attacking God, all gods, anything and everything supernatural, wherever and whenever they have been or will be invented" (2006: 36). Some of these new secularists are even ready to go as far as saying that "religion poisons everything" or is the root of all evil (Hitchens 2007). Most secularists would of course not go nearly as far, but—as noted above—the core idea is that we should actively strive to minimize the influence of religion first on politics and eventually on society as a whole.

This strategy of critical engagement has been developed in different ways. Let me here merely distinguish between a scientific or rather a scientistic[3] and a philosophical version of it. Again, Dawkins would be a good example of a spokesperson of the *scientistic secularist strategy*. He maintains that science is the only way to understand the real world, and since there are no scientific reasons which support religion in any way—rather, the available scientific evidence conclusively points in the other direction—it is not rational to be a religious believer today. The Nobel Prize laureate Steven Weinberg agrees and even maintains that "anything that we scientists can do to weaken the hold of religion should be done, and may in fact be our greatest contribution to civilization" (2006). It is or should be a central part of the scientific mission to be against religion. Others, such as the philosopher Massimo Pigliucci, think this move is bad for the secularist movement. This because it has the potential of undermining public understanding and damaging the reputation of science, since not all facts are scientific facts, since the best arguments against religion are philosophical and not scientific in nature, and since science cannot give us values—and therefore any argument which appeals to values is disqualified from the start (Pigliucci 2013). There are, Pigliucci argues, besides scientific reasons, decisive philosophical reasons and moral reasons which must be permitted to play a central role in secularists' critical engagement with, for instance, moderate Jews, Christians, and Muslims, as well as in their arguments against religious fundamentalism. What we can call the *philosophical* or *value-inclusive secularist strategy* is, from this perspective, to be preferred over and against the scientistic one.

A recent development of the secularist reasoning strategy is also worth our attention. Typically, the secularist strategy has been a negative one, with the aim of merely showing that religion in all its varieties is false, irrational, and dangerous to a democratic society, and that therefore we should actively strive to minimize the influence of religion first on politics and eventually on society as a whole. Thomas Nagel (a secular person but not a secularist) focuses on the intellectual challenges that secular people face and asks what secular philosophy has to put in the place of religion when it comes to the "question of making sense not merely of our lives, but of everything" (2010: 4). Can a consistent and comprehensive secular worldview, or what he rather would call a naturalistic worldview, be constructed? Is there a way to live in harmony with the universe, and not just in it? Philip Kitcher pays more attention to the practical challenges which secularism has to respond to. He talks about not merely the challenges *of* secularism to religion but the challenges *for* secularism: "An adequate response to these challenges requires moving beyond secularism as a merely negative doctrine, and offering something to replace the functional aspects of traditional religions. Secularism needs to become secular *humanism*" (2011: 24). The secularist strategy has to be positive and cannot merely be negative. Secularism has to fill the gap that religions leave behind.

So, the secularist's advice is that when we, in the public debate or within the academy, critically engage with religious people, we should try to convince them of the irrationality of all forms of religious belief, behavior, and practice. (And, as we have seen, some of them would add that we should also offer a proper substitute, an alternative worldview, to these religions.) We should do this by employing the principles that constitute a scientific approach to the world and by appealing to philosophical reasons and to secular values. We have to make them understand that (natural or social) science can explain religion and replace religion as the explanation of the natural world. An enlightened democratic society must, unfortunately for some people, reject religion. The public task for scientists, philosophers, scholars of religion, and so forth to undertake within this strategy of reasoning is to formulate the arguments for the irrationality of all religions so that they are as convincing and as accessible as possible, so that as many as possible in our society drop religion like a hot potato. In short, the best way to put an end to religious opposition, extremism, and violence is by convincing religious believers to become secularists or naturalists and leave their religions behind.

The Restrictionist Strategy

The *restrictionist strategy* is the second strategy of critical engagement on religious matters I would like to focus on. Restrictionists do not think that it is religion as such that is the problem. Some forms of religion, for instance, are committed to democracy and have evidently promoted democracy in the past, so why oppose them and think that they lead religious people into destructive and evil patterns of behavior? Instead, restrictionists typically maintain that it is religions in the form of religious fundamentalism or religious exclusivism which constitute the real problem. It is these forms of religious orientations that can and do lead some people to destructive and evil patterns of behavior. They would be inclined to agree with Charles Kimball when he writes, "When zealous and devout adherents elevate the teachings and beliefs of their tradition to the level of *absolute* truth claims, they open a door to the possibility that their religion will become evil" (2002: 44).

Restrictionists might think, as secular people like Jürgen Habermas do, that secular Western societies need the moral and spiritual resources of religion to not to cut themselves off from key resources for creation of meaning and identity. What we need to overcome is a narrow secularist consciousness and instead take religious contributions to contentious political issues seriously, and not see religions as "archaic relics of pre-modern societies" and lacking "any intrinsic justification to exist" (2006: 15). Or they could be more restricted and, like Richard Rorty, embrace anticlericalism; they could believe that despite all the good ecclesiastical institutions do, these institutions are dangerous to the health of democratic societies, but still maintain that religion is unobjectionable as long as it is privatized (2007: 33). Or restrictionists might themselves be religious believers and maintain like Robert Audi does that even scientifically oriented, educated people in the Western world can have far-reaching religious commitments and still be fully rational (2011).

Despite these internal differences, what is characteristic of this strategy of reasoning is that those who advocate it believe that certain *restrictions* must apply to the public critical engagement on religious matters in a secular democratic society, and these apply of course to discussions with people who are engaged in destructive and evil patterns of behavior as well. The problem, as restrictionists see it, is that the sorts of reasons that religious people use—especially those by religious fundamentalists and exclusivists—do not have enough epistemic merit because they do not convince beyond the boundaries of their own religious communities; we need to have access to reasons that also secular people can accept. So, we have to establish a common platform between secular people, moderate religious people, and religious fundamentalists to be able to reason about religious matters or even more acutely about militant religious extremism. This means that the religious reasons that people give to justify their behavior must, in the critical debate with the surrounding democratic society, be translated or transformed into public reasons or left out of the debate. Public reasons are, roughly, reasons that can convince also beyond the boundaries of religious communities; they could appeal to the majority of people in a secular and pluralistic society.

Philosophers and other scholars can within the framework of this strategy fulfill an important constructive role because and in contrast to what the secularist strategy allows, they can take the truth claims of religions seriously and they can provide crucial help in translating religious reasons into public reasons. As scholars, we can appropriate elements from religious worldviews and make them accessible so that they, in a second stage, can be the object of criticism or of learning something new that hitherto eluded the notice of the secular, democratic society.

On this construal, there are then essentially two differences between the first two strategies. The first is that secularists take religion *as such* to be irrational and dangerous to a democratic society and aim with their strategy of reasoning to convince as many people as possible that the only reasonable option is to become atheists and secularists. Restrictionists, on the other hand, take only *some* forms of religion to be irrational and dangerous to a democratic society and see no need at all to promote a nonreligious society; they might even think religions can make a vital contribution to a well-functioning democratic society. The second difference is that whereas secularists reject religious reason-giving out of hand, restrictionists think that there is or that there might be some truth in it, but reason-giving can be taken seriously in public critical engagement only if those reasons can be translated or transformed into public reasons. (Some minimal restrictionists might like to qualify this restriction even further.) But despite these differences, what the secularist and restrictionist strategies have in common is that they require or expect that the reasons or arguments to be used when we cultivate ways of critically and constructively engaging with one another on these urgent religious matters must be external to the religious communities in question.

The Open Strategy

Essential to what I call the *open strategy* is that its defenders reject the requirement of externality and thus allow religious reasons in their own right to play a crucial role in the justification of religious beliefs and behavior in the public life of a secular democracy. It does not require that all reasons, in order to be appropriate, must be translatable into external, public reasons; it is permitted to appeal also to internal reasons. I suggest that this strategy is the most fruitful one to use and I will try to explicate and defend it in what follows.

The open strategy is very generous in that it allows people in a critical debate in our society to put on the table almost any kind of reasons they might actually have for what they are thinking and doing. (But it also allows the opponents to religions or to specific religious beliefs and patterns of behavior to use whatever philosophical, scientific, moral, or secular reasons they might have to criticize these religions or these religious beliefs or patterns of behavior.) Defenders of the open strategy—call them *non-restrictionists*—think that the best strategy of reasoning to use in a critical debate, even with people who we regard as engaged in destructive and evil patterns of religious behavior, is to hear them out on their own terms. By permitting or even encouraging religious reason-giving, we can get a good grip on why deeply devoted religious believers think and act like they do. As philosophers or concerned citizens, we would then be able to offer a form of criticism which would, most of the time at least, be significantly more effective than the external criticism of offering public reasons or of appealing to scientific evidence or to secular values.

So, if we for instance find out that an essential part of the justification some Muslims give of their use of violence and terrorism against civilian population in Western democracies consists of passages in the Quran such as "Fight in the cause of God those who fight you, but do not begin hostilities; for God does not love such injustice. And kill them wherever you find them, and drive them out from the places where they drove you out; for persecution is worse than slaughter; but fight them not at the sacred mosque, unless they [first] fight you there; but if they fight you, slay them. Such is the reward of infidels" (Quran, 2:190–91), then we should look for internal grounds or religious reasons to oppose this idea. To use internal reason against people in such cases could be to point out that such verses should be understood in relationship to the passages that affirm that Jews and Christians are People of the Book, who, just like Muslims, are promised a place in the life hereafter. So, we can, for instance, read in the Quran that "believers, Jews, Christians, and Sabaeans—whoever believes in God and the Last Day and does what is right—shall be rewarded by their Lord; they have nothing to fear or to regret" (Quran 2:62). On the basis of these considerations, we should then construct as convincing arguments as we possibly can against such violent radical Muslim behavior. We appeal to some of their own values and beliefs to try to persuade them to change their minds. Things are of course more complicated than these two quick quotations from the Quran might suggest, but the way of arguing still exemplifies the open strategy.

Another example, taken from Charles Taliaferro, is the philosophy conference in which a Christian philosopher tried to develop a nuanced concept of the Christian belief in incarnation and she faced some serious objections. In this setting, another professor "raised his hand and said something like: 'Although I am an atheist, and I do not believe in the Incarnation, *if I did think that there was a God*, then an Incarnation might occur in the following way…'" (2009: xi). He criticized one understanding of the Incarnation but offers at the same time a way of improving, in terms of a philosophical explication, this core Christian doctrine.

If we in secular democratic societies really tried to understand religious people's way of thinking and let these people's worldview commitments play an essential role in our critical engagement, we could actually find (some) religious people wrong by the light of some of their own values and beliefs. To reason in this way is to use the resources provided by internal reasons. Internal reasons would not only be religion-based reasons that people give to support their religious views, but reasons we give to them that appeal to some of their own religious commitments in order to try to convince them to change their mind on evolution, violence, blasphemy, or other issues.

Concerned citizens would, as non-restrictionists, then be able to develop their skills as "immanent critics," and as Jeffery Stout points out, they would then "either try to show that their opponents' religious views are incoherent, or try to argue positively from the opponents' religious premises to the conclusion that the proposal [they themselves embrace] is acceptable" (2004: 69). In short, non-restrictionists' advice is that if we want to successfully influence religious people, especially those who are engaged in what we take to be destructive and even evil patterns of behavior or their tacit supporters, we should focus much more attention on developing internal criticism rather than external criticism. We should look for reasons that might appeal even to those who are deeply devoted religious believers or in this case are violent religious extremists. Again, non-restrictionists do not deny the existence of external reasons but do not think they would be particularly compelling against certain forms of religious fundamentalism.

This strategy is probably one that is bound to be disappointing to many secularists because it means finding religious people wrong by the light of their own values and beliefs and not by evidence or values that seem almost self-evidently true to secularists. Moreover, what we—if we embrace this strategy—have to oppose is the tendency in our secular democratic society to assume that if there are no successful external reasons or for that matter public reasons against religious violence and extremism, there is not much left by way of reason. Now it is true that there are no guarantees that internal reasons might be available, because it is logically possible that a religious worldview is perfectly coherent. But notice that it is sufficient for internal reasoning to get a grip on the fact that there are tensions or dissonances within the beliefs and values of a religious community; the set of beliefs and values do not have to be blatantly inconsistent or incoherent to be internally conflicting. It is, however, very unlikely, given the limited cognitive resources of humans and the actual predicament they find themselves in in this world, that different groups of religious people or for that matter of secular people would be wholly without tension or dissonance in their worldview commitments. And after all, all the open strategy says is that if want to increase our chances of convincing people—especially those who hold radically different life-orienting beliefs and values than we do—to change their views, we should focus on offering immanent criticism. It does not say that we never could or should use external reasons.

The Internal Strategy

Consequently, a purely internal strategy is also rejected by non-restrictionists. An *internal strategy* could essentially be shaped in two different ways or be a combination of the two. Either it says that the only acceptable reasons are those which belong to, or could be justified on the basis of, the commitments and values that are implied by the religion which is the target of the criticism. Or the strategy assumes that only people who belong to or are members of the religion in question have the right to raise objections against it or criticize it. A Christian and no one else can legitimately criticize Christian faith and expect that Christians should take the criticism seriously and perhaps respond to it. A third version would of course be one that assumes that both conditions must be fulfilled. For example, only a Muslim could legitimately criticize Islam, and only reasons which are acceptable within the framework of one's own worldview are warranted. This view is often called "fideism" within the philosophy of religion.

Advocates of the open strategy, as far as I can see, must oppose the idea that deeply devoted believers' viewpoints have no right to be expressed in a public critical engagement. We must reject the idea that if we listen to what they say, if we encourage them to express themselves on matters about which they care deeply (but on which we might strongly disagree), we allow these ideas to become publicly accessible within the framework of a democratic society, and that is unacceptable. This might to some be a price too high to pay, but as far as I can see it is unfortunately a price one has to pay if one embraces the open strategy. If deeply devoted religious believers do not have this opportunity, we will lose the chance, by using the resources of internal reason, to critically examine what they say.

The downside is of course that by using internal reasons, it is less likely that we will pose a profound challenge to the religious outlook being criticized. But then again, the open strategy does not deny us the right to use external reasons when criticizing religion. However, it is more likely that we will be able to connect with the target of our criticism in the first case. If we give others reasons to believe that they are failing according to their own way of thinking, then they will be more willing to change their beliefs, values, or behavior.

Concluding Remarks

To summarize, by critique of religion we mean an assessment or evaluation that is directed by someone (for instance an individual, a group, or an institution) against religion as such, against a religion as a whole, or against a part of it in order to reject it, question it, or point out that something needs to be changed in it. Critique is an expression of disproval of someone or something, and I have assumed that there is nothing special with critique that is directed at religion. It is merely an instance of a broader category.

Moreover, I have distinguished between four overarching critical reasoning strategies we could use or merely assume when we criticize religion. What I have proposed and tried to defend is the idea that we should analyze much more thoroughly and systematically what resources there are within religions themselves to deal with, for instance, religious violence and to support tolerance and if available—which they typically are—to use these resources in our construction of arguments against the religious views which lead to violence.[4] The identification and construction of religious reason-giving or religiously informed arguments (i.e., arguments that include and draw essentially on religious premises), and insight into how to assess them and how to evaluate responses to them, could be an important contribution that philosophers of religion, and other scholars of course, can make to the surrounding secular Western societies in which many of us live. My conviction is that within secular democratic societies, it must be both possible and justified to criticize religions as an outsider, but the biggest success will probably the criticism that is constructive and employs internal reasons or arguments; this is particularly so when the target of our critique is a religion or a particular form that religion takes that diverts substantially from the religious or secular worldviews we have ourselves.

2

Secular Criticism of Religion

Stephen LeDrew

Criticism of religion in recent years, at least in the popular realm, has been dominated by a group of thinkers advancing a school of thought known as the New Atheism, represented most famously by the Oxford biologist Richard Dawkins. While this movement has waned after a period of significant public interest starting with the 2006 publication of Dawkins' *The God Delusion*, it has had a lasting impact on public debate, and also on organized secularism, which consisted of mostly invisible and very small organizations that suddenly grew exponentially after Dawkins and other New Atheists like Christopher Hitchens and Sam Harris became minor celebrities and persistent media figures.

These atheist and secularist organizations constitute a new social movement (LeDrew 2015). While the New Atheism has faded from the spotlight in the general public sphere, the movement persists, despite some years of turmoil. A major feature of the contemporary secular movement in Western societies is an internal tension between people who emphasize scientific authority and religion as an enemy of science (this is the part of the movement most closely aligned with the New Atheism) and others who oppose religion more for its perceived harmful social and political influence, and work to promote social justice more so than science. These groups are in tension for a number of reasons, but most significantly, because the New Atheism side is seen by the others to be politically conservative and overly concerned with the supposed conflict between religion and science.

Without venturing into the details of this conflict within the secular movement, I want to highlight the different schools of thought at the root of it, mainly to identify an alternative tradition of secular criticism of religion that is very different from the New Atheism and its historical antecedents. Dawkins and other New Atheists see themselves as the inheritors of a tradition of Enlightenment thought represented by figures like Hume and Voltaire, but these thinkers were actually deists rather than atheists. The thinker they are most closely aligned with—though they themselves may not be aware of it, since they never reference him—is Baron d'Holbach, a French intellectual whose book *System of Nature* in 1770 was a watershed event in the history of atheism. D'Holbach is considered by many scholars of atheism to be the first professed atheist in the Western tradition. David Berman (1988), for example, considers *System of Nature* the first published work of "avowed" (i.e., explicit and publicly stated) atheism in

Europe. D'Holbach's criticism of religion may be distilled down to three essential points: (1) it is unscientific and its teachings are contrary to scientific truth, (2) it supports a corrupt social order by diverting attention away from the here-and-now and instead toward the afterlife, and (3) it is not a useful foundation for morality. These points refer to three dimensions of critique: epistemological, political, and moral. These in turn correspond to the three categories of the Enlightenment critique of religion as outlined by Jose Casanova (1994): "cognitive," "practical-political," and "subjective expressive-aesthetic-moral" (which might be more simply stated as the moral-subjective critique).

D'Holbach's emphasis was on the cognitive critique—that is, the irrationality of religious faith in consideration of the advancing knowledge produced by modern science. This is the form of critique that characterizes the New Atheism, which includes discussion of morality and (to a significantly lesser extent) the political nature and impacts of religion, but focuses primarily on the perceived conflict between scientific knowledge and religious accounts of creation and the nature of material reality. The practical-political dimension of critique was arguably more important during the Enlightenment, when opposition to religion was firmly attached to its connections to political power more so than its relationship to science. But this has become somewhat of a lost tradition in contemporary atheist thought (again, at the level of public debates), even though many people within the secular movement espouse ideas that are mostly in line with this tradition. This chapter explores this "lost" tradition through an examination of two of its major exponents: Ludwig Feuerbach and Karl Marx, who constructed complex critiques of religion that situated it within a social and cultural context, recognizing the inextricable nature of the relationship between religion and society.

These thinkers provide a source of critique for and by secularists that offers a more constructive approach in that it emphasizes positive social changes, rather than aggressive attacks on the irrationality of religious belief. This is not to say that they were "soft" on religion relative to the popular atheists who have made waves in contemporary debates about the role of religion in modern societies. Marx in particular held great scorn for religion, but the crucial distinction is that his scorn was directed at religion as an ideological manifestation of the alienation produced by social inequalities, not at religious believers themselves, for whom he expressed great compassion. For him religion was the cry of the oppressed—the poor masses seeking a sense of justice in a world that appeared to contain little of it. The ideas presented here, then, are not exactly "constructive" in quite the same sense as the term is used in most of the chapters in this collection, which is natural given that these are secular critics of religion who do not seek to reform or improve religion, but rather to argue that a world without religion would be better—or, more precisely, a better world would be one without religion, since for these thinkers religious belief would naturally fade out if the right conditions were in place, namely a more just and equal society. While Marx and Feuerbach may appear to be as militant in their opposition to religion as a figure like Dawkins, they are highly divergent thinkers in terms of their understanding of religion, why it is a social problem, and most crucially, what should be done about this problem. For Dawkins and other New Atheists, the Western liberal-capitalist social order is not in question. They believe that this social structure is legitimate and that the only obstacle to modern progress toward an earthly utopia is religion, which must be eradicated through scientific education. Feuerbach and Marx, conversely, believed that religion is a cultural manifestation of unequal social relations—part of the superstructure, which is determined by its underlying socioeconomic foundations. They therefore advocated for social transformations aimed at mitigating social inequality, or eliminating it altogether in Marx's theory of communism, in which case religion, as ideological support for unequal social relations, would simply vanish. This approach to religion is more constructive because it does not directly target religious belief, and individual believers, but rather, the social structure that gives religion its power. These ideas therefore offer atheists and secularists a more constructive and pragmatic program of action that emphasizes positive social changes, rather than hostile attacks against those who profess religious beliefs of any kind. They could be read to emphasize cooperation and mutual understanding, rather than conflict and the division of the world into two groups—religious and nonreligious—and demanding that the former submit to the authority of science or a secular worldview.

The New Atheism

Atheist thought (at least of the popular variety that is relevant to the public) has been shaped and dominated in recent years by the New Atheism, a group of bestselling authors of works that are highly critical of religion, most famously represented by Richard Dawkins, evolutionary biologist and former Professor of the Public Understanding of Science at the University of Oxford. Dawkins' 2006 book *The God Delusion* launched a wave of unprecedented public debate about the place of religion in modern society, and with it, unprecedented levels of interest and participation in atheist and secularist groups of various sorts. The other original members of the New Atheism (a host of other figures emerged later, but originally there were the so-called Four Horsemen) were Sam Harris (2004), Daniel Dennett (2006), and Christopher Hitchens (2007), all of whom expressed slightly different ideas about religion and what should be done about it, while agreeing on certain core principles of criticism.

These core principles can be illustrated with reference to Dawkins' critique as delineated in *The God Delusion*, which is the key text of the New Atheism movement. The foundation of his critique, and his entire view of religion (more precisely monotheism, and even more precisely Christianity, which is his most direct target), is the idea of the "God Hypothesis," or the idea that "God" is in essence a scientific hypothesis about the nature and origin of the universe and everything in it (the ultimate grand theory). This hypothesis can be tested, he argues, by subjecting the claims made in the Bible to scientific scrutiny. If the Bible's account of creation is incorrect, then the God Hypothesis fails, and the existence of God himself should be discounted.

This is a version of the argument that God is a plug used to fill gaps in scientific knowledge. Wherever a mystery concerning the natural world persists, God is used to explain it. As scientific knowledge advances, there are fewer gaps to fill, until eventually God is left out of the equation altogether. As far as Dawkins is concerned, Darwin's theory of evolution filled the last major gap in our understanding of nature by providing an explanation for human life, though even at this level this is a disingenuous argument, as Dawkins knows perfectly well that, while evolution provides an account of the emergence of human life, it has no explanation for the emergence of the primitive forms of life that humans evolved from. But Dawkins nonetheless believes that evolution has provided enough of an explanation that the God Hypothesis has proven false, and therefore it is almost certain that God does not exist.

The other major element of Dawkins' thought on religion is that it is a "natural phenomenon" in the sense that religious belief is a product of evolutionary forces (Daniel Dennett's book *Breaking the Spell* is entirely concerned with this idea). As the theory goes, evolution has hard-wired us for a religious impulse, which is likely a by-product of another underlying psychological propensity that is, or at one point was, a useful adaptation. Dennett (2006) offers a more specific account of this process, theorizing that our early ancestors developed a tendency to attribute agency to all natural phenomena, which was a useful adaptation because it encouraged caution. The by-product of this adaptation was a primitive form of animism, which gradually evolved into polytheism as human thought became more sophisticated, and eventually monotheism. Dawkins, meanwhile, envisions a more insidious by-product, arguing that children are programmed by evolution to trust their elders, again because of the obvious survival advantages such a propensity confers (a child who heeds her elder's warning not to eat a poisonous plant will survive to produce offspring—the one who fails to resists temptation will not). The unfortunate by-product here is vulnerability to infection by "mind viruses," which are ideas or beliefs that are transmitted from one individual's mind to another's in a process analogous to genetic replication (Dawkins 2006: 176). Religion is simply the most ubiquitous and pernicious mind virus in history, with its own built-in survival mechanism: the demand to surrender to faith, and the prohibition on criticizing it. This is a specific instance of Dawkins' general theory of cultural evolution, as outlined in his career-making early work *The Selfish Gene*, where he explained that "memes" (ideas that act like genes) that replicate and evolve are responsible for guiding human thought and action (it is notable that for this theory, which he has stuck to for four decades, Dawkins feels no need to provide the evidence that he demands from religious believers to justify their own beliefs).

The critique of religion outlined here centers on an individualistic conception of religion, God, or gods as things that exist within the human brain and are transmitted from one brain to another via Darwinian processes. Even the idea of the God Hypothesis, which treats God as a pseudoscientific theory, centers on belief at the individual level (each individual must "test" the hypothesis for herself by weighing the evidence). In this view, religion is an outright competitor to science in the quest to explain nature, and as such is strictly a matter of beliefs. The social nature of religion is almost completely ignored by these thinkers, and along with it, social-scientific approaches to understanding religion, which are considered unnecessary additions to Darwinistic frameworks that only serve to obfuscate the matter.

In the context of the three dimensions of Enlightenment critique identified by Casanova, the New Atheism is primarily an extension of the cognitive critique. These thinkers do have much to say about religious morality, and a bit less regarding the political dimensions of religion, other than to say that religion is the major cause of political violence and terrorism. But the heart of their critique—and almost the entirety of it for Dawkins—has to do with religious beliefs as sets of truth claims about the natural world, claims that are essentially primitive pseudoscience which have been surpassed by modern physics and biology. So while the New Atheists claim to represent Enlightenment thought and values, they are selective in which aspects of Enlightenment thought they choose to emphasize (primarily because their main objective is not to rid the world of religion, per se, but to enhance the political and cultural authority of science). For a more nuanced and constructive critique that focuses on the political dimensions of religion and how it is related to the social world in a more practical, everyday way, we must look to thinkers representing another tradition of Enlightenment thinking.

Anthropological Atheism

In the mid-nineteenth century a very different kind of atheism was developing that diverged from the Enlightenment cognitive critique that culminated in the scientific atheism of Victorian Darwinists like Thomas Huxley, and more recently, New Atheists like Richard Dawkins. David Berman (1988) refers to it as an emerging "anthropological approach" to atheism because it emphasized social and cultural forces and processes with which religion is interconnected. It is best encapsulated in Karl Marx's view, drawing on Ludwig Feuerbach, of religion as an ideological manifestation of alienation. This tradition of criticism was very influential for a long time, and appears now to be much more relevant given what contemporary theories of secularization say about the causes of religious decline—namely, that religious belief appears to decline in societies that are more highly developed, and more importantly, that exhibit a high general standard of living and socioeconomic equality (Norris and Inglehart 2004; Bruce 2011). The key insight in this perspective, which is where it diverges from the Enlightenment and Darwinistic traditions, is that religion is a social phenomenon that must be understood in relation to its social, cultural, and political context. Assuming the nonexistence of God rather than seeking to prove it, these thinkers were interested in why religion persisted despite its apparently irrational nature. Their answer was that religion is not a rational pursuit of knowledge that can be eradicated by science, but a fundamentally irrational response to social conditions and existential crisis.

Feuerbach is rarely mentioned today in popular or scholarly religious criticism, but his work was deeply influential on a host of major thinkers of his time, most importantly Marx. In his major work on religion, *The Essence of Christianity*, Feuerbach makes a distinction between the "true" essence of religion, which is anthropological, and the "false" essence of religion, which is theological. This distinction forms the basis for the division of the book into two parts:

> In the first part I prove that the Son of God is in religion a real son, the Son of God in the same sense in which man is the son of man, and I find therein the truth, the essence of religion, that it conceives and affirms a profoundly human relation as a divine relation; on the other hand, in the second part I show that the

Son of God—not indeed in religion, but in theology, which is the reflection of religion upon itself—is not a son in the natural, human sense, but in an entirely different manner, contradictory to Nature and reason, and therefore absurd, and I find in this negation of human sense and the human understanding, the negation of religion. (1841: xxxvii)

In this passage we see that Feuerbach agrees with the cognitive critique (religion is "absurd" and "contradictory to Nature and reason"), but he wants to investigate religion more deeply and reveal its "true essence" so that criticism can be directed at the real sources, functions, and consequences of religious belief. For Feuerbach, the truth of religion is in the human social relations that are disguised by the notion of humanity's relationship to the divine. This divine character and metaphysical claims regarding God's role in nature—that is, theology—constitute religion's false essence.

Feuerbach's principal contribution to the development of atheism was his notion of God as the hostile antagonist of the human and the debasement of humanity. This debasement is a result of the projection of the human onto the divine, which is a projection of alienation: "Religion is the disuniting of man from himself; he sets God before him as the antithesis of himself" (Feuerbach 1841: 33). Michael J. Buckley offers a useful summary of Feuerbach's argument:

God is the alienation or estrangement of the human from the human. The human subject projects onto this imaginary subject what belongs properly to the human essence. The attributes ascribed to God—as a false subject—are always taken away from human beings. In this way, the human being is stripped of that which one attributes to God. God is holy, human beings are sinful; God is pure, human beings are corrupt; God is wise, human beings are foolish and ignorant. God is thus the estrangement of the human from itself, the despoiler of all that is dearest about human beings and their ideals. Thus, everything attributed to God—whether in thought, words, or values—is really alienated from human beings. In this zero-sum game, the human subject and the divine subject are antithetical. To ascribe something to one is to remove it from the other. One must perish if the other is to live and flourish. (Buckley 2004: 85)

The simple truth of religion for Feuerbach, then, is that God is secretly man, and that man has projected his best qualities onto the divine, leaving for himself only sin and vice. This rupture within man is the alienation of man from himself. For this reason Feuerbach wanted to turn theology into anthropology, to replace the science of God with the science of Man, since God is really a reflection of the human: "He reconceived theology as anthropology, regarding the traditional attributes of God as the best and highest attributes of humanity, personified and projected into infinity to produce what has become known as theism. Our doctrine of God, therefore, is really a disguised or coded doctrine of humanity" (Hyman 2007: 36). His philosophical project is to repair the division with the human, the alienation that is wrought by religion, by revealing the secret or true essence of religion, which is that it is not God that is worshipped, but humanity alienated from itself. This would thus "enable humans to reclaim responsibility for their own world by exposing the psychological origins of religious dependence" (Beckford 1989: 5–6). Feuerbach's project seeks to reclaim the divine properties for humanity by getting rid of God; thus the basis of his atheism is not a scientific-rationalist discrediting of the tenets of scripture and theology as false explanation, but rather a recognition of the essentially human character of God and the need to eliminate God in order to resolve the division within the human being and to restore dignity to humanity. This insight formed the basis of the atheism expressed by some of the major intellectual figures in the next hundred years, most significantly Marx, who reconfigured Feuerbach's approach by defining more precisely the nature of the human experience that was projected onto God; that is, alienation.

Marx's goal in his discussions of religion was "to expose the illusory character of religion, to strip away the distorting layers of religious ideas about social life and to expose the underlying interests sustaining religious institutions," and the dominant theme in his work is "a categorical denial of the possibility that religion could be analytically separated from 'the world'" (Beckford 1989: 18–19). In his analysis religion could not somehow be siphoned off from social context. Engagement with religion was not engagement with an abstract realm of ideas, but rather with the material conditions of social life. He accepted Feuerbach's theory of God as projected alienation: "The basis of irreligious criticism is: man makes religion, religion does not make man. Religion, indeed, is the self-consciousness and the self-esteem of the man who has not yet found himself or who has already lost himself" (Marx 1845: 115). The alienated man is the one who makes religion. This is the basis of Marx's atheism and his rejection of religion as a manifestation of the oppressive and dehumanizing conditions of social life. His ideas about religion are best expressed and summarized in this famous quote:

> Religious suffering is at once the expression of real suffering and the protest against real suffering. Religion is the sigh of the oppressed creature, the heart of a heartless world, just as it is the spirit of spiritless conditions. It is the opium of the people. The overcoming of religion as the illusory happiness of the people is the demand of their real happiness. The demand that they should abandon illusions about their conditions is the demand to give up conditions that require illusions. The critique of religion is therefore in embryo a critique of the vale of tears, whose halo is religion. (Marx 1845: 115–16)

The "opium of the people" line from this passage is very well-known even to mass audiences and frequently used as a shorthand in contemporary popular religious criticism. In context, the words refer to religion as an ideological condition resulting from oppressive material conditions. Whereas the eighteenth-century Enlightenment philosophers objected to religion because it didn't stand up to reason, Marx didn't bother with the question of religion's truth (its falsity was taken to be obvious to any rational person) and instead critiqued it as a social phenomenon arising out of the forces and relations of production. For Marx religion is an ideological manifestation of alienation, a mechanism for coping with the dehumanization and powerlessness experienced when subjected to oppression (specifically capitalist exploitation); it is an expression of, and protest against, earthly human suffering—and yet it is an ideological system that quells this revolt. The alienated self, buried by oppressive conditions, is projected onto the divine figure, which in turn promises relief from this oppression in the next world. Marx chooses to use the Christian concept of the "vale of tears" as a descriptor of our world; this and the notion of religion as the "sigh" of the oppressed are references to the first verse of the Salve Regina, a Roman Catholic prayer:

> Hail, holy Queen, Mother of Mercy,
> Our life, our sweetness, and our hope.
> To thee we do cry, poor banished children of Eve;
> To thee we do send up our sighs,
> Mourning and weeping in this vale of tears.

The "vale of tears" is the idea of the world as a place of sorrow and suffering from which one can escape only through divine salvation; sighs and cries of the miserable "poor banished children of Eve" are sent up to heaven. Marx uses this idea to indicate where exactly anti-religious criticism should be directed, which is not at the concept of God or heaven, but rather, at the "vale of tears" itself—the place where the "mourning and weeping" happen and which requires that sighs be sent up to heaven. In other words, the critique of religion is really the critique of a world that is characterized by sorrow and suffering: "Thus the critique of heaven turns into the critique of earth" (Marx 1845: 116). In other words, the critique of religion is a critique of a real world so unjust that it makes belief in another just world a necessary psychological coping mechanism.

Marx's description of religion as the opium of the masses and the heart of a heartless world serves to elucidate what Feuerbach meant by the "true" anthropological essence of religion as opposed to the "false" theological essence. Religion is, in fact, "true" not in its theological claims, but in the sense that it is a real expression and manifestation of the human experience of oppression and suffering. The "truth" of religion is not in any fantastical story about omnipotent beings and earthly miracles, but in the human social relations to which it corresponds. It is true in the sense that it is the heart of an otherwise heartless world, and thus it serves a very real purpose. The point for Marx, however, is that the world is indeed heartless and this is why religion exists in the first place—if the world were recreated according to his socialist vision it would have a heart of its own, and religion would be reduced to a vestigial organ, eventually to be left in the dustbin of history along with capitalism.

Marx also agreed with Feuerbach that the elimination of religion is necessary for human beings to be restored to their humanity: "The criticism of religion ends in the teaching that man is the highest being for man, hence in the categorical imperative to overthrow all those conditions in which man is a debased, enslaved, abandoned, contemptible being" (Marx 1845: 119). Like Feuerbach, Marx expresses the humanistic viewpoint that religion is fundamentally antihuman in its debasement of man in relation to the divine through the projection of the best human characteristics onto the figure of God—religion takes our real humanity, that from which we are alienated, and makes it into God. The conditions that it is imperative to overthrow, from the above quote, are the exploitative conditions of labor under capitalism, as this is the principal cause of the debasement of man. He is also talking about religion, though, as religion is to be seen as a symptom of oppression, and also one of the "conditions" which must be overthrown. It is, in fact, no less than a "categorical imperative" to do so, indicating that, for Marx, the abolishment of religion is no less than an ethical imperative for humanist philosophy, as well as a practical-political imperative for the ultimate emancipation of the working class. Marx thus carries on the practical-political element of Enlightenment criticism, which saw religion as a political obstacle to emancipation in its conservative support for traditional authority.

Marx diverges from the Enlightenment tradition in his outline of the method for the abolishment of religion. For him, when the oppressive conditions that necessitate religious belief are transformed, the comforting illusion of religion will no longer be necessary, and it will simply disappear. Giving up these illusions will only happen when we give up conditions that require illusions. In other words, the transformation of material conditions is necessary for a real transformation in consciousness. With the right material conditions in place (i.e., the abolishment of the class structure and its replacement with socialism), the comforting illusion of religion will no longer be necessary—the ideology will vanish after being rendered ineffectual when its material foundation crumbles.

To be fair to the Enlightenment tradition, the notion of religion as "opium of the people" was not entirely new when Marx wrote these words. The notion of religion as a soma-like sedative was already very much present in the atheist conversation. Having noted this, Marx took the critique to an entirely new level, situating it within a much more specific outline of the nature of oppression and its relationship with, and dependence on, religion and its institutions. It is not simply that religion is a sedative, but that it specifically reduces the incentive to revolt against the earthly class-based social order through the promise of a far more just heavenly order; in Owen Chadwick's words, "Heaven and hell are indispensable to class society, because they produce hope of imaginary justice later and thereby emasculate the longings for real justice now" (1975: 65). This might not quite be tantamount to divine justification of social inequality and exploitation, but it does at least offer consolation for it. While many—even some Marxists, including Terry Eagleton (2007)—have described the character of Jesus and Christianity in general as revolutionary, there does seem to be some support for capitalist ideology within the Christian doctrine of faith, hope, and charity. The promise that the meek shall inherit the Earth might be a revolutionary idea, but for Marx the real promise of Christianity is "blessed are the sick and the poor"; this is the "hope" it offers (Christopher Hitchens [1995] argued that this ideology was at work in Mother Theresa's celebration of the suffering of people in her care as a reflection of the suffering of Christ). Charity itself might be considered a repressive ideal that fits into a capitalist ideological framework quite neatly. There is no problem with a highly unequal distribution of wealth as long as the ones who have the wealth exercise the Christian virtue of charity. It is these false promises of divine justice and false hopes for earthly charity that Marx derides with the notion of religion as the opium of the people.

Marx also, for the first time in atheism's history, developed a program for dealing with religion that did not rely entirely on intellectual engagement. He recognized the fundamentally irrational nature of religion in a way that his Enlightenment forebears did not. For him, engaging in rational debate on questions regarding God's existence and his role in nature was futile, since religious belief simply lies outside the lines of rational "proof," at least from the perspective of the believer, who is surely aware to some extent of the inherent irrationality of his faith. Furthermore, the question of "true or false?" is not important for Marx; the important question is whether religion is desirable for society and why these inherently irrational beliefs exist in the first place. He focused on the political, economic, and social foundations of religion, suggesting that it was a manifestation of these social relations and should thus be dealt with at that level.

If we were to put it in the terms of the three Enlightenment critiques of religion, Marx's approach would be to focus on the practical-political line of critique, while claiming that the cognitive critique is not useful since it does not address the real source of religious belief, which is suffering and oppression, not ignorance. Owen Chadwick summarizes Marx's program for secularism: "If we want to change men's ideas, or to dissolve their illusions, we shall not do it in preaching atheism, or in undermining their beliefs by philosophizing. We shall change their conditions of work and life. To make religion vanish, we need not science but social revolution" (1975: 59). While the Darwinist scientific atheists were focusing on the cognitive critique and the notion of religion as a product of ignorance, then, Marx took a different approach, focusing on the social foundations of belief and the requirement that these material conditions must be changed before faith could finally disappear. A rational analysis of religion's transcendent ideas would do nothing to transform the earthly human social relations that constitute their foundation.

But religion is not simply a symptom of exploitative social relations, or a trivial cultural manifestation of economic relations. For Marx, as for Feuerbach, religion reifies alienation by projecting it onto a divine, unquestionable, unalterable, eternal order; it makes alienation natural. This is why it is a major obstacle to radical social change: it makes the conditions of life more bearable and legitimates the debasement of the vast majority of humanity before its earthly rulers, thus tempering the will to revolt against this apparently natural state of affairs: "They are even forced to recognize and acknowledge the fact that they are dominated, ruled, and possessed as a privilege from heaven!" (Marx 1845: 173). In this understanding of the relationship of oppressor and oppressed we will see a general agreement with Nietzsche on the effects of religion. On this view it might seem reasonable to conclude that attacking religion itself might be a useful, and even necessary, strategy to initiate revolution, since it plays a large role in weakening the revolutionary spirit and accepting the conditions of life as the will of some divine order. Marx, however, argued that the strategy of rational deliberation was bound to fail because it did not address the true essence of religion, which, as Feuerbach noted, is human social relations, and not its theological claims and their purported abrogation by science.

Just as Feuerbach wanted to turn the science of God into the science of Man, Marx similarly argued that the critique of heaven necessarily becomes the critique of Earth, and that "the religious reflex of the real world can, in any case, only then finally vanish, when the practical relations of everyday life offer to man none but perfectly intelligible and reasonable relations with regard to his fellowmen and to nature" (Marx 1845: 164). This shift in perspective reflects a new understanding of the essence of religion; it represents a deeper engagement with religion than that of the Darwinists, who never bothered even to attempt to understand religion as anything but ancient superstition that conflicted with a scientific worldview, most particularly with an evolutionary account of the origins of human life. Marx's thought on religion signals a progressive development in atheist thought, moving from rational-scientific refutation of theology (as expressed by d'Holbach) to consideration of religion as a social phenomenon, including the sources of belief and its social and political consequences. It also signals a point of divergence among different schools of atheist thought—the Darwinist, scientific atheists continued the cognitive line of critique in the tradition of d'Holbach and other eighteenth-century atheists, while virtually ignoring Marx's more sociological and anthropological brand of criticism. For Victorian Darwinists, as for contemporary New Atheists, the issue was science more so than religion. They sought to defend science, and particularly the theory of evolution, from attack by religious forces, and in doing so set up the religion/science dichotomy that dominates atheist thought to this day.

Conclusion

The historical split between the cognitive-oriented critics of religion and the anthropological variety is mirrored in organized secularism today, which is characterized by tensions between groups espousing essentially these same positions. Returning to Casanova's three dimensions of Enlightenment criticism, Dawkins and the New Atheists focus primarily (though not exclusively) on the cognitive critique (i.e., religion as the antithesis of science, and an irrational, prescientific explanation of nature). A critique of religion's moral status is also a feature of this line of thought, but it is secondary.

The branch of the atheist movement that connects secularism with a concern for social justice, meanwhile, takes a different approach. It is more engaged with the practical-political critique: that is, religion's relationship to social oppression and inequality. While not explicitly referencing the ideas of people like Feuerbach and Marx, they take roughly the same approach. For them the major problem with religion is not a conflict with scientific truth (though they may consider that a problem), but that religion, as they see it, promotes various kinds of bigotry, justifies discrimination (especially against homosexuals in the American context), and generally supports established hierarchies of power and authority that they want to subvert.

The Dawkins brand of scientific atheism is not constructive, since its purpose is precisely destruction—that is, the eradication of religion through scientific education. Dawkins is as critical of multiculturalism and liberal norms of tolerance and religious and cultural accommodation as he is of religion (Eagleton 2007; LeDrew 2015). The scientific atheism he endorses is a universalistic utopian ideology that allows no space for competing ideas, or for the possibility of different cultures to coexist. In the society

Dawkins imagines, there is really to be no such thing as cultural differences, since politics and morality are all subsumed within scientific authority. Culture, identity, and nationality are all to be eradicated along with religion and replaced with a set of norms, values, and political prescriptions for creating a good society that are all based on the authority of science, and scientific experts (like himself). To put it a little more crudely, though no less accurately, atheism for people like Dawkins is essentially an argument that scientists should have the authority to tell people how to live. The tradition of anthropological atheism has much more to offer in terms of a constructive critical engagement with religion. We see this at play in the social justice branch of the contemporary atheist movement, which places concerns about social inequality, discrimination, racism, sexism, etc., on equal footing with concerns about more negative or destructive qualities of some forms of organized religion (LeDrew 2015; Simmons 2017).

This brand of atheism makes more sense in light of some major recent theories of secularization, notably Pippa Norris and Ronald Inglehart's (2004) claim that "existential security" is the key factor to consider when trying to understand secularization. Existential security refers to a general standard of living: people who live in societies that have greater income equality, gender equality, better education and health care, less war and violence, and so on are more "existentially secure" and generally speaking, also less religious. One could argue that these facts support the criticisms advanced by Feuerbach and Marx, which posit that religion is an expression of the alienation produced by living under oppressive, dehumanizing social conditions, and that it is the absence of such material conditions, rather than the acceptance of abstract principles of scientific rationality, that create a situation where religion can, and will, fade out.

In terms of how secularists have adopted this general approach and put it into practice, it results in a more constructive approach because it is not a totalitarian belief system that rejects all other forms of belief; rather, it is more a prescription for the good society that could accommodate many different kinds of belief, provided that they do not conflict with the basic humanistic values of freedom and equality. It is only when religion takes a form that does not support these values—most notably for the atheist movement, the American Christian Right, which is notoriously patriarchal and hostile to sexual minorities—that religious belief itself becomes a problem, according to this perspective.

3

Academic Feminism as Immanent Critique: Three Feminist Theological Critiques of Patriarchy

Ulf Zackariasson

Critiques of religions are certainly nothing new: religious traditions like Christianity and Islam constitute themselves partly by critiques of the traditions that they take themselves to have superseded, and in Western Europe and North America various politically and ideologically motivated critiques of religion have been part of the public debate at least since the Enlightenment era (LeDrew 2015). In recent times, a vocal right-wing populist critique directed particularly against Islam has gained much attention, particularly in North America and Europe.[1] However, religious traditions have always also brought forward many critics within their own ranks, calling for change from within.

I understand critique as an activity aiming for change. Critics typically present some standard that, they claim, the criticized party fails to meet. Such standards can be derived from epistemology, from what the critic takes to be revealed truths, from moral considerations, political visions, and so on. The force of any critique depends to a significant extent on how sound the standards it relies on are—but not only, as I suggest later. *Internal* or, as I will call it, *immanent critique* (of, for instance, religion), seeks to derive the standards used in critique directly from the commitments of the criticized party (in my case, the religious tradition itself). The focus of my paper is one such form of critique, exercised by feminist academic scholars.

Purpose and Research Question

The purpose of this chapter is to improve our understanding of immanent critique of religion via a study of one of its branches, namely, feminist theological academic reflection on religious traditions. I will connect the mainly philosophical discussion of immanent critique with a study of *exemplars* of academic feminist immanent critiques of Islam, Judaism, and Christianity, respectively. I will explain what I mean by exemplars and my reasons for opting for this approach in the next section, where I also present the exemplars I will work with.

Method and Material

In *Exemplarist Moral Theory*, Linda Zagzebski argues against the typical philosophical impulse to demand that any serious discussion of some phenomenon like, say, courage, should begin by defining the concept. Very often, she holds, we are actually much more certain about—and in agreement on—various instances, or *exemplars*, of, for instance, courageous behavior, than we are about how to define courage. Zagzebski develops this idea via Saul Kripke's and Hilary Putnam's work on reference in the philosophy of language (Kripke 1980; Putnam 1975). According to Kripke and Putnam, we often fix the referent of a concept via ostensions: we point and say, "that's water," or "*that's* what I call courage!" Indeed, if we did not have such concrete examples to start from, it is hard to see how we could get very far in our reflections on, for instance, what courage is (Zagzebski 2017: 11–13).

Kripke and Putnam applied their theory of reference primarily to natural kinds such as gold and water. Zagzebski expands the theory to evaluative terms like "courageous" and suggests that our reflection on virtues such as courage, too, should start with exemplars—concrete persons who, we agree, have showed great courage, and that we identify with the help of the emotion *admiration*.

"Constructive" is a similarly normative term, and I take Zagzebski to show that choices of exemplars are always located within some moral universe and thus inextricably related to a vague yet substantive conception of human flourishing, what human life may be like at its best. This helps explain why I choose academic feminists rather than, for instance, Christian fundamentalists, members of the Islamic State, or militant Jewish settlers as interesting exemplars: certainly, one reason is that I wanted to focus on academics specifically, but another equally important reason is that I seriously doubt whether the latter groups qualify as *constructive* critics of anything. You need not agree with each thinker's critiques in detail to appreciate them as suitable exemplars, but the very choice of some critique as an instance of constructive critique is, I take it, in itself a kind of acknowledgment (I return to the complexities of analytic categorizations such as "constructive" in the concluding section).

The exemplars I work with are Asma Barlas' *"Believing Women" in Islam*, Kwok Pui-Lan's *Postcolonial Imagination and Feminist Theology*, and Rachel Adler's *Engendering Judaism*. Barlas, Adler, and Kwok are all well-established academics firmly situated in Western academic culture, and their work has not only religious but also academic ambitions. This establishes certain frames for their critique: it must meet the academic standards of their respective disciplines. On the other hand, their position also offers them a platform which, although it certainly does not confer any *religious* authority, nevertheless might have some such weight, since religious traditions are generally concerned about and cherish study, teaching and—more generally—the pursuit of truth. What makes the thinkers I study particularly interesting is that they explicitly identify themselves as religious believers committed to the future of their tradition. To make their case, they negotiate their roles as academics (and thus as "outsiders" in a way) and religious believers (and thus "insiders"), seeking to make this double role an asset rather than a handicap.

Theory: Immanent Critique and Tradition

The concept of immanent critique is intimately connected with the Frankfurt School, which saw it as an activity aiming to uncover the contradictions and tensions inherent in primarily bourgeois liberal democracies, but today, the concept is often understood and used more broadly to refer to what Arvi Särkelä (2017) calls transformative practices in intellectual traditions, societies, and so on. I limit my discussion here to such transformative practices that are interesting for my purposes.

For something to be "immanent," there has to be something—like a tradition—with respect to which it *can* be immanent (Moore 2012, 89). Immanent critique is impossible without a rough consensus among agents that sets them apart from others. Henceforth I call this a *tradition*.

Immanent critique thus needs to situate itself as within, and at the same time in tension with, a tradition and its way of working. A conception of traditions that present them as homogenous, tightly knit entities will leave very little space for critique, but amorphous conceptions make the target unclear and threaten to make immanent critique impotent (Sabia 2010; Green 2004). Immanent critics need a conception of tradition that finds a middle ground between these extremes. Thus, a first question concerns how the critics *constitute tradition* both in terms of what they take to be wrong or misguided about its current ways of functioning and what we should consider its *properly* constitutive elements.

My second question concerns what Lövheim and Stenmark call the *form of critique*; that is, the concrete *forms* immanent critique takes in each theologian's work. Here, the literature on immanent critique offers a range of options. Jeffrey Stout, inspired by Robert Brandom (1994), proposes a *linguistically oriented* immanent critique where participants' reasoning is a public and rule-governed activity that outsiders, too, can study and engage in (Stout 2004, chaps. 2–3). Linguistically oriented immanent critique aims to show that the members of a tradition fail to abide by their own inference rules, and Stout holds it to be the only really effective critique once we reject universalism and admit that there are only historically constituted and situated standards to appeal to (Stout 1989).

Anthony Sabia, on the other hand, problematizes this straightforward understanding by pointing out that if immanent critique were only a matter of directly employing "dominant understandings and norms" within, for instance, a society or a tradition, critique would almost invariably be conservative and serve the purposes of already established authorities (Sabia 2010: 686). A more *comprehensive* immanent critique, as I will call it for lack of a better term, would enable critics to call into question the very inference rules and standards of a tradition by "somehow drawing on [other] resources internal to the society or culture of which they are a part."[2] Sabia admits that "[t]his makes immanent critique something of a mystery" because it must find in the tradition itself, and without straying *too* far from "dominant understandings and norms," resources that allow us to question these very norms and inference rules (Sabia 2010: 687).

I will treat Stout's and Sabia's conceptions of immanent critique as situated on a continuum, where Stout to a relatively higher degree stresses the possibility to use established inference rules, while Sabia emphasizes the possibility to reconstruct them via changes at a more fundamental level. On this continuum, there is also room for in-between positions, and I will discuss the way the central critical thrusts of each critic fit on this continuum.

A third question—closely related to the second—concerns what Lövheim and Stenmark call the *actors*, or *agency*. What does it take to establish oneself as an *immanent* critic worth taking seriously, and how can you combine that status with the more detached role of an academic scholar? Naturally, the answer to this question differs depending on the conception of immanent critique with which you operate. Stout, for instance, is relatively optimistic that more or less anyone able to learn the publicly accessible inference rules of a tradition can engage in immanent critique, which means that both insiders and outsiders can partake on relatively similar terms.[3]

The further we move, however, along the continuum toward Sabia's conception, the more difficult it becomes to see how outsiders could play any prominent roles. Green points out that with comprehensive immanent critiques that challenge dominant norms and standards, there is always the difficulty of determining if, and how, a proposed change constitutes an improvement—after all, the very standards of improvement are also under negotiation. This means that the agent's reliability becomes important, and that reliability depends, at least in part, on factors such as identity, motive, and purpose. Put succinctly: if you cannot trust a critic to be knowledgeable enough and sufficiently committed to the tradition, why take her critique seriously (Green 2004: 516)? So perhaps a more apt way of putting the question about agency is: *what forms of immanent critique are available to different types of agents?*

The question of agency becomes particularly interesting here given the institutional context of the academic feminist theologians, and their ambition to combine their roles as believers and academic scholars. Of course, positivistic ideals about value-free research and strict norms for justification are less prominent than before. There is, arguably, an increasing emphasis today both within the academy and elsewhere on the multitude of forms of knowledge that exist, and the need to acknowledge (more explicitly than before) the epistemic legitimacy of academic methods of inquiry other than the strictly scientific (McKenna 2015). Kenneth Gergen also traces a shift of academic ideals (at least in the social sciences) from "mirroring to making"—rigorous research methods are, though not abandoned, modified so they can be used not just for the purpose to *describe*, but also to help change, the current state of society (Gergen 2014: 194). Scholars are, in other words, increasingly agents and not just spectators, and this fits, of course, well with the ambitions of Barlas, Kwok, and Adler.

The more you stress these shifts toward a broader conception of knowledge and the active roles of scholars, the more natural it also becomes to reflect on questions about the agents—their goals, motives, and competences to engage in such "making" activities. This brings us, once again, back to questions concerning agency and about how to situate oneself as a competent immanent critic worthy of attention.

Analyses of the Material

Barlas

Barlas situates herself as a "believing woman" in the Muslim tradition. With regard to my first question, then, on what constitutes tradition, in her view believers are those persons who fully adhere to the claim that the Quran is God's complete and ultimate revelation (Barlas 2002: 19, 33). Barlas' conception of Islam thus makes hermeneutics a central discipline, because the tradition is constituted by its privileging of the Quran as sacred *text* and she sees no need (or possibility) to move outside the core of Islam itself to criticize its current patriarchal forms (Barlas 2002: 3).

Barlas' claim that the Quran is a complete and ultimate revelation is very far-reaching, and this is due to her special use of the tradition of hermeneutics. As Barlas uses the term, hermeneutics is "the theory, method and philosophy of interpretation" dealing with questions about how we "interpret texts, what counts for a con/textually legitimate reading and the role of preunderstanding in the interpretive process" (Barlas 2002: 211).

Barlas' claim that the Quran is God's ultimate and complete revelation allows her (now turning to my second question) to argue that unlike other texts, its divine origin ensures that it supplies the hermeneutical principles necessary to understand it correctly and as a whole—that is, the way God intended. Barlas uses this unorthodox hermeneutical move to accomplish two important tasks. First, she seeks to avoid a relativism about interpretations that would reduce her reading to a reflection of *her* interpretative community's interests just as patriarchal readings would simply reflect the orthodox community's interests. Second, she aims to eliminate the problem of evil that looms in relation to the question how God's revelation could be open to (for instance) misogynic interpretations. The fact that the text itself disproves such understandings is, she argues, further evidence of the text's divine origins (Barlas 2002: 204f).

Islam as a religious tradition is hence properly founded on the view of the Quran as revealed by God. Barlas' argument is that Islam in its contemporary forms fails to fully acknowledge the Quran's divine (and thus complete) status, which is signified by the flawed hermeneutics of what she calls conservative readings. In this argument, she draws on elements of hermeneutic thought while she still withstands the potentially relativistic implications of accounts of interpretation that emphasize the situatedness of the reader/interpreter.

Conservative readings employ, according to Barlas, an atomistic hermeneutic that isolates verses and statements in the Quran from the whole of which it is part. In order to interpret these isolated statements, they then turn away from the Quran and toward sources such as accounts of Mohammad's *Sunnah* and early interpretations and applications gathered in the different schools of *Tafsir*. This reveals another fundamental error of conservative readings, Barlas argues, namely, the assumption that people living in spatial and temporal proximity to an act of revelation are also its best interpreters.

According to Barlas, this assumption subjects God's revelation to a time-bound interpretative pattern (Barlas 2002: 58). It will not help to take recourse to the Prophet's *Sunnah* either, she argues, because critical studies of the way the *Sunnah* was established reveal that Islamic scholars have favored the *hadiths* that fit their own outlook, even when the historical support for their authenticity is weak. A particular time-bound interpretation operating with sources other than the Quran itself has set "an Islamic stamp on pre-Islamic misogyny," and this is only possible because scholars have neglected the Quran's own hermeneutic principles (Barlas 2002: 65). Authorities within the current patriarchal order are of course, she points out, keen to defend their positions even by arguing for the insufficiency of the Quran, but according to Barlas this amounts to a kind of lack of faith in the Quran and ultimately even in God (Barlas 2002: 68f).

Barlas' immanent critique thus takes as its goal that the Quran should be restored to its proper place in Muslim tradition. This also means that she must reject a substantial amount of current inference rules in Islamic communities—while drawing on others. According to Barlas, the proper hermeneutics which she derives from the Quran stresses first that an adequate understanding of the Quran must respect the unity (*tawhid*) of God and, hence, that there can be no sovereignty besides God's. The Quran's message is thus strongly egalitarian. Second, the Quran also teaches that God never does or teaches *Zulm* to anyone; that is, God never transgresses individuals' rights, nor does God entitle anyone else to do so. Hence, we can know that the Quran never teaches "misogyny or injustice" (Barlas 2002: 14).

Third, the Quran teaches that God cannot be represented in anthropomorphic terms, and this entails, for Barlas, that no gender can be closer to God, more God-like than the other, or more entitled to power and influence. Descriptions of God in male terms are, Barlas argues, heretical. Combined with the egalitarian element contained in the first principle, this means that it is not possible to read the Quran as legitimizing, for instance, physical abuse of women, forced marriages, veiling, and other pre-Islamic practices that have become Muslim practice only through the faulty hermeneutics of atomistic readings of the Quran.

Barlas' immanent critique (to address my second question) thus claims to represent a more genuinely Islamic stance than currently dominant forms by virtue of its faithfulness to the Quran's message. This leads naturally to my third question, concerning agency: that is, what it is that puts her in a good position to make the latter claim. She insists that a legitimate and effective immanent critic must acknowledge the Quran as divinely revealed. It is also clear, however, that from her point of view her way of deriving a hermeneutic from widely accepted Islamic commitments enables her to critically expose problems with contemporary Islamic hermeneutics.

From the point of view of a secular academy, this rather unorthodox application of hermeneutic theory may pass as just another interpretive tradition among many. However, what Barlas describes as the shared Muslim view of belief in the Quran's status as divinely revealed and thus infallible helps her avoid a looming relativism as well as the conservative readings she primarily opposes. Despite their differences, both these approaches reveal a similar lack of faith in the Quran.

Given the central role that Barlas assigns to the Quran, it is only natural that she also takes the Quran itself to supply the appropriate measure of the extent to which we make progress. Since she understands the Quran to be deeply egalitarian, it follows that increased equality (for instance, between the sexes) becomes the primary measure of progress.

Kwok

Kwok is deliberately less explicit about what she takes to be the constitutive elements of a properly Christian tradition (my first question). In fact, from her postcolonial feminist point of view, attempts to pin down some essence or clear criteria of an authentic Christian tradition are problematic, and if they are to be undertaken at all, they need to highly inclusive. The major problem with Christianity in its classical as well as contemporary forms is, however, easier for Kwok to pinpoint: it concerns the relation to *empire*. According to Kwok, "the most important contribution of postcolonial feminist theology will be to reconceptualize the relation of theology and empire through the multiple lenses of gender, race, class, sexuality, religion, and so forth" (Kwok 2005: 144). The major vice of Christianity is, then, the preoccupation with empire, and that can only be exorcized through a relatively radical critique.

The relation to empire is a pervasive problem for Christianity because, Kwok argues, from its inception Christian theology has either sought approval from a secular empire (such as the Roman or the Western nation-states) or aspired to create an empire in its own right (as the Church in the Middle Ages). This prepossession with power and empire makes Christianity, Kwok claims, an excellent religion for colonizers (Kwok 2005: 15ff).

Turning now to my second question, regarding the form of immanent critique, Kwok insists that constructive immanent critique of Christianity requires that Christians begin to listen to the many Christian "subalterns"—primarily neglected women and various marginalized and colonized groups and peoples—and learn about *their* conceptions of piety, Christology, interreligious dialogue, and so on. These resources are already present in the tradition, though they fly under the radar of more traditional theologies. We can thus say that Kwok's immanent critique also has a synchronic (rather than diachronic) element: the immanent critic needs to return not to some golden age in the past free of aspirations to empire, but to the reflections, actions, and rituals that take place among "subalterns" today as well as in earlier times.

The postcolonial conception of tradition at work here, then, sees Christian traditions as constantly tempted to submit to the desire for domination through homogenization and oppression—and most of the time, religious authorities have not managed to resist that temptation. As an illustration, Kwok argues that theologians have traditionally defined "reason" in ways that favor abstract disembodied reasoning at the expense of a more practical and contextual reasoning, a definition that allows their claims a much broader reach than they could otherwise have. Other individuals' and groups' thinking and reasoning can, at the same time, be dismissed as parochial and uninformed (Kwok 2005: 70–76). Gender is one, though far from the only, important category in these exclusion and domination processes.

There is also, though, from early on, a Christian emphasis on resistance to domination, purity, and oppression. Kwok argues that *postcolonial imagination*, which acknowledges that it is the "female subalterns who experience the intersection of oppressions in the most immediate and brutal way" are best suited to articulate more inclusive theologies (Kwok 2005: 127). In other words, agents who benefit the least from Christianity's preoccupation with empire should have the most influence over the restructuring of Christian traditions. This privilege is conditioned, however, on the egalitarian acknowledgment that there is not one, but many, different subalterns that should all be given a voice. Instead of simply substituting a new hierarchy for the old, we need to move away from hierarchical thought-structures.

The concrete strategy Kwok describes is a postcolonial imagination that operates in at least three different modes. First, *historical imagination* involves learning imaginatively about (and from) the many different forms of life and thought that colonialism and other forms of political and religious oppression have obliterated or marginalized. Second, *dialogical imagination* involves letting different "stories" speak with one another in a mutual exchange where, previously, the colonizers' and Western Christianity's stories dominated. Third, *diasporic imagination* "recognizes the diversity of diasporas and honors the different histories and memories" of migrants of various sorts, a recognition that is particularly important in a world of increasing migration (Kwok 2005: 49). All forms of imagination, Kwok holds, enable us to find axes of overlap between modes of oppression but also, importantly, overlaps between ways of resisting oppression and domination.

Kwok thus draws heavily on postcolonial thought, a strong current in contemporary research, not least in religious studies. She is, however, careful to point out that egalitarianism and concern for the marginalized are in no way alien to the Christian tradition. The kind of "colonizing ideology" she finds in Christian prepossessions with empire is thus only part of the story (Kwok 2005: 83). All over the world, subalterns adopt and reconstruct Christian rites, myths, and beliefs and mingle them with other religions and other practices, and this too is Christianity, Kwok argues. Hence, postcolonial scholarship is an academic entry point that helps Kwok detect and draw attention to what she claims are tendencies already present within Christianity once we look beyond its institutional authorities and formal hierarchies. That is, for Kwok, the only (though important) form of authority that her academic position gives.

One problem for Kwok's antihierarchical and heterogeneous approach to theology is that it becomes relatively hard to know whether states of affairs are improving or not. It is not sufficient that previous subalterns gain power, because that could happen at the expense of other subalterns. This means that for Kwok, as I read her, the judgment that things are progressing can only be made by an appropriately widened community that does not aim to speak with a single voice.

With regard to agency, Kwok's conclusion becomes that the agents must be practicing subalterns, and relatively privileged persons like herself should primarily function as *facilitators* of immanent critique. Here, the very notions of "insider" and "outsider" become contentious, because for privileged parties it will be tempting to adopt a narrow conception of "insiders," while subalterns seeking recognition will naturally seek to broaden and nuance it. However, this does not mean that questions about the facilitator's agency and identity are unimportant: it takes a particular position as partial insider and partial outsider to be able to see both the problems with the current form of Christianity and where to look for the proper means to solve them.

Adler

Adler takes *tradition* to be the central concept of Judaism. Traditions function as bridges between past and future, and between theory and practice (Adler 1998: xv). With regard to my first question, Adler suggests that traditions operate with *epistemologies*, that is, a set of norms that help identify which sources to consider authoritative and which forms of reasoning subjects may draw on. Epistemologies thus offer resources but also set limits for immanent critique. In Judaism, the dominant epistemologies have a patriarchal character that consistently neglects women and women's perspectives and experiences. Still, Judaism cannot exist, Adler holds, without tradition and its epistemologies; hence, critics need to work with those epistemologies in order to revise, rather than reject, them.

The current epistemologies' male-dominated character prevents them, however, from functioning as bridges between past and future for contemporary Judaism. They therefore stand in need of reconstruction. Reconstruction requires, Adler proposes, that we distance ourselves from the tendency among both Orthodox and Reform Jews to treat tradition as a kind of artifact shut off from society and immune to change. Tradition can, in its proper form, "inform itself with lived realities," and it "commit[s] its adherents to a moral vision in which these realities are contingent and open to transformation" (Adler 1998: xxii).

Adler's academic entry point is narratology and narrative analysis, and this is relevant for my second question regarding the form of immanent critique. She takes narratology to be particularly important for readers who wish to understand yet resist the temptation to "assume the text's perspectives and objectives so completely that I temporarily forget my own identity and investments as a woman" (Adler 1998: xxiv). On a narratological approach, texts have no complete and fixed meaning until there are recipients who can react to and negotiate with them. Jewish tradition is hence created ever anew as it is reiterated in new forums and with partially new audiences. Sources like the Torah, Talmud, and so on are the sources a feminist theologian must work with, and the Jewish community cannot change these sources, but it *can* change the dominant epistemologies that regulate which parts of these texts it should emphasize and what recipients can do with them. Adler writes: "Theology's task is to allow the texts of the tradition and the lived experiences of religious communities to keep revealing themselves to one another so the sacred meanings both of text and experience can be renewed" (Adler 1998: xiv). Once the sphere of listeners grows to include women, Judaism's commitment to justice (that applies even to the relation between listeners) can be appealed to as an imperative that obliges us to redress gender inequality wherever we find it. So even a small shift in the direction of a more inclusive Judaism can be the start of a self-reinforcing process.

Adler's analyses result in the conclusion that the current epistemologies of Jewish tradition are only seemingly sophisticated, because they effectively stunt rather than display the richness of input from experience, and then they use this stunted input to legitimate themselves (Adler 1998: 34ff).

One example of Adler's approach is her immanent critique of *Halakhah*, Jewish law. She stresses the need for *law* as a means of identity and continuity for Jewish tradition and its communities, yet rejects classical *Halakhah* for its refusal to acknowledge the importance of context and experience (Adler 1998: 45). Jewish law, like other elements of tradition, is not to be seen as a set of fixed rules focusing on prohibitions, but as a set of guidelines for how to orient oneself.

To make that case, Adler emphasizes how narrative is already constitutive of *Halakhah* in the sense that narratives from the Tanach legitimize many laws (such as against idolatry). However, that very dependence on narrative, and thus on recipients, reveals the need for *Halakhah* to be sensitive to the situation of modern Jewish women and men, and the possible futures to which they may aspire. There is no "original sense" that we can use as a measure for all later interpretations, but there is a continuity in reception that cannot be completely disregarded either.

Adler's diagnosis is therefore that as long as one retains the view of law as a set of prohibitions of, for instance, idolatry, it will be very hard to reform it. However, that very conception of *Halakhah* arose as a response to a particular context and set of problems that are different from the ones Jews face today. She writes: "The purpose of a feminist Jewish hermeneutic is not to reject either text or law but to seek ways of claiming them and living them out with integrity. It keeps faith with texts by refusing to absolve them of moral responsibility. It honors *Halakhah* by affirming its capacity to be created anew" (Adler 1998: 58). On a narrative approach, the way to create *Halakhah* anew is to let Jewish men and women today partake together in the identification of what kind of law a religious community living in modern liberal societies today needs, and how such a law can be derived from the texts and narratives constitutive of Jewish tradition (Adler 1998: 52). The path forward that she sees is a conception of law where it becomes a synthesis of Jewish *praxis* rather than a detailed regulation of a set of practices. This would entail an overarching vision of what Jewish life is like at its best. Such overarching visions need, also, to be presented in narrative form, and thus they can function as legitimizing narratives of new forms of *Halakhah*. Since women's experiences have been particularly marginalized, their presence in this constructive work is particularly important (Adler 1998: 40).

To fend off any relativistic implications, Adler argues that not just any narratives can be told in the name of tradition. The ideas of a covenant between God and the Jewish people, and an unrelenting commitment to justice are, she suggests, nonnegotiable components of these narratives. However, that very commitment to justice cannot tolerate, she holds, a preferential treatment of any group or gender, and this means that attempts to describe God as masculine, for instance, are unacceptable (Adler 1998: 85).

Adler's narrative approach makes—turning now to question three—the question of agency revolve around the issue of which people we consider the proper *recipients* of narrative, because recipients are never passive, but have a say on the way narratives unfold and what moral we should draw from them. Much like Kwok, Adler's competence allows her to combine a role as immanent critic of the status quo with a role as facilitator of critique. Adler seeks to reconstruct epistemologies in such a way that they should become more inclusive, because people committed to the tradition, thus abiding by its narratives, are its best critics. That claim is, of course, itself disputable, and here she draws on both her academic competence and her intimate relation to Jewish tradition to make her case. Although her account does not state that agents practicing immanent critique *must* be Jewish, it suggests that the agents need a nuanced understanding of the kinds of critique current epistemologies despite their conservative character nevertheless make possible, an imaginative narrative grasp of possible Jewish futures and a deep commitment to the tradition. The demands on an outsider thus become rather high.

Discussion: Learning via Exemplars

Instead of rehearsing all the points I have made above, I want, before I close, to concentrate on some more general conclusions of my study of exemplars. A first thing to note is that all the thinkers stress the egalitarian element of tradition that they believe is an inherent feature of monotheism. This, in turn, gives them leverage to criticize past and current hierarchies and power structures as *religious* shortcomings. The inherent egalitarianism in traditions that acknowledge no sovereignty except God's allows them to take a relatively orthodox view of the relation between God and human beings, while at the same time ruling out hierarchies, discrimination, and exclusion, including gender inequality. This element of egalitarianism helps, in different ways, each theologian to launch an immanent critique of their tradition.

Turning secondly to the forms that immanent critique takes for each thinker, it deserves notice that their projects are all mainly oriented toward the comprehensive form of immanent critique advocated by Sabia, because they all seek to effect substantial changes in current norms and understandings. Barlas is, to be sure, relatively close to Stout in that she explicitly refers to something like inference rules when she constructs her case that Islam's constitutive commitment is to the divine character of the Quran. However, the changes she proposes on that foundation would require that the Islamic community should not only reconstruct, but even abandon, very many of its currently accepted inference rules.

Adler is probably the one who pays most attention to external social changes such as increased gender equality and what they imply for a viable religious commitment. Nevertheless, those external forces are, for her, consonant with Judaism's main commitments; hence such forces are perhaps *causally*, but certainly not *epistemically*, external. If they were, there would be no hope of salvaging Judaism in a modern context. So impulses from the outside can bring out, and help us reemphasize, excluded and forgotten elements that are concealed by the currently dominant epistemologies; but this does not alter the fact that change comes, and must come, from within. Like Sabia, the thinkers I study seek resources within the traditions that are, currently, neglected and/or misunderstood, and once we broaden the view of traditions beyond what Stout calls inference rules, immanent critique along the lines sketched by Sabia are perhaps not "something of a mystery" after all.

Another interesting feature of the arguments recounted above concerns the way each thinker also characterizes tradition and its proper ways of working so that their partial status as outsiders—that is, as academic scholars—becomes a significant asset, a competence that gives their critique special weight. Academic authority does not, I pointed out, automatically translate into religious authority. However, each critic is careful to argue that given the shape of each tradition and its major shortcomings, the competences they have acquired in the academy *rightly* offer the critics unique opportunities to offer fair and important critiques of the status quo. Their status as insiders is also important here, because without that nuanced understanding of tradition, they would not qualify as competent critics. Still this is, at the same time, not *sufficient:* the knowledge they have gained from academic research is the decisive component for the particular type of critique they offer. This holds even when Adler and Kwok present themselves as primarily facilitators of critique; you still have to be an agent that comes across as fit to suggest the appropriate changes tradition needs to develop and flourish.

This leads to the most complex set of questions, those concerning agency, and not least to the relation between agent and critique. By and large, Barlas, Kwok, and Adler all aim to use resources from within the tradition itself to bring about change. To accomplish that task, they establish themselves as concerned and competent insiders with a stake in the future of the tradition (a well-earned right to reconstruct each tradition), and as willing to live with the changes they propose.

This means that Green's observations about *trust* become relevant. Green emphasizes that it is as a rule difficult to determine whether the transformative practices wherein we turn tradition upon itself, and venture into partially unknown territory, will really lead to improvements from the tradition's own point of view. To be trustworthy, an agent needs to come across as both *competent* and deeply *engaged*, which includes that they are willing to live with the changes they propose. Barlas' critique of the use of *Tafsir* and *hadiths* as interpretative tools is, for instance, rather radical. She defends that radicalness with the proposal that she is really urging Muslims to return to something even *more* Islamic, namely, the Quran itself, but also by appeal to her academic competence. For the thinkers I have studied, then, it becomes important that they be able to engage in a more far-reaching critique than the linguistically oriented immanent critique of Stout's type. Further, the close connection between agent and critique helps explain, I believe, how we can understand the "mystery" Sabia pointed to, namely, that immanent critics find within the tradition means to criticize current norms and understandings. There is more to being an insider than being familiar with certain inference rules: traditions contain images, rites, symbols, myths, stories, institutions, and much else that, arguably, can be understood and appealed to in different ways and for different purposes.

Here, we also encounter a complicating factor regarding analytic categories such as insider and outsider, or immanent and external critique (cf. Hartman 2005). Not only do judgments about how to categorize critique depend on perspective, and the conception of tradition with which you operate, as I have already pointed out; more importantly, such categorizations can function as ways to dismiss critique as too radical and thus insensitive to tradition. That is, ascriptions and self-ascriptions serve a number of normative purposes in discussions both within and outside the tradition itself. Just as it is difficult to characterize critiques as constructive without tacitly assuming some conception of human flourishing, it may be equally difficult to make disinterested and uncontroversial judgments about whether to classify some critique as immanent rather than external. This is not to say that such ascriptions are arbitrary; it means, however, that the analytical categories themselves become parts of the debate over the proposed changes.

A similar point holds with regard to "insiders" and "outsiders." Given the central role of trust, it becomes important for someone who wishes to come across as a trustworthy critic to position herself as an insider (and her critique as restorative rather than revolutionary). Categorizing someone as an "outsider" is likely part of a dismissal of that person's critique. For persons belonging to some traditionally marginalized group such as women, it almost certainly takes more than it would for persons higher up in the hierarchy to actually be perceived as competent insiders. Grace Jantzen has documented that in the Christian Middle Ages, female mystics were viewed with much suspicion and they had to establish themselves as trustworthy through extreme asceticism and piety that were not expected (to the same degree) of male mystics (Jantzen 1996). And of course, the more radical the critique, the more pressing the question of insider versus outsider becomes.

This normative dimension applies even to the very concept of immanent critique. To acknowledge something as immanent critique (rather than intrusions from external agents and sources) is to already assign it a particular status. "Immanent critique" is hence a kind of *achievement term*. To illustrate with a simple example: to *perceive* something is an achievement because it is not sufficient to happen to be at a particular place and having functioning sense organs to perceive a state of affairs—you can still fail to perceive for a number of reasons. In a similar fashion, it takes competence and commitment to qualify as an immanent critic of the kind capable of moving beyond the use of established inference rules. Whether you are suitable for the task or not will be one of the questions that immanent critics with such ambitions will have to expect.

From this it also follows, of course, that one fast and cheap defense against immanent critique is to question the agent, her competence and, not least, her motives. This risk is probably most obvious for a theologian like Barlas, because her position as a scholar at a Western university—with no traditional connections to religious institutions as is often the case with, for instance, Christianity—can lead people to suspect that she is influenced by Western and "un-Islamic" views of gender and sexuality. The same critical points can, though, certainly apply to the others as well: critiques of Christian universities are, for instance, not uncommon among Christian theologians, to take just one example (Hauerwas 2010). Hence it is not surprising that Barlas, for instance, works hard to establish herself as a reliable insider both competent and engaged enough to work in accordance with, rather than against, tradition by picking up on and reinforcing already received views about the sacred status of the Quran. Hermeneutic theory functions, in this argument, as a way of explicating, not reconstructing, Islamic commitments.

The forms of immanent critique that my exemplars practice are hence such that it becomes hard to separate judgments about whether the critique is constructive and worth taking seriously or not from judgments about the agents presenting the critique. This is somewhat frustrating for a philosopher like me, who prefers to concentrate on arguments regardless of where they come from, but I think my study reveals that an insider can practice a wider range of immanent critiques, but the price she must pay is that her own motives, position, and competence become part of the debate.

However, it is worth remembering that the method I have chosen has its limitations, and one such limitation is that it leaves open the possibility that there are other forms of immanent critique (not to mention other forms of constructive critique) that can be much more accessible to outsiders. Such critique could take inspiration from Stout and seek to point to contradictions and tensions within a religious tradition's ways of working and making inferences.

I believe, though, that as long as we discuss *comprehensive* forms of immanent critique, it seems likely that questions about the agents' competences, motives, and commitments—regardless of whether the critics *want* the discussions to circle around such questions or not, and regardless of whether we think this is fair and fortunate or not—will have a prominent role. And, ironically, it seems likely (though this is a matter I have not studied in detail) that when it comes to questions of competence and being a trustworthy agent, feminist critics such as the ones I have discussed will be judged more harshly than many others, given the very lack of gender equality that they so forcefully oppose.

4

Internal Critique in Muslim Context

Mohammad Fazlhashemi

A common perception, of apologetic nature, is that religious criticism is not possible within Islamic theology and jurisprudence. It is based on the notion that in Islam the Quran is regarded as the word of God and thus forever constant. Likewise, the prophetic tradition is seen as something to be followed by Muslims because Muhammad was chosen by God and thus inalienable. It is impossible to ignore the fact that these beliefs have had a firm grip on Muslim thinking, especially in theology and Sharia jurisprudence, but the question is whether they have prevented disparate interpretations and critique within Islam. A look back on the history of Islam shows that Muslims have been involved in a long dispute concerning the supremacy of interpretations in many areas like theology, philosophy, jurisprudence, and even sectarian disagreements. The critique has been expressed in rather harsh words against the opposite camp, which in some cases has gone as far as stamping each other as heretics and renegades.

The critique within Islam is not limited to contemporary Muslim thinkers. We find many historical examples of critical views within Islamic theology and philosophy as well as the broad literary tradition of the Muslim world. Criticism has been designed in different ways. Common to the criticism is its internal character, that is to say, the critics are Muslims themselves. However, one cannot ignore the fact that much of the criticism has been inspired by external factors, such as the changes that Muslim societies have undergone during different ages, especially during the modern era. The criticism is pointed at different recipients. It contains criticism of Muslim authorities, criticism aimed at Sharia laws and Islamic jurisprudence, and also anticlerical criticism. In the latter case, the critique has been aimed at Muslim authorities for their shortcomings or because they wanted to force a rigid form of religious beliefs or lifestyle on people. Another category of internal critique has concerned the interpretation of justice and its basic idea of considering Sharia law as eternal and unchangeable. The purpose of this criticism has been to modify and improve the interpretation of the law, since it has been perceived that they were based on conditions which are not compatible with today's life. The internal critique has been formed through interactions between Muslim thinkers and ideas and conditions that they have been dealing with historically and today.

The internal critique of Islam has not been monothematic; rather, such critique has focused on different targets. Some Muslims, as we will see, have criticized limitations on women's rights in Islam and patriarchal structures, others the ban on homosexuality and Sharia laws. Other targets of the internal criticism have been the anti-rationalistic tendency of Muslim orthodoxy, the dogmatism and blind faith of religious authorities, and their rejection of political secularism.

The ambitions of the internal Muslim critique have been unmistakable. The purpose has been to reform established interpretations. This ambition is not limited to any particular direction, but is more or less in both Sunni and Shiite Islam. However, it is not a matter of equal distribution among all directions within Islam.

All research shows that we do not meet any uniform interpretation of Islamic sources. The diversity depends on many different factors, such as different schools of law in Sunni and Shiite Islam, their different methods for interpretation, the different principles they use in Islamic jurisprudence, and the extent to which they allow the use of reason and critical thinking.

An important component of the interpretation of the law has been the principle of consistency or coherence, *Ijma'*. Everything that falls outside what has been agreed by a majority of jurists/scholars has been rejected as deviations. This principle has at the same time served as an effective barrier rendering any kind of change very difficult. Parallel to this, the Islamic legal tradition opens up the possibility of contesting and giving a separate and dissimilar interpretation. Anyone who has achieved a sufficient level of education is also entitled to raise his/her own interpretations and perceptions. This means that you may be entitled to your own interpretations, which necessarily do not have to follow the majority opinion. This right has created the opportunity to challenge the authorities. Against the vertical hierarchy throughout the history of Islam, a horizontal form has been established which has contradicted the current interpretation. This has meant that it has not been possible to prevent divergent opinions. However, this plurality of voices regarding legal interpretation has not yielded profound change.

The contemporary critical voices do not risk remaining divergent and individual voices that only receive response in intellectual and academic milieus. Globalization, the increased level of education among young Muslims, and the revolution in information technology help these voices evoke empty responses among the broad Muslim public. They have rather opened up new opportunities for these critical views to reach an ever-increasing group of Muslims. There has also been a change at the level of players. Today, there are young and highly educated women from middle and upper classes participating in this process (Bano and Kalmbach 2012).

In the contemporary discussions, we meet a polyphonic debate concerning the Sharia laws and other vital principles in Islam. The critique challenges the already established interpretations of the Quran and the prophetic tradition. It claims that these views and interpretations are in disharmony with current cultural references, global social structures, modern political ideas, modern human visions, and international conventions and legal frameworks. The critique is aimed primarily at the Sharia laws, which advocate restrictions on individual civil rights, gender equality, minority rights, etc. The representatives of these critical views do not let themselves be limited by presumptions like the eternity and immutability of the Quran. Their ambition is to modify, reform, and in some cases completely change those Sharia laws and Islamic traditions/beliefs that exclude or oppress people and deny them their human and civil rights on the basis of their gender, faith, lack of faith, etc.

The purpose of this chapter is to discuss the actors and motives for the internal Muslim critique. The essence of Muslim internal critique seems to be the challenging of the universalism of Muslim traditions as if they were eternal and unchangeable. These critics try to show that many of these laws have been influenced by premodern social structures and cultural, economic, and historical references. For this purpose, they use various methods such as hermeneutic interpretation and text-critical, contextual, norm-critical reading of the texts, etc., to demonstrate different methods for critical reviews of stereotypical, schematic, and categorical representations.

Norm-Critical Reading

The Moroccan sociologist Fatima Mernissi (1940–2015) discusses the historical circumstances under which Islam's prophet Mohammad made his statements and actions. In her mind, Mohammad was a historical character, a reformer whose actions were influenced by contemporary references.

Mernissi discusses Islamic Sharia laws that allow for the restriction of women's rights. She emphasizes that previous traditional intertextual and contextual studies of these regulations must be supplemented by norm-critical reviews such as a gender perspective. She takes, for example, the Quran's ordinance which gives women less inheritance compared to men. According to Mernissi, this is because women were excluded from power because of the patriarchal structure. In the absence of women, men abused their opportunities to create rules that gave them benefits at the expense of women. They created a kind of gender order that cemented inequality between men and women. This gender inequality became the foundation for laws and institutions whereby inequality was maintained through the history of Islam.

Mernissi's criticism is directed at the perception that Sharia laws cannot be changed. She believes that the fact that often it is people who have established these laws means that they are of human nature and thus may be interpreted, questioned, or dismissed. This paves the way for a reform of Sharia law by way of the conclusion that these laws, although derived from the Quran, were adapted to human relations in the first century and for that reason, they must be modified and developed so that they are harmonized with today's reality. This means, therefore, a kind of adjustment with the present situation and its social structures, cultural references, and human perceptions.

Mernissi is not satisfied with some controversial Quranic verses. One example is the Quranic verse that calls for assault on women.[1] She combines a gender perspective with historical contextualization in her review of this Quranic verse. Her point of departure is that the view of women expressed in this verse is based on the social structures and cultural references of the Arabian Peninsula, which are incompatible with today's equality thinking. Mernissi is critical of previous interpreters' understanding of this verse, which defends in one way or another its misogynist message. She believes that it should be understood based on contextual circumstances and rejects the idea that the message is to be defended or promoted. She points out that, despite his basic pro-female approach, and despite the fact that Mohammad was chosen by God, he was a human who acted in a socioeconomic, cultural, and historical context. Mernissi believes that Islam's early history testifies that Mohammad had to interact with the sociocultural and political context of the Arab Peninsula in the 620s and 630s. Mohammad's goal was to lay the foundations for a new society based in Islam, but it also happened that he was forced to adapt to current conditions. Sometimes he was forced to retreat and sometimes he managed to compromise.

Mernissi considers that there is historical evidence that shows that Mohammad had to give way to the demands of his male companions regarding women's rights. The male elites were afraid that their position of power would be undermined by women's new position in the young Muslim community. Therefore they demanded a reintroduction of pre-Islamic patriarchal traditions, such as the man's right to decide on his wife and his right to use physical violence to get his will through. If Mohammad had opposed their demands, the continued existence of young Muslim society and Islam could have been endangered. For example, they could choose to unite themselves with the enemies of Mohammad and thereby threaten his position. It was in these circumstances that Mohammad was forced to give up his pro-female ambitions. Today, such threats do not exist, Mernissi says, and thus they can overlook such misogynist messages and consider them as invalid.

Islamic Theological Ethics

The purpose of norm criticism seems to be the foundation of a kind of theological humanism. It wants to explore if respect for the particularly religious assumptions can be united with respect for humankind. It concerns assumptions such as the Muslim belief that God has created all the people of the same substance and that God breathed into them of his own spirit.[2] This idea is used as a basis for a kind of natural justice equality system that assumes that all people are equal and criticizes those interpretations that legitimize inequality. Some Muslim thinkers, such as the Sudanese law professor Abdullahi Ahmed an-Naim (born 1946), interpret the Quran's idea that God has blown his spirit into humanity as evidence that God attributes humanity a specific individual dignity that may not be violated.

An additional perception based on the Quran that reinforces this protection is that the human is God's deputy on earth, writes an-Naim (Quran, 2:30, 35:39). In order to be able to live up to this responsibility, all people need an irreversible protection that creates the prerequisite for people to live up to their commitments (an-Naim 1990: 19).

It is interesting to note that the basis for this protection is based on natural law arguments that are in turn reinforced with ethical issues. From an internal Muslim tradition, the proponents of this idea talk about an intrinsic human ethical compass, *fitra*, with which God has equipped the human being since birth. This is a natural ethical navigation device that helps people to distinguish between right and wrong, good and evil, and act to fairly (Quran, 30:30).

One cannot ignore, however, that there are major gaps between the traditional interpretation of Islamic Sharia law and international conventions such as the UN Declaration of Human Rights. The question is whether it is possible to bridge the gaps in any way. Jurisprudence and interpretation have traditionally been the way through which Muslim thinkers have tried to solve the problem, but the legal model is not always the most optimal way. The theological ethics and the criticisms that have been arisen from this point of view against traditional interpretation are highlighted as the best way to create protection for the irreversible dignity of the human (Sachedina 2009: 118, 174–75).

Kecia Ali (born 1972), professor of religion, uses this model in her discussion about sexual ethics in Islam. She believes that Muslim scholars' legal interpretations and reasoning are in many aspects contrary to gender equality based on ethical justice and natural law. She discusses the changes that legal interpretation have undergone and their consequences from a legal and ethical perspective. Ali discusses what it is that makes certain sexual relationships represented as legal and others as illegal. She emphasizes that the view of legal sexual relations has changed in Islam during the course of history. An example is the view on sexual relations with slaves; while previously, it was allowed to have sex with slaves, the possession of slaves and sexual relations with them are forbidden in all modern Muslim legal systems. The only exception is the terrorist groups like Daesh/ISIS or Boko Haram, who still apply the sex slave system. Ali believes that this example shows that the view on sexuality and what are considered as legal or illegal relationships has changed in Islam. She raises the question of whether this changing approach, which has taken place through new interpretation, and because of social and political pressure, can also cover other areas. For example, she mentions women's rights, the separation between females and males that is applied in public places in Muslim countries, or the views on homosexuality.

Gender equality issues and women's rights have been discussed since the late nineteenth century in the Muslim context. They have led, among other things, to new interpretations and some, although limited, legislative improvements in some Muslim countries, but the issue of homosexuality has remained controversial and taboo-based. With reference to Islamic sources, homosexuality is classified as illegal in the Islamic jurisprudence. Ali writes that it is impossible to ignore the legal ban on homosexuality, but wonders whether this ban is compatible with the idea of divine justice in Islam. Given the assumption made by Muslim scholars that homosexuality is innate and thus has not been chosen by the individual, the prohibition becomes incompatible with divine justice. It is God who is the cause of this kind of sexual desire of homosexual people. Ali emphasizes that according to Islam, sexuality is a natural instinct of human beings, actually a very strong instinct that can or should not be suppressed.

Ali states that since marriage in Islamic jurisprudence is defined as a legal agreement between women and men, it is impossible to legalize homosexuality within the framework of this institution. The question she asks is whether it should also be considered as unethical. She discusses the legalization of homosexuality from an ethical point of view and takes as her starting point the changing view of sexual relations with slaves. In all schools of Muslim law today, slavery and sex slavery are classified as illegitimate and unethical—even though this form of sexual relations from a strictly legalistic perspective is permitted according to the Quran and is not legally prohibited. Ali believes that Muslims can use the changing view on sex with slaves in the case of homosexuality. The reason why Islamic law schools have banned slavery and sex with slaves is that they are considered ethically unacceptable. A majority of Muslim lawmakers have come to the conclusion—with support from international conventions, and with help of the principle of legal methodology of consensus, *ijma'*—that these phenomena are incompatible with Islamic ethics. Concerning homosexuality, there is therefore a clear legal ban on it in Islamic jurisprudence, and a majority of Muslim jurists regard it as unauthorized. However, Ali asks, does homosexuality necessarily entail being unethical? Should we not recognize a difference between legal and ethical, she asks? In the case of slavery and sexual relations with slaves, Muslim jurists have made this distinction. Ali states that since God has created all human beings, it would be contrary to God's justice to deny one group of people their sexual rights.

Unthought, Unthinkable, Untouchable

Another criticism is directed toward the approach to what is called the Islamic tradition. The criticism is aimed at Muslim authorities' view of the status of the Quran as the word of God, as something that should be considered as eternal and unchangeable—an idea that also includes the statements and actions of Islam's prophet Mohammad. Criticism is aimed at the uncritical and almost nostalgic approach to these Islamic sources. The late Algerian-French professor of the history of ideas Muhammed Arkoun (1928-2010) was one of those who demanded a critical, humanistic-scientific reading and approach to the Islamic sources.

Arkoun distinguishes between the classic era of history of Islam (the period between the seventh and thirteenth centuries) and the time thereafter. After the classical era, Muslim intellectual life suffered from a lack of critical thinking, according to Arkoun. A consequence of this development has been the uncritical relationship with Muslim authorities and what they honor as Muslim heritage and Islamic tradition. In characterizing Muslim thinking during this period, he talks about the thought, the unthought, the thinkable, and the unthinkable. The unthought is the part of the Muslim legacy which for various reasons has not been the subject of thinking among Muslim thinkers. Religious and legalist prohibition have caused a kind of fear among Muslim thinkers to approach these specific areas. He believes that there is usually no religious prohibition. But in cases in which such bans have existed, he wants to examine the religious, ideological, cultural, and political reasons for these prohibitions. The fact is that these prohibitions have restricted Muslim intellectual life by classifying issues and areas as unthinkable and creating what can be called as unthought issues/areas. The purpose of examining these obstacles is to reduce the unreachable and unthinkable issues/areas.

His main criticism is directed against Muslim thinkers who are stuck in dogmatism and blind faith in religious authorities. They have prevented a critical approach to the attitudes of Muslim authorities and to Islamic sources. Dogmatism and blind faith in Muslim authorities have also been used to legitimize various forms of political ideologies, including political Islam. Instead of dogmatism and blind faith in authorities, Arkoun calls for a critical review of the Quran. He wants, however, to anchor the critical approach in Islam, particularly by emphasizing the critical thinking that existed in Islam. He highlights the theological and philosophical traditions during Islam's classical era, which gave critical thinking a special position in Muslim thinking. In addition to the most famous Muslim theologians and philosophers, such as al-Kindi, al-Farabi, Ibn Sina (Avicenna), Ibn Rushd (Averroes), etc., he particularly emphasizes the Persian Muslim philosopher Ibn Miskawayh (932–1030) as a representative of this critical tradition. However, this critical tradition was pushed back by Muslim orthodoxy and the emerging dogmatism. One of those who Arkoun blames for this is the Persian theologian Abu Hamid al-Ghazali (1058–1111), who in his book *Tahafut al-falasifa* (*The Contradictions of Philosophers*), directed harsh criticism against Islamic philosophy and thereby cemented the decline of the philosophical tradition in Islam.

Arkoun accuses Muslim orthodoxy of having a close relation to and being allied with the representatives of power. Influenced by Foucault's ideas of hegemony, he claims that Muslim authorities for long periods after the classical era gave their support to those who had the political power. This has resulted in some areas remaining as unthought, unthinkable, and thus beyond critical examination by Muslim thinking. Arkoun calls for a theological and philosophical innovation, which is necessary for any form of change in Muslim communities. Parallel to this, a change in mentality is also needed to challenge the perceptions that exist in the minds of the population. This challenge and change is necessary because this mentality, along with authority and lack of critical thinking, has been used by extremist or conservative forces to manipulate Muslims. The uncritical approach has been used in areas such as the interpretation of the Quran, the history of Islam, the concept of Jihad, ideas about non-Muslims and their rights, and conceptions about those who have been classified as unbelievers and about the land of unbelievers, *dar al-kufr*.

Arkoun believes that the optimal way to become acquainted with the key components of Muslim thinking is by "removing the clothing" from existing Muslim thinking and Muslim inheritance, rendering it naked. Arkoun was inspired by the postmodernist thinker Jacques Derrida and his theory of the need for the deconstruction of tradition. When he talks about the undressing of the Muslim legacy and thinking, it is precisely this type of deconstruction he is aiming for. He wants to deconstruct it to get away from a constant reproduction of the tradition.

According to Arkoun, the Islamic tradition and the Muslim legacy have been developed by the actors who have been involved in designing of the tradition. These actors, in turn, have been influenced by their contemporary ideas and specific conditions, such as social, cultural, and historical references. With deconstruction as a method, he wants to distinguish between the different layers of ideas that have been stacked together in Muslim thinking and inheritance. He is driven by the idea that it is possible to distinguish between context-based thinking and what he describes as key components of Muslim thinking.

The starting point for Arkoun is that the Islamic tradition is text-based and should therefore be studied as such. It is based on the Quran and the prophetic tradition (and in Shia Islam on the traditions of Shiite imams). To these texts come the exegetical interpretations that have been reproduced in Islamic jurisprudence for centuries. By emphasizing that tradition is nothing but a text, he opens the possibility of relating to tradition and heritage as historical texts that can and must be subjected to hermeneutical and other forms of historical interpretation.

Arkoun emphasizes that the Quran is a text whose different parts differ from one another. They have different characters and convey different types of messages. The Quran is a text that has a clear sender, God; a recipient, the people; and a mediator, Mohammad. However, Mohammad, who acts as a messenger and mediator, appears in some sections as the addressee of the text. In addition to Mohammad, the language and the historical and cultural traditions and references affect the medieval world. The relationship between God and people is not a one-way directed conversation. There are texts that show that God interacts with people, revels in their wonder, and answers their questions. All this places the Quran in a specific position, which Arkoun calls the hermeneutics of the holy text.

It is precisely this specific character of the Quran that makes it possible to use hermeneutics for a contextual interpretation of its content. He prefers the hermeneutical model instead of philological analysis because the later tends to get lost staring at extreme linguistic details. This was what affected the philologically educated orientalists.

Arkoun argues that the scientific tradition and critical thinking are not foreign to Islam. With reference to the development of classical philosophy and theology in the early history of Islam, he concludes that the prerequisites for a humanistic-scientific approach are potentially within Islam. However, this tradition was obsessed with orthodoxy and Sufism.

The most distinctive feature of Arkoun's work is that it does not stop at the classic era of Islam. This era was influenced by its contemporary socioeconomic, cultural, and historical references. For Arkoun, it is not enough to just revitalize their tradition of thinking: Muslims need to move on and complete the traditions of classical philosophers and theologians with the tools that modern humanities offer. It should be studied by use of hermeneutical, linguistic, historical, sociological, theological, religious, and other modern methods and theoretical models. There is no area excluded from these studies. This approach applies to everything from the faith in God to those dichotomous views that place people in different compartments: believers – non-believers/unfaithful; those who have salvation – the misguided; pure – unclean; path of light – path of darkness; male – female; etc. In this regard, Muslim thinkers can be inspired by the models that modern Christian thinkers applied in their analyses of central dogmas in Christianity, he considers.

Arkoun talks about Islam as both a religion and a thinking tradition. It is important for him not to begin to determine what the Islamic tradition is. The Quran as well as the tradition must be studied critically. It is only through a critical reading that we can distinguish between different interpretations of Islamic sources, that is, the orthodox and nonorthodox traditions. This assumes that all who call themselves Muslims through the history of Islam must be part of a comprehensive study of the Islamic heritage and its traditions of thinking. According to Arkoun, only one way comes from the locked situation that orthodoxy and Muslim authorities have created. This solution is critical thinking and questioning of central dogmas. This, however, requires freedom of expression so that everyone can make their critical questions and that all views can be presented. It is only in this way you can solve the problem of the unthought, the unthinkable, and the untouchable, which have been some of the greatest obstacles of Muslim thinking.

The Complexity of the Muslim Heritage

Another thinker who actualized the need for a critical attitude towards the Muslim tradition and the Muslim legacy was the Moroccan philosopher Mohammed Abed al-Jabri (1935–2010). He was not only critical of the relation to the Muslim tradition, but also of the tradition itself. This is characterized by a limitation of critical thinking, where all forms of thinking are limited to a textual and intertextual interpretation of the Quran and the prophetic tradition. The problem is that reason and rational thinking do not get free play space but are controlled within certain limits.

Al-Jabri assumes that the limited space that the Islamic tradition gives to reason through analogous conclusion, *qiyas*, is far from adequate because everything must still be anchored in what is called the word of God. To try to find a connection between what reason has found and what is found in the Quran and the tradition of the Prophet is nothing but a limitation. This model leaves a very small space for reason. The situation worsened even more when the Islamic mysticism, Sufism, and its intuitive knowledge penetrated the philosophical mindset. Intuition did not leave room for rational argumentation. Al-Jabri wants to revive the legacy of classical Muslim philosophers and thereby replace the obstinate traditional mindset. What distinguished the classical philosophers was that they broke with the perennial need to balance between religious and rational thinking. They considered that the recurring reconciliation between reason and revelation made it impossible to develop ideas based on new scientific perceptions.

Al-Jabri believes that the relationship with the Islamic tradition has to change. The tradition is an inseparable part of the history of ideas of Islam. The solution is not to abandon the tradition, but to use a critical perspective. It is about reviving a philosophical tradition that had a central position in Muslim thinking during the classical era of Islam. This critique should be seen as a renewal of thought that takes its starting point in the conditions and references of the contemporary world.

He distinguishes between what he calls *La raison constituante*, the constituent reason, and *La raison constituée*, the designed reason/mindset. The latter consists of a collection of thoughts and ideas that have been established and have taken their shape and components from a certain period of time and under specific social structures and cultural references. They should therefore be regarded as time-limited. The constituent reason/thinking has to do with what is happening in our contemporary age. The problem has been that the constituent reason/thinking has stepped aside for the designed mindset or Muslim legacy. Instead of reviewing this legacy and examining whether it can answer to the challenges that Muslims face today, the main issue has been to defend the legacy. Al-Jabri criticizes Muslim authorities and thinkers who seek answers to the questions in the legacy itself. Their attempt to reconstruct the tradition is doomed because today's Muslim societies differ from the premodern Muslim societies. Muslims should examine their history, their traditions, and their legacy with new eyes. A first step is to break the influence of the authorities and to release themselves from the burden of tradition, without breaking the contact with their history.

Al-Jabri notes that it is important to underline that the constituent thinking is not unfamiliar for Islam, but it requires the freedom to have a critical relationship to the Muslim heritage. It is neither possible nor wise to completely cut all bonds with the history. However, maintaining the contact of the present with the past and tradition does not mean to equate them; it is more about a renewal of thinking that looks at the Islamic tradition through the conditions and references of the modern world. An uncritical approach means to deal with the issues and dilemmas that today's Muslims are facing with solutions that have their roots in a premodern reality. This means to try to adjust the present to the past.

Authorities and Secularity

Another Muslim thinker discussing the necessity of critical thinking within Islam is the Iranian philosopher Abdulkarim Soroush (born 1946). He writes about the need for a scientific approach to the beliefs associated with the Islamic tradition. His critique is directed against religious authorities and their power over Muslim thinking. He seeks the background for the lack of critical thinking in the setbacks for the Aristotelian-inspired Muslim philosophy, which coincided with the emergence of orthodoxy and Sufism in the 1200s.

Soroush criticizes the traditional view of religious knowledge that has come to be considered as holy. According to Soroush, there must be a distinction between Islam's transcendent norm and its concrete design in religious practice. Inspired by Karl Popper's (1902-1994) evolutionary epistemology, he defines knowledge as hypotheses that have undergone testing (falsification) and conform to reality. Religious knowledge—theology and jurisprudence—is, according to this definition, of the same historical character as other profane knowledge. This means that religious knowledge should be considered as inadequate and hypothetical knowledge, which means that it can be subject to the same scientific criteria as other humanities.

He distinguishes between different levels of secularity. The most important thing is the secularization of the state and a strictly rational interpretation of religious texts. He thus distances himself from the deterministic element in the discussions about secularization and emphasizes that it should not be perceived as the vanishing of religion under the pressure of modernization. To underline that this distinction is not strange to Muslim thinking, he emphasizes that there has been a secular tradition within Islam. The essential thing is to find the balance between the religious and secular in Islam and make sure that they do not interfere with each other's areas. One area where secularity appears in a clear way in Islam is the responsibility of every individual in her/his religious beliefs and practice. The secular in this context is that religiosity and faith are an affair between the individual and God.

A very prominent dimension in Islam is to seek to overcome social, economic, political, and other forms of injustice and create a world characterized by security, legal certainty, freedom, and justice. Soroush interprets this as evidence that Islam is a worldly religion that values the good life of this world. The secular in this context is that Islam is not a religion that rejects this world and a good life in favor of the world beyond. Muslims are urged to take their share of this worldly life (Soroush 1997: 167–70). The most prominent aspect of Islam is, according to Soroush, its philosophical secularism. The origins of its philosophical ideas were contacts with ancient Greek philosophy. In the field of science, the open reception and further development of the scientific heritage of the Babylonians, Indians, Persians, and other highly developed cultures constituted the basis for the progress of Muslims. Soroush describes the ideas of the Mutazilits, early Muslim philosophers and theologians, as arising from a secular mindset that approached the most vital issues in Islam in a non-confessional way. They had a rational starting point.

There is, however, an area where the secular tradition has been absent in the Muslim world, namely, political secularism, a separation between the state and religious institutions. Soroush believes that Muslim thinkers have been struggling with major problems in this area. His main point is that theocracy has no support in Islam, because religiosity and ruling are legally two completely different things in Islam. Political secularism means that the state does not allow itself to be ruled by religious institutions. He believes that the lack of political secularism in modern times in Muslim countries stems from two circumstances. One is based on a misunderstanding of the definition of this term: political secularism has been perceived as an anti-religious tradition and an attack on religion. This is mainly due to the secularization campaigns that took place in Muslim countries in the 1920s and 1930s and that authoritarian state-owned forces and secular intellectuals supported. These campaigns entailed intense attacks on religion and its representatives.

The second reason for the lack of political secularization is an outdated view of the legitimacy of political power. During the premodern era, rulers gained their legitimacy in religion, and they were to follow the orders and prohibitions of religion. In today's modern world, legitimacy is based on the votes of the citizens in free and democratic elections. The relations between the state and citizens are governed by civil law, writes Soroush (1997: 423).

It is only through political secularization that a state can guarantee freedom and diversity in society. In a pluralist society, it is the individual, the citizen, who decides whether they want to be or not to be religious. It is based on individuality and volunteering and the choice between a multitude of interpretations. Characteristic of this society is that it is nonideological and hence free from official interpretations of religion as well as interpreters who represent the state (Soroush 1999: 49). Soroush explains that the absence of political secularism was a result of the decline of the philosophical approach. That was also the reason of the lack of distinction between civil rights and religious duties (1999: 424–27).

It is therefore a mindset that does not look at society as a divine creation, where everything has been assigned a predetermined place by God. Human society appears rather as a study object that can be quantitatively and qualitatively examined by human and social sciences. Viewed from this perspective, society, politics, the economy, and the laws have arisen from human activities. He emphasizes that nothing in the field of politics avoids trial. Politics becomes a profane and thus a "non-holy" arena, and dealing with it does not risk infringing the area of religion (1999: 428–29).

Criticism against Sharia

Characteristic of many contemporary Muslim thinkers is their criticism against Muslim Sharia law with the motivation that many of these laws are in direct conflict with basic modern human rights. One example is Tanzanian professor of religious studies Abdelaziz Sachedina (born 1942), who explores the possibility of finding support for human rights in Islam. He admits without any reservations that the traditional Islamic interpretation is in contrast with human rights. He states, however, that it is possible to find some form of harmony between Islamic justice and respect for human rights. A prerequisite to this is a "re/new-interpretation" of these laws. He takes as an example the discrimination against women in Sharia laws. He presents an alternative interpretation based on the narrative of creation in the Quran, which claims that God created humans (regardless of gender) of the same substance. He believes that based on this narrative, one can support the idea of equal value and rights, regardless of gender, faith, and other reasons (Sachedina 2009: 175).

Sachedina believes that with the help of such alternative interpretations, it is possible to replace discriminatory Sharia laws against women, religious minorities, or other groups. He believes that structural problems are one major obstacle for alternative interpretations. Another reason for the discriminatory Sharia laws is the interpretation of men, who have made a gender and power order that disadvantages women.

One way to deal with the structural problems is that proposed by the Iranian theologian Mohsen Kadivar (born 1959). He launches the model of teleological (purpose-oriented) interpretation of Sharia laws. He believes that there are basic and noble values in Islam that must be safeguarded. These are values like justice and human dignity. These basic norms and values, however, have been interpreted on the basis of pre-modern social structures, cultural references, or other factors that make them inconsistent with today's human perceptions and values. One should not throw out the baby with the bathwater, he writes. He wants to protect these basic values by creating harmony between the interpretation of these and modern human perceptions of and respect for human rights.

An-Naim challenges that the traditional interpretation of Sharia law arises against individual rights. An-Naim believes that Sharia laws should be seen as a collection of legal and ethical principles compiled by Muslim lawyers based on their interpretations of the Quran and the Prophet's tradition. It began as an oral tradition and took about 200 years to compile. In other words, Sharia is a human design, and the first lawmakers did not intend to create a static application and understanding of them. He also emphasizes that these interpretations have been strongly influenced by historical, economic, cultural, and social references. Instead of the traditional and literary interpretation, he wants to base the interpretation on a pattern that can be recognized from other Muslim thinkers, that is, natural rights and theological ethics. An-Naim would rather see Sharia as a kind of pointer for a good Muslim life. It should not be seen as a generally applicable legal system (an-Naim 1990: 17–19).

Another criticism that an-Naim addresses towards traditional interpretation is that earlier scholars usually discussed Sharia on the basis of the problems that people confronted as individuals. Their interpretations were not primarily intended for civil institutions or the relationship between state and society.

His main criticism is that Sharia is the result of over fourteen hundred years of interpretations. Many of the rights that are taken for granted today were not even envisaged. Today, we talk about fundamental individual rights for every person, regardless of background, faith, gender, etc. Many Sharia laws are based on religious or gender affiliation. This leads him to the perception that the traditional interpretation of Sharia cannot be applied today because it violates basic human rights. However, he does not want to reject Sharia per se and rather calls for a modern and creative interpretation of the records that takes the modern rights perspective as its starting point.

The Iranian theologian Mohammad Mojtahed Shabestari (born 1936) aims harsh criticism against Islamic legal interpretation based on an anthropocentric perspective. According to him, modern human rights are based on values beyond the traditional model of interpretation. They are based on values derived from the conditions and structures of modern society, while the traditional legal interpretation was designed long before human society was influenced by the structural changes of modernity and its new human perception.

Mojtahed Shabestari is also critical of the view that regards regulations in the Quran as the words of God and therefore forever valid. According to him, they cannot be raised to a level of meta-historical laws, because they are based on social, cultural, and other pre-modern structures and conditions that are not compatible to today's conditions. For example, he mentions the distinction made in Sharia law between people because of their gender, religion, and other reasons. Inspired by the theories of the German theologian and religious philosopher Friedrich Schleiermacher (1768–1834), Mojtahed Shabestari sees the interpretations of religious scholars as human reflections. These reflections have been influenced by historical and social structures and by the language, which, in its turn, is penetrated by cultural references and a variety of different factors (Mojtahed Shabestari 2004: 47–49). His point is that in the Islamic tradition, the interpretations of Muslim scholars and their sources are exempt from a critical, historical, and phenomenological review. These laws and regulations, whose roots go back to the pre-Islamic era and have been influenced by contacts with other cultures and religious traditions, must be examined through a critical perspective based on scientific methodologies and theories (2004: 43–47).

Conclusion

Internal criticism of Islam is based on both epistemological motives and a critical attitude towards Islam's records. In some cases, the criticism has targeted different issues in Islam. In other cases, i.e., anti-clerical criticism, the target has been Muslim authorities, who have been blamed for their shortcomings and hypocrisy. Yet another part of criticism has taken its starting point in philosophical and theological questions. This criticism, which can be regarded as radical, is directed at some basic beliefs in Islamic doctrine or Sharia laws, because the latter are seen as incompatible with modern norms and basic human rights. The latter category of criticism has been designed through interaction with more current ideas flowing through history and in our contemporary times. Muslim authorities have been challenged by Muslim feminist theologians and Muslim liberal theologians, who have accused them of upholding notions that are in disharmony with the structures of modern society and international conventions.

The tradition of internal criticism has existed throughout the history of Islam. However, the outcome has not been clear; there are elements of both negative and constructive criticism. The critical voices within Islam have involved theology, philosophy, jurisprudence, literature, and other fields. They have not been complete traditions of ideas from the beginning, but have rather been constructed, reconstructed, or negotiated through interactions between different individual actors, institutions, and groups. These processes have taken place in different contexts. This includes, for example, ideas, social structures, cultural references, economic structures, legal traditions, religious and political institutions, etc. This shows that critiques of Islamic theology and jurisprudence have not been founded in a vacuum. Interpretations of the legal system and Sharia laws have actually developed through dialogue between human actors, the religious and legal sources (texts), and the tradition (the religious experiences), which have been far from uniform. These interactions have taken place in different contexts, which in their turn have affected the dialogues. Many Muslim authorities emphasize that their beliefs are based on uniform and forever-valid interpretations. From their perspective, Islamic theology and jurisprudence are closed entities. However, their points of view have met internal criticism, skepticism, and, in some cases, sarcasm.

Apart from the negative internal criticism, the ambitions of internal Muslim critique have been unmistakable. Criticism has played a corrective role as critics have provided constructive views with the stated purpose of reforming the established traditions of interpretations. This ambition is not limited to any particular direction, but is more or less in all directions within Islam. However, it is not a matter of even distribution among the different directions.

Another issue concerns the role that internal criticism has played in Muslim contexts. The question is whether it has lived its own isolated life within Muslim intellectual institutions, or whether it has affected or may affect what is described as mainstream Islam. In fact, the criticism has played a role and has had an impact. All research on both contemporary Islam and Islam's history shows that we do not meet any univocal and unambiguous interpretation of Islamic sources. The diversity is due to many different factors, including the existence of different directions like Sunni and Shia and their associated law schools. This diversity is also due to the existence of critical voices that have questioned and expressed doubts about the perceptions of religious authorities. Traditional representatives of Islamic institutions may have rejected much of what Muslim feminist and liberal theologians have put forward. However, they have been forced to take a stand on issues like new models of interpretation of Islamic sources, the lack of gender equality in Sharia laws, human rights, etc.

The responses to the criticisms have been of different natures. One of the main reasons behind the differences has been the dissimilarities between different schools of law concerning the extent to which they allow the use of reason and critical thinking. The more of the latter, the greater the desire for a critical review of established thoughts and perceptions of the Muslim authorities. The law schools that have given reason and rationality a realistically free space differ significantly from those which do not recognize or which limit the space for reason. The latter, in turn, has lain the foundation for the emergence of authority in the legal interpretation. This does not necessarily mean a conflict or dichotomy in the relationship between reason and revelation, as many of the advocates of reason actually attach their positions to the revelation. Reason is presented rather as something that God has equipped the human with to help to investigate and understand fundamental theological, legal, and philosophical inquiries and existential questions.

5

Criticism and Christianity

Charles Taliaferro

There is a story from *The Desert Fathers* about a brother who commits a fault. The community assembles and sends word for Abbot Moses to join them in order to settle the matter. The abbot does not want to come, but when the brothers beseech him, he relents. When he comes to them, he is dragging behind him an old basket full of sand. The brothers ask him about the meaning of the basket, for the basket has holes and the sand is spilling out as the abbot walks. The abbot replies: "My sins are running out behind me, and I do not see them, and today I come to judge the sins of another!" Hearing this, the brothers pardon the one who was at fault.[1]

In this chapter, my intent is not to address the practice of criticism from a neutral point of view (what Thomas Nagel might call *the view from nowhere*). Rather, I offer a philosophy of criticism from a broadly Christian point of view, *broad* in the sense that it is not limited to one Christian tradition (Anglican versus Lutheran versus Roman Catholic, Eastern Orthodoxy, and so on) or to the art of criticism or disputation in the academy. The project is more broad and proposes that there are at least six principles that define constructive criticism from a Christian point of view: (I) the primacy of loving the good, (II) the importance of self-criticism prior to the criticism of others (a principle illustrated in the story about Abbot Moses), (III) the golden rule, (IV) the avoidance of schism and persecution, (V) openness to criticism from non-Christian sources, and (VI) Good Samaritan virtue. I suggest that these principles are important primarily between individuals, but I believe they also apply when institutions, such as a church or monastery or school, engage in criticism from a Christian point of view. After exploring each, I address a domain or type of criticism where there is some serious disagreement among Christians. Some Christian philosophers advance the faith in terms that are personal, challenging individuals to be transformed in relationship with Christ, while others make a more general, less individualized case for Christian faith.

Before addressing the five principles and the topic of personal (or less personal) criticism, here is a brief prelude.

In what follows, I assume readers have basic Biblical literacy, though not necessarily expertise in Biblical scholarship. Regarding a New Testament admonition not to judge ("Do not judge lest you be judged yourselves," Mt 7:1), it will be assumed that this is a warning about what may be called *judgmentalism*, an excessive drive to find fault in others, and not a prohibition against the forming of any judgments whatsoever about the value of persons, beliefs, arguments, purported ideals, and so on. The Christian Bible and tradition contain abundant cases of ostensibly sound judgments and criticism. Consider Jesus' judgment about the Pharisees (Mt 23), the establishment of the different creeds in Christian tradition, and classic cases of when Christians have advanced even harsh judgments about professing Christians who are believed not to be faithful to Christian values (a very incomplete list might include Augustine's *The City of God*, Erasmus's *In Praise of Folly*, Kierkegaard's wide-ranging, severe criticism of the official Danish church, and Bonhoeffer's *The Cost of Discipleship*). Moreover, critical arguments and the cross-examination of different theological positions have been at the heart of Christian education in the tradition of the *ars disputandi*. This practice reached its zenith in the work of Thomas Aquinas, who would ask a question, assemble reasons for answering the question one way, and then, after citing some authority, provide reasons for answering the question differently. This methodology is thoroughly fueled by critical evaluation and the exercise of incisive judgments. While this methodology was (and to some extent is) a formal, academic undertaking, I believe that the presenting of arguments, counter-arguments, objections, and replies has had a robust role throughout the (general) history of Christianity.[2]

In this chapter, I shall also assume a common-sense understanding of when criticism is appropriate and inappropriate. This understanding is quite independent of Christianity or any other religious tradition. In general, I will assume criticism is inappropriate when based on what are knowingly false premises or misinformation, when directed against those who are impaired and unable to understand or respond to criticism, and so on. I suggest it should be common sense to think criticism is inappropriate when it involves logical fallacies like begging the question (assuming the very thing one sets out to argue for). Some forms of criticism can be so bad that they fail even to be about the object of criticism; for example, someone using deeply racist language in criticizing another person may simply be exposing himself as a racist without making *any credible claim whatsoever* about his target people. Criticism is also inappropriate or at least tainted when it is dishonest, as when I might criticize a colleague's book as poorly researched when my real goal is not to enforce high standards of scholarship, but to shame him. There is an amusing, short account by Thomas Nagel about how ill feelings can lie just underneath the social, polite interaction between academics. He imagines two persons, A and B: A has just reviewed B's book. Here is Nagel's sad, but amusing look at what academics might be really thinking (but not expressing) when they encounter each other:

> B: You son of a bitch, I bet you didn't even read my book, you're too dimwitted to understand it even if you had read it, and besides you're clearly out to get me, dripping with envy and spite. If you weren't so overweight I'd throw you out the window.
>
> A: You conceited fraud, I handled you with kid gloves in that review; if I'd said what I really thought it would have been unprintable; the book made me want to throw up—and it's by far your best. (Nagel 2004: 11)[3]

Clearly when criticism is given and received with such ill will, something has gone wrong!

Moving to more positive cases of sound criticism, I assume criticism is appropriate in abundant cases, as when one reproves professionals who, due to negligence or recklessness, have endangered others, or leaders who deliberately lie for nefarious purposes; criticism is (rightly) expected when persons enter into relationships for the purpose of education through critical evaluations; criticism is essential in peer-reviewed projects; and so on. While many (but not all) of the cases I refer to as cases of criticism involve identifying shortcomings, failings, or matters needing improving, I assume that *criticism* as a term can also rightly be used positively as when someone claims that a book meets someone's critical praise.

Having this broad, common-sense background in place, let us consider six dimensions of criticism from a specifically Christian point of view.

I The Primacy of Loving the Good

As Nietzsche points out in his *The Genealogy of Morals*, sometimes a religious or moral stance can appear to be based on positive values when, in reality, the stance is based on envy and resentment. In my view, in his book *Ressentiment* Max Scheler definitively shows (contra Nietzsche) that Christian values are thoroughly positive, but Nietzsche's analysis should prompt Christians to ensure that their use of criticism should be primarily motivated by a love of the good. There are abundant Biblical precepts to the effect that evil is to be overcome not with evil, but with goodness (Rom 12:21, I Thes 5:15, Gal 5:22). We are invoked to love enemies (Mt 5:4) and told that hating others puts us at enmity with God (1 Jn 3:15).

By stressing the primacy of loving the good, one will naturally be led positively to purify one's motives behind the practice of criticism. This would involve the renunciation of vices such as vanity (the inordinate desire for preeminence), malice, jealousy, envy, resentment, (inappropriate) anger, or rage. I suggest Scheler appropriately points out one of the dangers of moral motives that privilege hate more than love. Consider a police officer who is principally motivated by her hatred of injustice or a doctor who hates disease. Scheler proposes that in both cases the agent's life is defined by what they oppose, so much so that if there were no injustice or illness, the officer's and doctor's lives would lack meaning. Their lives are, in a sense, parasitic on that which they despise. Far better, according to Scheler, for the officer to love justice and the doctor to love heath. The officer and doctor may still hate injustice and illness, but this is best rooted in a deeper love for justice and health. Perhaps an example closer to home for some readers would be to compare a teacher who loves wisdom and knowledge versus a teacher who principally hates foolishness and ignorance. Personally, I would prefer the first as I imagine the teacher who loves the goodness of wisdom and knowledge taking pleasure in the growth of her students versus the other teacher who becomes less and less loathing as his students become less foolish and ignorant.

One reason I propose that the first precept in a Christian approach to criticism is the love of goodness rather than, say, love of truth, is that (I suggest) our love of truth should be driven by the love of goodness. It is because of goodness that we should pursue self-knowledge, the knowledge of others, the world, the divine. The horror of living with a false understanding of reality is (in part) because it cuts us off from the goodness of relating to ourselves, others, the world, and God. Love of the good should also impede the harm that can be done in the name of the truth, as when a cruel person might insult others in the name of honesty, e.g., imagine a stranger tells someone with a disability, "To be perfectly honest with you, I am glad I do not have that disability. Oh, and by the way, you have irritating body odor."

I suggest that it is largely because of the Christian stress on the primacy of loving the good that there is a strong stress on reconciliation in Biblical and subsequent Christian ethics. Consider the many precepts on seeking to correct another person with gentleness (e.g., Prv 15:1 and 18, Ps 37:8, Col 3:16) and to offer criticism in non-ostentatious privacy (Mt 18:15). I believe it is because of the primacy of loving the good that we can see a sharp distinction between healthy critical exchanges versus mere quarrelling (Jas 4:1–2). We might also see some sense in the precept that love can cover a multitude of sins (1 Pt 4:8) insofar as exposing the sins of persons should be governed by an authentic love of the good of others and oneself. I am not suggesting that Christian values should disincline persons from important, critical, desirable confrontations (e.g., confronting a person with a drug or alcohol addiction or abusiveness, and so on); I only suggest that caring for the good of the beloved (from a Christian point of view) should disincline one from an officious preoccupation with finding faults.[4]

II The Importance of Self-criticism Prior to the Criticism of Others

This is an element in the story from the *Desert Fathers*, cited at the outset of this chapter. What moved the brothers to pardon their erring brother was the abbot's theatrical admission that he himself was a sinner. Perhaps the clearest New Testament admonition to prioritize self-critical evaluation is Matthew 7:3–5: "And why do you look at the speck in your brother's eye, but do not notice the log that is in your own eye?" Interestingly, Jesus does not undermine the motive of a brother to assist a brother in correction or healing, but only after the one seeking to aid the other undergoes self-examination and self-purification:

> Or how can you say to your brother, "Let me take the speck out of your eye," and behold the log is in your eye? You hypocrite, first take the log out of your own eye; and then you will see clearly enough to take the speck out of your brother's eye. (Mt 7:3)

Confessing one's sins, in both the Old Testament and the New, is a colossal element in a redeemed, reconciliatory relationship with creatures and Creator. Some of the cases of sinners calling on Christ to have mercy are likely the foundation for the Jesus Prayer in wide use in the Orthodox Churches: "Lord Jesus Christ, Son of God, Have mercy on me, a sinner." The Lord's Prayer (Mt 6:9–13; Lk 11:2–4) enjoins us first to acknowledge our own sins (trespasses, faults) and then to observe or reflect on the extent to which we have forgiven those who have sinned against us. In fact, the prayer gauges our supplication for forgiveness to the extent that we practice forgiveness with one another. These practices are evidence of the priority of individual self-scrutiny and of admitting one's own sin.

The importance of the practice of self-examination and confession is widely testified to in Christian liturgy. In the Eucharist (sometimes referred to as Mass, Communion, the Lord's Supper), in most forms in Christian tradition, confession takes place prior to the reception of the elements (consecrated bread and wine). Some liturgies have communicants (or penitents) making a public, general confession, but some are personal ("forgive me Lord, for I have sinned").[5]

Furthermore, the priority of self-examination or self-criticism over and against the criticism of others is evidenced historically and today in the many manuals used by both laity and clergy in the practice of confessions and absolution. In one such manual in use in the Episcopal Church (the USA branch of the Anglican Communion), *Saint Augustine's Prayer Book*, there is a thorough guide to examining when one has engaged in the different dimensions of the seven deadly sins (pride, anger, lust, envy, sloth, avarice, and gluttony); but note that this is a guide for an individual to use in her *self-examination*, not one that penitents are urged to use in their judging other persons.

In Judaism, the great prophets (Isaiah, Jeremiah, Amos, among many others) all highlight the central act of self-examination and repentance (essentially involving a criticism of oneself and behavior, one's acts and omissions). This is taken up in Christianity, beginning with John the Baptist, through the Apostolic age, and to present times (think of Dr. Martin Luther King calling on white Christians to examine their conscience and faith). The importance of self-examination comes especially to the fore in Christianity when it teaches that Jesus was put to death by his own people (through Roman military means), who were blind (or ignorant) of Jesus being the Christ or Messiah. While the relationship between Judaism and Christianity is being reconceived since World War II, the New Testament narrative preserves the charge that Jesus's own people chose not to be open to the person and teaching of Jesus (the Gospel of John). Returning to Jesus's criticism of the Pharisees (Mt 23), they are taken to task for their capricious criticizing and for placing burdens on others, as well as for their failure to engage in humble self-examination which should lead to a renunciation of their prideful arrogance.

Two further aspects of self-examination as a form of self-criticism in Christian perspective are worth noting. One is that self-criticism can be excessive. Linda Zagzebski (2012) has plausibly argued that self-trust is foundational to all our cognition; once we abandon self-trust in our own powers of inquiry, we are imperiled and perhaps become subject to the manipulation of others. Excessive self-examination can also be a symptom of narcissism or vanity.[6] Second, Christian tradition has stressed that the motive behind confession and repentance that follows self-examination should be the love of the good, not fear of (for example) punishment. Thus, this second principle about self-criticism should be understood to be subordinate to the first principle of loving the good.

III The Golden Rule

I suggest that a third principle guiding criticism from a Christian point of view should involve the golden rule, doing unto others what you would have them do to you (Mt 7:12). Because of the pervasiveness of the golden rule in other traditions, this might be deemed part of what I described at the outset of as the common-sense approach to criticism. For that reason, it perhaps requires the least amount of explication. Still I cite it here because a Christian would have not just a common-sense reason for only criticizing others the way she would wish to be criticized herself (if the roles were reversed) but also a sacred reason for doing so (acting in accord with the teaching of Jesus). In *The City of God*, Augustine records a fellowship he had with his friends in which disagreements were treated with the greatest care for everyone's mutual benefit. The following, from Augustine's *Confessions*, may serve as an ideal case of treating others with mutual care:

> There were joys to be found in their company which still more captivated my mind—the charms of talking and laughing together and kindly giving way to each other's wishes, reading elegantly written books together, sharing jokes and delighting to honour one another, disagreeing occasionally but without rancour, as a person might disagree with themselves, and lending piquancy by that rare disagreement to our much more frequent accord. We would teach and learn from each other, sadly missing any who were absent and blithely welcoming them when they returned. Such signs of friendship sprang from the hearts of friends who loved and knew their love returned, signs to be read in smiles, words, glances and a thousand gracious gestures. So were sparks kindled and our minds were fused inseparably, out of many becoming one. (1961: 79)

Combining the primacy of the love of the good, the prioritization of self-criticism over and against criticizing others, and the golden rule, may aptly serve as a frame and support the Swedish theologian Krister Stendahl's three rules of religious understanding:

(1) When trying to understand another religion, you should ask the adherents of that religion and not its enemies.
(2) Don't compare your best to their worst.
(3) Leave room for "holy envy."[7]

The curious, but admirable, third rule involves one's appreciating how a religion different from one's own might have some sacred and desirable virtue which is lacking (or is not as evident) in one's own religion. A Christian might, for example, concede that, today, most Muslims show more systematic discipline in their prayers than most Christians. (This is advanced as a hypothetical supposition.) In any case, I suggest that adherence to the golden rule would support these three rules: I myself, as a Christian, would want my critics (whether Christian or non-Christian) to treat me with the three-fold reciprocal respect Stendahl endorsed.

IV The Avoidance of Schism and Persecution

Obviously, criticism of another person or group sometimes does not always remain peaceful; it can be a prelude to divorce, expulsion from a community, the declaration that a former "believer" is now an apostate, condemnation, or violence. Tragically, criticism in the history of Christianity has played such ugly roles. This may seem surprising given the New Testament teaching on peace and peace-making (e.g., "Blessed are the peace-makers" Mt 5:9), the call for forbearance (Gal 5:22), the command to forgive others (Mt 18:21–22), the value of not being divided (Mt 12:22–28; Mk 3:25), and so on. There have been historically pacifist churches, and in fact the early church was at least ambivalent about whether Christians could serve in the military. Still, Christ cleansed the temple (Mt 21:12–17) and one needs to balance a verse like "Put away your sword" (Mt 26:52) with others ("Think not that I come to send peace on earth, I am not to send peace, but a sword." Mt 10:34). The church was persecuted at its inception (and is still persecuted in places), but Christians and their churches have themselves engaged in persecution and violence: think of the Inquisition and Witch Trials; the abundant cases when, historically, so-called Christians killed Christians in the great religious wars of Europe, including the sacking of Constantinople in the Fourth Crusade; and the shameful, great violence against the Jews by so-called Christians prior to World War II. Think also of the beheading of Thomas More by a Protestant king, as well as of the burning of the Oxford martyrs by a Roman Catholic monarch, the burning of Bruno, and so on.

Looking over such a tragic history, one needs to appreciate how destructive all such violence in the name of Christianity has been. I suggest the historical legacy of such violence needs to caution the Christian practice of criticism. In the contemporary context, when non-Christian groups have been persecuted, dispossessed, and made vulnerable to violence, I suggest that philosophical and theological criticism of the relevant non-Christian traditions needs either to cease altogether or at least be suspended until stable, just conditions are established. When groups are in a crisis, it is time for Christians to show solidarity with the oppressed, regardless of whether this involves protecting communities who may be quite hostile to Christianity.

V Openness to Criticism from Non-Christian Sources

Earlier, I referred to Nietzsche's *The Genealogy of Morals*. While I believe Scheler successfully rebutted Nietzsche's claim that Christianity is based on negative emotions (such as envy and resentment), I suggest that it is vital for Christians to take seriously such charges, as well as the criticism of Christian beliefs and values from a variety of perspectives (that of Karl Marx, Freud, non-Christian feminists, environmentalists, advocates of race theory, and more). Not all criticism of Christianity is well motivated or fair; some of the critiques by so-called New Atheists seem wide of their mark. However, their work has led many Christian philosophers to publish excellent responses to Richard Dawkins et al.[8]

The most engaging and dramatic moment in terms of the Christian community in the United States responding to external criticism involves the environmental movement, which began in the 1960s and still has momentum today, notwithstanding the election of Donald Trump and his effort at overturning progressive ecological legislation and treaties. From its inception, environmentally oriented philosophers and ethicists blamed Christianity for fostering a domination view of nature in which the natural world was deemed a realm in which humans may use it without seeing nature (including all nonhuman animals) as valuable for its own sake. The case against Christianity is abundant among philosophical environmentalists (Paul Taylor, J. Baird Collicott et al.), but nowhere is it more explicit and articulate than in the famous article "The Historical Roots of Our Environmental Crisis" by Lynn White in 1967, widely anthologized in environmental ethics textbooks. Regardless of whether White (1907–1987) was himself a Christian, the article encapsulated the judgment of non-Christians who saw Christianity as dangerous and to blame for Western exploitation of the natural world. There is ample reason to believe that it was White's essay that stimulated a massive, creative response from Christian philosophers and theologians who sought to find the resources within Christianity to recognize and treasure the innate goodness of the created world. A kind of green Christian ecological movement and literature came about with contributors including Wendell Berry, Wes Jackson, Robin Attfield, Holmes Rolston III, Andrew Linzey, and many others. Linzey, an Anglican priest, founded a Christian vegetarian movement, as well as founding the Oxford Centre for Animal Ethics. Linzey and others acknowledged the legitimacy of the critique of how Christian tradition had been used to exploit the natural world, and yet they urged that Christianity had great resources to condemn such exploitation and to provide a theological foundation for environmentalism.

A model of a critical engagement by a major twentieth-century atheist and the Christian community is Albert Camus's presentation in 1948 to a Dominican monastery on what the world expects of Christians. Camus positively calls on Christians to be in solidarity with all those who oppose violence against children and human persons in general. While positive in tone and substance, the talk and subsequently published paper may be read as critically cajoling those Christians who do not recognize or act on their obligation to such solidarity. Here are the opening comments:

> Inasmuch as you have been so kind as to invite a man who does not share your convictions to come and answer the very general question that you are raising in these conversations, before telling you what I think unbelievers expect of Christians, I should like first to acknowledge your intellectual generosity.

I shall strive not to be the person who pretends to believe that Christianity is an easy thing and asks of the Christian, on the basis of an external view of Christianity, more than he asks of himself. I believe indeed that the Christian has many obligations but that it is not up to the man who rejects them himself to recall their existence to anyone who has already accepted them. If there is anyone who can ask anything of the Christian, it is the Christian him/herself.

What the world expects of Christians is that Christians should speak out, loud and clear, and that they should voice their condemnation in such a way that never a doubt, never the slightest doubt, could rise in the heart of the simplest man. That they should get away from abstraction and confront the blood-stained face history has taken on today. The grouping we need is a grouping of men/women resolved to speak out clearly and to pay up personally. (Online)

This case is so profoundly different from the current rhetoric by "New Atheists," blaming Christians (and other theists) for mindlessly cultivating delusions and so on.

VI Good Samaritan Virtue

The parable of the good Samaritan, which appears in Luke 10:25–29, is about how a stranger comes to the aid of a traveler who has been beaten and robbed. The rescuer, a Samaritan, provides direct care and even pays for refuge for the victim to recover. I suggest that there can arise cases when a non-Christian person or community is unfairly and cruelly criticized by others when a Christian can and should intervene to protect the person and community. Imagine a Muslim community in a country which is largely non-Muslim is being wrongly criticized for being superstitious and, for whatever reason (a language barrier or a culturally embedded Islamophobia), the community lacks the resources to effectively rebut the criticism. If a Christian person or community can effectively protect the Muslim community, I believe it is their Good Samaritan obligation to do so. There may be inappropriate ways to provide aid (e.g., through condescension or patronizing), but it seems to me that such aid might be done without vice and perhaps even involve courage on behalf of the Christian.

Summary, so far: The six principles guiding criticism from a Christian point of view are related. The first principle is the most important: loving the good should lead us to avoid the peril of presumptuousness and hypocrisy by prioritizing self-criticism over the criticism of others; it is good to exercise the golden rule; it is good to avoid schism and persecution; it is good to be open to external sources of criticism; and it is good to assist others (whether or not they are Christian) who are being improperly criticized.

While I believe the above proposals are backed up in a great deal of Christian scripture, literature, and practice, one needs to recognize when self-identified Christians have flagrantly violated all of them. A modest survey of the way Christians have unfairly martyred each other would provide ample evidence of this sad fact. Rather than close with lamentation, I turn now to an area where there is disagreement among Christians, especially Christian philosophers, on the extent to which welcome criticism is or should be personal.

Probably the most prominent Christian philosopher working today who takes what I am referring to as a personal approach to critical engagement is Paul Moser (2019). Foreswearing natural theology (arguments from the cosmos such as the cosmological argument or from history such as an argument from miracles that may persuade an impartial inquirer to become a theist), Moser contends that persons should be challenged to freely accept the Lordship of Jesus Christ as revealed in the New Testament. By yielding to the (believed) reality of Jesus and living out a life of agape-love, persons may come to find evidence that their beliefs are indeed true, based (in part) on the recognition that one's life has a newly transformed depth and profundity. Moser's methodology is personal insofar as he sees it as essential that the philosophical presentation and assessment of Christian faith involve a decision by the inquirer as to whether she is willing (and does) commit herself the loving Lordship of Jesus Christ. He disparages the projects of natural theology which traffic in what he calls spectator evidence. What is the use of knowing about the God of Christianity if that has no impact on how you live? (Moser 2019). In terms of the history of Christian philosophy (or philosophy by Christians), Moser would be aligned with Pascal and Kierkegaard.

On the other hand, there are Christian philosophers today who seek to justify Christian faith on grounds that do not require such a personal challenge to commit to Jesus prior to assessing the merits of Christian faith as a whole. Without a doubt, Richard Swinburne is the paradigm philosopher in this school of thought. He has advanced a massive cumulative case for Christian faith accessible to impartial inquirers without challenging them to personally commit at the outset to the Lordship of Christ. Swinburne develops a huge number of interconnected arguments that begin with making a case for the coherence of theism, then a case for the reasonability of theism, then a case for the veracity of Christian revelation, followed by a case for the reasonability of believing that Jesus of Nazareth is fully God, fully man, followed by an argument for the reasonability of belief in the Resurrection, the Atonement, an afterlife as depicted in the New Testament and Christian tradition, and more. To engage Moser's metaphor of being a spectator, a follower of Swinburne's method is sympathetic to spectators: assuming we are spectators of two teams, why should we feel obliged to join a team without watching them from a distance and then choosing which team to join? If Moser is more akin to Pascal and Kierkegaard, Swinburne is closer to Thomas Aquinas and Joseph Butler.

There are middle positions. For example, John Cottingham relies on some natural theology but his main philosophical case for the vindication of Christian belief seems to be an appeal to how Christian faith provides a convincing understanding of the meaning of life. Alvin Plantinga and Reformed Epistemologists might also be in a middle position. While some of them allow for Swinburne's natural theology, they also allow that Christian faith can be warranted as a basic belief not supported by discursive reasoning and evidence. I suggest this is a middle position insofar as it does not tie itself to natural theology nor does it necessitate the personal, critical engagement proposed by Moser.

While I deeply admire Moser, I am more aligned with Swinburne. This is partly because I accept some of the main theistic arguments of natural theology (versions of the cosmological and teleological arguments, an argument from religious experience—which Swinburne has advocated—and even a version of the ontological argument—which Swinburne does not accept). Still, it should not be a mystery that Christian philosophers are deeply concerned about persons and the personal. Some of the arguments from natural theology pay quite a bit of attention to persons and the personal (there are theistic arguments from the emergence of consciousness, from the recognition of moral and aesthetic values, from religious experience, and so on). Orthodox Christianity recognizes that God exists in Three Persons (though this is differently interpreted by the West and East). Moreover, Christians believe that the person Jesus Christ is the incarnation of God.

I conclude then by noting that while contemporary Christian philosophers differ in their views about the personal nature of criticism, most Christian philosophers would (I hope and trust) resonate with the way the six principles outlined in this chapter influence how Christians approach criticism.

Part Two

Law, Politics, and Education

6

Courts as Critics:
Nuancing the Insider/Outsider Binary

Effie Fokas

A great deal of scholarship on the intersection between religion and law has observed an increasingly expansive judicialization of religion (Koenig 2012; Foblets et al. 2014; Fokas 2015; Mayrl 2018). Religious majorities, in particular, have often been recipients of "critique" from a legal perspective by courts, given the counter-majoritarian nature of courts as institutions and the fact that it is minorities (whether religious or secularist) most frequently taking their religion-related claims to courts. The effects of such case law in terms of the curbing of religious majorities' privileges have been addressed by socio-legal scholarship (most recently regarding the European context by Temperman, Gunn and Evans 2019). But we know relatively little about how these groups receive what may be considered as critique by courts. How do religious actors react to judgments which are issued by courts calling somehow for a limitation on particular practices of theirs? Are such judgments received as messages of critique? And to what extent may such critique be considered constructive, in terms of leading to an alteration of certain practices? Further, to what extent may such critique be *perceived* as constructive by the religious groups in question, given that courts are, by their nature, sites of conflict?

The messages courts communicate about religion through their decisions in a given case may leave a powerful mark on the religious groups in question (see Foblets et al. 2014 and Beaman and Lefebvre, Chapter 8 in this volume). This chapter draws on research considering the impact of European Court of Human Rights (ECtHR or, the Court) engagements with religion-related issues on grassroots-level social actors.[1] From this broader research, the chapter explores specifically the dynamic of critique of religion issued by the ECtHR in the form of its judgments, on the one hand, and religious majorities' reception of such critique, on the other. In so doing, it entails a further elaboration of the conceptions of insider versus outsider critique set out in the introduction to this volume; it also complements the contribution of Pia Karlsson Minganti (Chapter 7) on courts as sites of conflict.

Of course, there are certain specificities about international courts in general and the ECtHR in particular which must be brought to bear on a broader discussion of "courts as critics." Thus, the chapter first begins with a consideration of the latter specificities. Second, it presents the research methodology and some of the empirical data underpinning the chapter before turning, third, to a broad-brush consideration of religious groups in relation to courts and specifically to the ECtHR. A fourth section focuses on an ECtHR case that arose within the Greek context and on local-level reactions to the critique embedded in that case; the example helps us to nuance the terms "insider," "outsider," and "constructive" when it comes to the critique of religion.

Critique by and of the European Court of Human Rights

The ECtHR is today an important institution in the shaping of religious freedoms globally (Moravcsik 2000; Keller and Stone Sweet 2008; Durham and Kirkham 2012). It is a venue where some of the most contentious questions related to religion in European society are being addressed, including whether religious symbols can be worn or displayed in public spaces and in employment contexts, whether exemption from military service or religious education may be defended on conscience-based grounds, and whether states can require tax contributions to state churches. The scope broadens significantly if we consider also issues of special interest to religious and/or secularist publics though not directly related to religion, such as social and bioethical issues (e.g., same-sex marriage, assisted reproductive technology, euthanasia, etc.). In a truly broad range of issues related to the freedom of belief and worship, but also to rights to non-discrimination based on religion, freedoms of expression and of association and assembly, and other religion-related issues, the Court hears the cases of individual citizens claiming that their rights have been breached by the states in which they reside.

Beyond its topical jurisdiction, the geographic breadth of the Court's influence is also immense. The ECtHR bears direct relevance for over 800 million people across 47 states:[2] any right won in any of these 47 states automatically becomes a right for which a citizen in any of the other states may contend at the ECtHR. The reach of its "indirect effects" relevance is far greater, in the sense that the ECtHR is a standard-setter for human rights globally and a reference point for national and international courts well beyond the European context.

The ECtHR was rather slow to engage actively with religion-related claims that arose before it: in its first three plus decades of operation from its establishment in 1959 until 1993, the Court did not vindicate a single claim raised on religious grounds.[3] This changed in 1993 with *Kokkinakis v. Greece*, a case brought forward by a Greek Jehovah's Witness challenging the proselytism ban in that country. The Court did not go so far in *Kokkinakis* as to call for an end to that ban, but it did find the Greek state's rigorous implementation of the latter in violation of the right to religious freedom. And in so doing it opened the floodgates, so to speak, for what may be described as a rapid judicialization of religion: the Court went from 0 violations found in religious freedoms cases in its first 34 years, to nearly 80 in its subsequent 25 years (Fokas 2015; Ringelheim 2012; "Violations" 2018).

This rapid judicialization of religion is not limited to the ECtHR or to the European setting but is, rather, a more general phenomenon (Mayrl 2018). Particularly important in the context of the present discussion of critique of religion, though, is a consideration of what the increasing judicialization of religion means for a *supranational* court addressing nationally sensitive issues, as are most legal issues to do with religion, in a time of heightened particularism and new nationalisms proliferating across Europe. The ECtHR, like other European institutions, is facing a legitimacy crisis amid nationalist backlashes against perceived threats to national sovereignty and national identity. One rather vivid example of the latter is the case of *Lautsi v. Italy*. In 2009 the Court decided in favor of an atheist mother (Soile Lautsi) who claimed that the display of the crucifix on Italian school walls violated her right to educate her children in accordance with her own philosophical or religious beliefs (a right enshrined in Art. 2 of Protocol 1 of the European Convention on Human Rights, which the ECtHR defends). After appeal by the Italian state, the Court reversed that decision, moving from a 7–0 chamber decision in 2009 to a 15–2 Grand Chamber decision in 2011. That dramatic reversal followed the (quantitatively and qualitatively) unprecedented interventions from other national governments (among other interventions) in favor of the Italian state's right to decide in such matters to do with national identity (Mancini 2010; Liu 2011; Ronchi 2011). It may be argued that the Court treaded rather more carefully in religion-related cases for some time "in the shadow" of the *Lautsi* case, not least because of "lessons learned" regarding how states may mobilize in the face of unwelcome critique on sensitive issues such as those related to religion (Fokas 2015, 2016).

In short, the standing of an international court such as the ECtHR to issue critique against "national religions," in the current context of *global* nationalist backlash, is rather precarious. And yet it continues issue such critique so, albeit more cautiously. States react in different ways to what may be perceived as critique by the Court of their handling of religion-related matters: in some cases states implement the Court's decisions, in others they refuse to implement the decisions, and in still others they mobilize other states and various social actors in calls for reversal of the Court's decisions. But how do religious groups themselves react to the Court's critique? Insights into this question may be gleaned from research conducted on grassroots-level awareness of and engagements with ECtHR case law, to which topic I now turn.

The ECtHR and Religion at the Grassroots Level: Research Aims and Methods

The vast potential impact of the ECtHR in the realm of religious pluralism prodded an in-depth five-year study of grassroots-level awareness of and engagements with that court's religion-related case law (Grassrootsmobilise 2014–2019; Fokas 2015, 2018, 2019). As one socio-legal scholar explains, messages communicated by courts do not "simply trickle down on citizens and state officials in a unidirectional, determinate fashion" (McCann 1992: 773); rather, judicially articulated norms must be understood "in the eye of the beholder," because they take a life of their own at the grassroots level. In Marc Galanter's words describing the "radiating effects" of the law, "the messages disseminated by courts do not carry endowments or produce effects *except as they are received, interpreted, and used by (potential) actors*" (Galanter 1983: 136; *emphasis mine*). Thus, it is important to ascertain how stakeholder actors interpret the messages courts produce through their decisions (Fokas and Richardson 2017, 2018). A more contextualized understanding is required of how court-produced messages of critique might be differently interpreted among different social actors and in different national and local contexts; the latter would also help get at the third question posed by Lövheim and Stenmark in the model presented in their introduction to this volume: "how is the criticism conceptualized and responded to by the target group?"

To this end, the Grassrootsmobilise research program entailed empirical research conducted in four European countries: Greece, Italy, Romania, and Turkey. The selection represents country cases in which religion is socially, culturally, and politically significant, and where the stakes are perceived to be relatively high in relation to ECtHR judgments on religion. The country cases are all marked by strong relationships between religion and national identity and between religion and state. But they represent different levels of democratization and "Europeanization," with two "older" members of the EU, one relatively recent, and one whose candidacy reflects a long and strained relationship. The selection thus allowed an exploration of the role of the latter factors into the ways and extent to which the Court's religion-related case law impacts upon grassroots social actors.

The research included a special focus on two issue areas found to be highly salient across the four country cases: religious education and the legal status of religious minorities. And it entailed a combination of research methods, with an emphasis on in-depth semi-structured interviews conducted with representatives of religious minority and majority groups, representatives of other conscience-based groups and NGOs (e.g., secularist, atheist, and humanist groups), lawyers representing religion-related concerns before courts, and government officials managing religion-related affairs. Other methods were also used (e.g., mass media and national high courts study), but most illuminating for the present purposes is the interview research, because it offers first hand insight into how religious groups react to what may be perceived as critique from the ECtHR.

Religious Groups and the ECtHR[4]

In most countries, there is a system in place distinguishing between rights and privileges afforded by the state to different religious groups, arranged in different forms of hierarchy in each case. Thus, the grievances each group may have are largely contingent on where in the hierarchy it falls and thus on what rights and privileges the group is denied, particularly in comparison with other religious groups.

Across the cases, we see certain patterns emerging in terms of the propensity of various conscience-based groups to utilize political or legal means to pursue their claims, and this in turn influences the extent to which and ways in which the ECtHR's case law will bear relevance for them. Among these patterns the tendencies of three groups stand apart as particularly noteworthy in their engagements, or lack thereof, with the ECtHR: Jehovah's Witnesses, Muslims, and atheist associations. Space limitations do not allow thorough attention to each (see instead Fokas 2018). But here I would like to focus attention on religious groups' and individuals perspectives on the act of taking a case to the ECtHR as somehow negative. The comment of one Muslim minority spokesperson is representative of the perspective found among many respondents: "Well, [the ECtHR] is indeed relevant for us, but I wouldn't want us to end up there." In both Greece and Italy, Muslim representatives express a fear of being perceived as confrontational, and from this perspective litigation is considered a particularly confrontational route to pursuing a group's claims. As one Italian respondent expresses it: "You can file a case to the court, of course but, in addition to the uncertainty of the outcome, it is already the 'hard way', it's confrontational, whilst we want to be moderate and responsible citizens." Muslim respondents emphasize the importance of the public image of Islam as a non-confrontational religion, particularly in the context of the political polarization around Islam-related issues. (The discussion in the following chapter in this volume by Pia Karlsson Minganti offers greater depth on this point).

Other groups too, particularly in the Greek, Romanian, and Turkish contexts, express a sense in which pursuing one's grievances nationally is one thing but at the ECtHR it is quite another, being perceived more as an act of betrayal of one's nation. As one Turkish minority faith respondent put it, "We are sons of this country; we don't want to complain about our country [to international institutions such as the ECtHR]." In Greece, one religious minority representative declared "discrimination against a religion is proportional to the 'noise' and trouble the respective religion makes." This is a direct reference to Jehovah's Witnesses, especially noisy in their long list of ECtHR wins against the Greek state, and particularly discriminated against in the Greek context. In fact, there is a tendency found among many respondents across all cases to speak about the act of taking a case to the ECtHR as fundamentally anti-national. References are made to wanting to be good citizens, or to avoid displaying "our dirty laundry" in Europe. The latter point helps to illustrate religious groups' perceptions of the ECtHR as an "outsider."

Insights from the *Papageorgiou* Case

I now turn attention to a particular ECtHR case that arose in the Greek context and which facilitates an exploration of the notions of "insider," "outsider," and "constructive" critique of religion. That case, *Papageorgiou and Others v. Greece*, offers, through the Grassrootsmobilise program's engagements with it (see below), a meta-analysis of religious groups' reactions to court-related critique, specifically, those of a group of theologians involved in religious education (RE) reform.[5] My exploration here begins necessarily with an overview of RE in the Greek context.

Religious Education in Greece[6]

RE is constitutionally enshrined in the Greek context: Art. 16(2) of the Greek constitution indicates that one of the purposes of state-provided education is "the development of their national and religious conscience," the underlying assumption being of course that the two go hand in hand. Greek RE has historically, until the reform discussed below, been mono-confessional in nature, focused principally on Greek Orthodoxy, and instructing the students in that faith (i.e., teaching Greek Orthodoxy rather than teaching *about* Greek Orthodoxy). RE is mandatory for all school children from the third year of primary school and throughout secondary school, with the exception of "non-Orthodox students" (a point to which I will return). The 1985 Law on Education currently in effect further indicates that RE should aid students "to develop into free, responsible, democratic citizens… in whom is instilled a faith in their motherland and in the authentic elements of Christian Orthodox tradition" (Markoviti 2018).[7] Greek RE also, until its relatively recent reform, paid little attention to other faiths and treated some of these disparagingly.

RE reform was initiated as part of a broader "New School" program launched in 2011 by the then-socialist government and entailing a series of proposals for the improvement of the current curriculum and of the educational orientations of the different school subjects, including RE (Markoviti 2018, 2019). The new RE curriculum spends proportionally much more time and space on other faith traditions, is not disparaging about any of the latter, and teaches more *about* religion in general with less of teaching Greek Orthodoxy in a confessional way.[8] As such, it comes far closer than was previously the case to the Swedish non-confessional RE presented by Löfstedt and Sjöborg (Chapter 10) in this volume. This curriculum was introduced into schools by the leftist Syriza government, which came to power in 2015 (though developed and piloted under the previous two governments in the 2009–2014 period), both reflecting and exacerbating an intense rift between church and the Syriza government over RE.

It should be noted here that long prior to a church-state rift over RE, there had developed a deep division within theological circles in Greece, with the Greek Union of Theologians gradually dividing into two theological unions, one more conservative in orientation (the Panhellenic Union of Theologians, or PETH), and the other more liberal (Kairos).[9] The Kairos theologians, broadly speaking, supported the reform in RE, and many of the latter were directly involved in the reform process and in particular underwrote the new RE curriculum for primary and middle school. Meanwhile, PETH in the main champions Orthodoxy-only RE. Both groups of theologians, though, advocate a mandatory RE course. The latter fact may have many explanations, depending on the theologian in question, including a principal concern for their employment status, as their training has, until recently, been for confessional teaching of RE; a concern to buttress Orthodox culture in schools, not least because low church attendance does not bode well for the latter; and/or a concern that students emerge from school better equipped to understand the increasingly religiously plural society around them. Certainly, both sides have noted a worry that if the course is made optional (i.e., there are no restrictions on exemptions), it will become obsolete. Regardless of the motives, this shared insistence on mandatory RE is important to emphasize because the process of exemption from RE is key to problems around Greek RE to be addressed below.

Greek RE under Legal Crossfire

Rather strikingly, the Greek system of RE was challenged in a Greek high court (the Council of State, or "*Symvoulio tis Epikratias*," StE), nearly simultaneously, from two different directions. One case, led by a particularly outspoken conservative Greek Orthodox bishop (Bishop Seraphim of Piraeus), claimed that the new system of RE is unconstitutional in that it is "not Orthodox enough" and thus fails to fulfill the constitutionally enshrined aim to develop students' "national and religious conscience." A second case, led by two atheist families (Papageorgiou and Anastasiadou/Raviolou[10]), claimed that the Greek RE continues to be "too Orthodox" to be mandatory, and sought exemption for their children on philosophical grounds. The exemption issue is rather important, because as indicated above, RE exemption in Greece is currently available only to the "non-Orthodox," which means the school requires a declaration of one's non-Orthodox identity for exemption (whereas according to EU directives regarding private data protection, a public institution ought not require declarations of faith or lack thereof).[11] Further, because students' religion was indicated on the high school diploma (another violation of EU private data protection),[12] the parents in the case in question had more reason to wish to avoid having to declare their non-Orthodox identity to the school in order to secure exemption from RE.

In March and April of 2018, the StE ruled in favor of the claim led by the Greek bishop in two separate rulings (one for primary and middle school, and one for high school, respectively), thus finding that the new RE program is in violation of the Greek constitution. This result has been met with incredulity expressed by many in the academic community in Greece and beyond. That ruling has also been challenged legally and is due to be revisited by the StE.

Meanwhile, in the case taken by the atheist families, the StE accepted initially to hear the case but postponed the date for this so many times as to render the case moot, given that the students in question by then were required either to attend the RE course or to seek exemption by declaring their non-Orthodox faith status (on this see Markoviti 2018). These postponements thus opened an opportunity for the claimants to take their case directly to the ECtHR, as they had effectively exhausted all national measures in their efforts to have their case heard in time for that academic school year. In April of 2018, the ECtHR accepted to hear the case of *Papageorgiou and Others v. Greece*, and it is currently pending before the ECtHR.

As hinted above in relation to the *Lautsi* case, the ECtHR offers an opportunity of third-party interventions (TPIs) to individuals or groups who have special insights or information relevant to the issue under consideration in a particular case, which insights or information might be helpful to the Court in its assessment of the case. In the US context, such interventions are called "amicus briefs" and the interveners are referred to as "friends of the Court": in other words, the "side" of the court is taken, not of a particular claimant or defendant in a given case. TPIs to the ECtHR must be neutral to the cases themselves and are not to address the details of the case; rather, the information provided is meant, among other things, to help the Court to better understand different sides of an issue at stake (on TPIs at the ECtHR, see Eydne 2013 and Bürli 2017). The procedure entails writing to the Court with a request to intervene, explaining in what ways one's planned intervention could be deemed helpful by the Court and, if such permission is granted by the Court, then the intervention must be submitted to the Court within a set timeframe. In the case of *Papageorgiou and Others v. Greece*, the Court gave permission to intervene to three particular groups: the UK-based National Secular Society (NSS), the Greek Helsinki Monitor (GHM), and the Grassrootsmobilise Research Team.

Papageorgiou goes to Europe[13]

Though RE in Greece has been the subject of political, and even legal, contention at the national level, the Europeanization of the issue, in the form of the *Papageorgiou* case before the ECtHR, takes the concerns of the theologians defending the new RE program (which group forms the focal point of this part of the chapter) to a whole new level, both literally and metaphorically, and in so doing yields a clearly defined "outsider" in this case (the European court). As noted above, there is something of the "anti-national" seen by many in the act of taking a case to the ECtHR. There is also a sense in which one's internal affairs seem suddenly "out of control," and in the hands of people (in this case, judges) who are unfamiliar with the national setting and its particularities. One such particularity in the Greek setting is the fact that reform of RE was the result of a long process of negotiations involving theologians' unions, various governments over time, certain leaders within the Church of Greece, individual theologians, and individual government officials, among others. As one theologian explained to me, "we have had to take baby steps. We took the reforms as far as we could at this stage." This fact is key: though theologians involved in the RE reform and "defending" the current RE program against the legal attacks that the latter has faced might themselves have wished to take the reforms even "further" (i.e., more scientific rather than confessional approaches to RE), the current RE program is as "liberal" as they were able to negotiate. In theory, over time there would have been the possibility of "opening up" the RE course even further. Timing is key, then, and there was a sense in which, for some of the theologians consulted for this study, the timing was unfair because major steps have been taken in the RE reform process, and more could be expected in the fullness of time.

But the timing of courts does not thus discriminate, and the *Papageorgiou* case reached the ECtHR at the particular point in time which it did, with the RE course "as open as it could be" at this stage in Greek socio-political reality. The latter is attested to by the fact that the Greek bishop-led case was successful before the StE in arguing that the RE course was "too liberal"/"not Orthodox enough." As expressed by one theologian respondent:

> the court (StE) in Greece has decided that not only is the [new RE] not confessional, but to the contrary it is secularized and "panreligious." This is the complete antithesis of all that the Papageorgiou family claims about the [new RE]. In the end what is actually the case? And this will be determined by yet another court, the European one?[14]

This presumption of the Court's inability to appreciate (or to know or understand) the internal-to-Greece struggles around RE seemed to render especially important (for the theologians in question) the existence and content of the two TPIs in this case from within Greece. As noted above, all TPIs to the Court are meant to be neutral to the particulars of the case. Yet in reality, in *Papageorgiou* and more generally, most TPIs by default support one "direction" or the other because of the specific information offered to the Court. The interventions of the NSS and the GHM in the *Papageorgiou* case could be assumed to be in defense of the atheist claim, while that of the Grassrootsmobilise team could in theory at least be less predictable. In fact, the Grassrootsmobilise intervention by default falls clearly on the "side" of *Papageorgiou*, because of its conclusion that

> RE as it is taught and managed in Greek public schools undermines the universality of Art. 2 of Protocol 1, in its applicability only to members of religious minority groups (and to those willing and able to declare their belonging to a minority faith to the school).[15]

As such, the intervention led to expressions of disappointment among some theologians who had been involved in the development of the new RE curriculum.[16] Though the intervention was focused especially—as suggested by the excerpt above—on the problem of discrimination in the exemption process, the intervention was still, by and large, received by some theologians involved in RE reform as a criticism of the content of the RE course itself. Whilst the two (content and exemption rights) are of course related, they are also distinctive issues, and this distinction tended to be overlooked or go unobserved altogether by some of the theologians in question. This fact points to a first takeaway relevant to the questions set out in the introduction to this volume: the potential for misinterpretation of critique by its recipients.

Related to the latter, the Grassrootsmobilise team's intervention was based especially on an assessment of Greek RE with reference to the ECtHR's previous case law relevant to RE. More specifically, the TPI focused on an analysis of Greek RE in the light of the case of *Folgero v. Norway* (2007). This point leads to a second takeaway: *the heightened potential for misinterpretation of critique when that critique comes in a form (in this case, legal reasoning) less familiar to those receiving the critique.*

Critically, this heightened potential for misinterpretation is not necessarily because of an inability or lack of interest among the theologians in question to engage in legal reasoning. Rather, it is at least in part to do with the fact that the legal reasoning of the Court, on which the critique rests, is not itself fully clear.[17] This, according to some scholars, is to be expected, given that religion "fits uneasily into a legal scheme that demands such categories and such expert certainty" (Sullivan 2005: 10; see also DeGirolami 2013). Thus, there was a disconnect between the detailed language of the Court's relevant case law, on the one hand, and on the other the in-depth experience of a reformed Greek RE, the gist of which seemed, for the theologians in question, to fully conform to ECHR expectations.

Nuancing the "Insider"/"Outsider" Binary

The "national-level" dynamics of the *Papageorgiou* case rather interestingly highlight limitations in the use of the categories "insiders" and "outsiders" when it comes to critique of religion—limitations also explored in this volume more or less explicitly in the chapters by Zachariasson, Fazlhashemi, and Beaman and Lefebvre. As suggested above, it is clear that the Court itself is considered an "outsider" critic: the Court is perceived by the theologians addressed by the present study as distant, *not knowledgeable* on the internal socio-political-historical intricacies of Greek RE, and somehow "dependent" on whatever information comes before it from the claimants and their lawyers, the respondent state (which may or may not be effective in laying out those intricacies for the Court), and, where applicable, from third-party interveners. Beyond this, though, the picture becomes more complicated and it seems there are different "insiders" and degrees of insiderness. For example, both the Greek Helsinki Monitor and the Grassrootsmobilise research program seem to be considered by the theologians defending the revised RE program as "insiders" in the sense that they are both based in Greece; this is because of the broader context of the case—i.e., the fact that it is a European court, so "insider to Greece" is attributed one type of "insider" status. And of course, it is their base in Greece which leads to the interveners having "insider insight" about the Greek context which they could share with the Court. As such, they are especially "on trial" (pun intended) by this group of theologians for the critique entailed by the *Papageorgiou* case, and differently so. The GHM, secularist in nature as it is, seemed to be perceived as acting as expected in its TPI, based also on its other interventions in the Greek legal and political scene. For example, its leader, Panayote Dimitras, took the Greek state to the ECtHR in the cases of *Dimitras v Greece 1, 2, and 3* (2010, 2011, and 2013 respectively) against the religious oath in courtrooms, and was involved in *Vallianatos v. Greece* (2013), which established the right to same-sex civil unions in Greece. Thus, the GHM's scrutiny of the Greek RE program could presumably have been expected to be rather critical and to find it "too religious." The GHM is an insider in the sense that it is Greek, and most importantly will be considered by the Court as an "insider" to Greece with special insight into the Greek context; however, it is an "outsider" for the theologians in question in that it is clearly a secular*ist* organization based on the specific causes it has championed.

Grassrootsmobilise, on the other hand, is less of an "outsider-insider" because it could be considered either "neutral" or "sympathetic," not least because of *its* leader's association with theological circles and the study of religion more generally. Greater neutrality on the topic of RE could also be expected based on its engagement with the study of religion-related rights more generally. Thus, there are "degrees of insiderness" within the category of "internal to Greece." Critically, attached to these differing degrees are different degrees to which the Greek Helsinki Monitor and the Grassrootsmobilise research team are held "responsible" by the theologians in question for their negative critique and for its potential consequences (i.e., impact on the ECtHR in its decision-making in the *Papageorgiou* case). For example, the Grassrootsmobilise team had extensive insider knowledge of the hard work theologians had put into the RE reform; they also knew details of the reformed RE program versus the previous RE curriculum and could thus be expected to appreciate the tremendous strides having been made in the direction of a less confessional RE. Overall, the resistance to RE in general from the GHM and from the claimants and legal counsel in the *Papageorgiou* case were more easily expected by the theologians in question, and thus accepted, than the critique perceived to be coming from the Grassrootsmobilise research team, because of its different position as *less* of an outsider.

Constructiveness in the Eye of the Beholder

As with the notions of "insider" and "outsider," the *Papageorgiou* case calls for a nuancing of the concept of constructive critique, depending both on the critic in each case and on the recipient. It is clear from the reactions of many Greek theologians consulted for this study that critique of the ECtHR would be considered "outsider" critique, and as such it is far less "problematic" than the insider critique of (a) the claimants in the case, (b) the legal counsel of the claimants, and (c) the internal-to-Greece interveners in the case. From the perspective of some theologians, in taking the *Papageorgiou* case to the European level and in intervening "in favor" of *Papageorgiou*, the insider critics preclude the possibility of constructive critique: they bypass direct communication, and it seems the nature of the litigation process as one of confrontation is rather consuming, even more so for European-level litigation. From the perspective of others, including those studying ECtHR engagements with religion-related case law and especially those studying the latter in relation to Greece specifically, the potential critique from the ECtHR is welcome, not least because it has been incredibly instructive in terms of leading to changes in legislation and practices. This prompts the following question: though the outcome of court-issued critique may be positive (in the eye of the beholder), if the means (litigation) is aggressive and confrontational, may the critique still be considered "constructive"? In other words, should the term "constructive" be nuanced to distinguish between means and ends?

Certainly, for some of the religious actors in question, much depends on the final outcome. For example, in the case of *Papageorgiou*, for some theologians who saw the "baby steps" in RE reform as an unfortunate necessity, in the event of the Court finding Greece to have violated the claimants' rights, it is *conceivable* that if this helps open the way to further reform, then the Court's critique embedded in its decision could be received by the religious actors in question as a constructive and positive development. Here, however, the complexities of law and politics enter the picture: because in reality state reactions to case law are rarely so immediate, positive, and straightforward (e.g., the chances of the Greek state reacting by saying "OK, clearly our RE needs to be even less confessional in order to be mandatory, so rather than lose RE from the curriculum in general, let's make that change" are slim), such a perspective on the Court critique as constructive is rather unlikely.

Conclusions

Socio-legal scholar Marc Galanter writes that "the masses will do better at reconciling reforms with their religious understandings if the courts disclaim any competence in religious matters and reiterate instead their claim to overriding authority in whatever touches upon public life." In so doing, he highlights the questioned competence of courts to engage substantially with religious matters and that critique from courts will be better received by religious actors influenced by their decisions if courts steer clear of claiming competence over "religious matters." One question this raises is what counts as religious matters: as illustrated with reference to the case of *Papageorgiou v. Greece*, religious actors were bothered by the ECtHR's (presumed) inability to comprehend the complicated socio-political-historical story of RE in the Greek context, and not just the even more difficult "religious matters" of doctrine and the like. Thus, this group of actors has questions as to how well Greek RE can be examined in the vacuum of court precedence and from the historical and cultural distance represented by Strasbourg.

Thus instead of (or at least, in addition to) the theologians' focus on the critique that might emanate from that court, the theologians have paid significant attention to the "insider critique" expressed by other actors involved in a particular case (in this case, the claimants and their legal counsel and the third-party interveners). In my attention to the latter perspectives here, I have highlighted the gray areas between "insiders" and "outsiders" when it comes to critique of religion, as well as the differing expectations held by the theologians defending the reformed RE of the actors representing different *degrees* of insider- or outsiderness (the Court, the claimant, the legal counsel, the "secularist" intervener, and the "neutral" intervener). Finally, the chapter also further complicates notions of "constructiveness" of critique of religion by adding attention to the means versus the ends of that critique. Overall, this chapter adds texture to much already existing scholarship on the complexities involved in courts' engagements with religion.

7

Framing Religious Criticism in a Secular Cultural and Legal Order: Subsidies to Muslim Youth Organizations

Pia Karlsson Minganti

Religious criticism can be externally formulated from a non-religious standpoint, which is certainly the case for much contemporary criticism of Islam in societies where Muslims live as minorities. Values like human rights, democracy, equality, and nonviolence are often at the forefront of this critique and also make up the basic conditions for governmental funding to religious organizations in Sweden. In this chapter[1] I will employ the concepts of secularist, restrictionist, and open strategies of critical engagement with religious issues (as elaborated by Stenmark in chapter 1) to explore how external criticism of religion as practiced by the state may (dis)enable constructive criticism and dialogue. Following the line of thought characterizing this book, I apply constructive criticism of religion as a dialectic process that promotes enhanced understanding and transformative learning, rather than increasing hostility and polarization. The inquiry is illustrated by the example of the Swedish state actions towards a youth organization with a Muslim profile. More precisely, the analysis draws on a legal process in the Swedish court system, concerning the Swedish Agency for Youth and Civil Society's (Myndigheten för ungdoms- och civilsamhällesfrågor, MUCF) decision in 2016 to deny governmental funding to the national umbrella organization Sweden's Young Muslims (Sveriges Unga Muslimer, SUM). MUCF's denial came after many years of approvals and was motivated by criticism against SUM for not living up to the democratic criterion for such funding (MUCF 2016).[2]

Young peoples' development of civic values and behaviors is important for national governing bodies and the focus of an extensive bulk of international research (Amnå 2012). The Swedish government's youth policy aims to create conditions for all young people "to have good living conditions, the power to form their own lives and influence over developments in society" (MUCF 2018a). The policy is defined in line with a global code of individual children's rights to be informed and involved, as for instance manifested in the 1989 UN Convention on the Rights of the Child, which nowadays also includes civic engagement, and the European Union Youth Strategy 2010–2018, which aims at supporting "young people's participation in representative democracy and civil society at all levels and in society at large" (EU 2009). Besides safeguarding individual rights, these policies also emphasize young peoples' role in strengthening the democracy and civil society organizations' role as schools of democracy (Van Der Meer and Van Ingen 2009; O'Toole and Gale 2012).

Thus, the Swedish government's youth policy reflects an internationally disseminated idea that civic engagement in adolescence constitutes a crucial societal resource and that this resource ought to be channeled through recognized civil society organizations. In Sweden, this is arranged in a rather unique model for the relationship between the state and civil society, which grants substantial governmental funding to organizations. Since the nineteenth century, the model has served to mediate interests between the state and various social and religious movements, such as the labor movement and the Free Churches; today, this model provides incentives for new ethnic and religious minority groups to take part in dialogue and decision-making processes (Micheletti 1995; Karan 2008).

Youth organizations can apply for governmental funding through MUCF (2018b) on the basis of the Ordinance on central government grants for child and youth organizations (SFS[3] 2011:65, previously 2001:1060). This is also true for youth organizations with a religious profile. Contrary to religious organizations, their rights to funding are not assessed by the application of the Act concerning faith communities (SFS 1998:1593), nor of the Act concerning state support to faith communities (SFS 1999:932). This means that, as I will highlight in this chapter, criticism against a youth organization like SUM does not necessarily deal with "religion" in an explicit way but is rather expressed within the frames of public debate over, for instance, democracy, equality, security, and the state–civil society relationship.

Like other European welfare states in transition, Sweden faces challenges to the relationship between the state and civil society organizations with regard to their pluralism and autonomy. In a way, the Swedish state's ambition to invite and support eligible organizations stands in tension with the principle of social movements as being independent of the established political order. From the perspective of youth civic education, professor of political science Erik Amnå stresses that "the more the development of civic engagement becomes dependent on initiatives from above, the greater is the risk that adolescents will be tamed and disciplined rather than empowered and skilled" (2012: 612). Extensive research demonstrates how religious, immigrant, and youth movements that try to organize in Sweden tend to adjust to a complex system of state grants, which imposes structural prerequisites and monitoring (Karan 2008; Enkvist and Nilsson 2016; Dahlstedt and Foultier 2018). In reaction to these dilemmas, there are suggestions to motivate organizations to decline subsidies in order to regain autonomy, or to cut public funding to civil organizations altogether. Simultaneously, public and political debates call for increased surveillance over new movements such as SUM and for continuous governmental funding, albeit on restricted conditions, in order for the state to maintain control over their development (SOU 2016, 2018).

Intimately linked to the call for restrictive policy implementation is the process in which religious engagement is becoming politicized and ultimately securitized, that is, defined as a threat to society. In the wake of the Islamist terrorist attacks in several European countries, including Sweden in 2010 and 2017, and of the recruitment of young Europeans by jihadist movements, the securitization of Muslims has increased. Professor of religion and politics Jocelyne Cesari (2018) has illuminated how the securitization of Muslims is not only a matter of state prevention of foreign political violence but is also aimed at Islamic religious practices which are interpreted as signs of political radicalism, such as sartorial and greeting practices. Some of these practices, like the covering and seclusion of female and queer bodies, point to a key area of tension in today's Europe: that is, the balancing of freedom of religion with gender and sexual equality. However, researchers like Cesari (2018) and Beaman and Lefebvre (chapter 8 in this volume) illuminate how valid criticism of religion can become subsumed by a complete rejection of religion or a specific religion such as Islam. Configurations of gender, sexuality, and "race"/ethnicity are today realigning in relation to contemporary trends of nationalism and securitization, respectively, and constitute an important driver of critique of religion. When such values as equality, democracy, and security are claimed to be European, Swedish, or secular liberal in contrast to Muslim, a consequence is that governments are granted greater means to control expressions of Islam and religions in general, which may threaten religious freedom and democracy across Europe.

In this chapter, I explore how a secular government agency interacts with a Muslim-oriented youth organization when affected by these aforementioned multifaceted developments within and beyond Europe. While focusing on a particular Swedish context, the chapter contributes insights to an international problem: in what ways are constructive religious criticism (dis)enabled when a secular government agency and other influential secular actors implicitly take on the task of religious criticism? When reacting to certain suspected problems within SUM, does MUCF articulate *negative* critique that undermines Islam as a religion, or *constructive* critique of religion that is comprehensible for SUM and thereby can open up possibilities for improvement in relation to those particular problems? Further, is governmental funding necessary to maintain constructive religious criticism? What other spaces for religious criticism emerge if state-supported organizations are dismantled, and with what implications?

The analysis draws on materials produced within the legal process between MUCF and SUM, and on knowledge produced during my fieldwork with Muslim organizations, including SUM (see for instance Karlsson Minganti 2007, 2012, 2016, 2017). The first three sections of this chapter offer chronologically arranged insights into MUCF's reviews of SUM with points of departure in two selected cases: one in 2010 and another that was initiated in 2016. Briefly, in the 2010 case, MUCF reviewed SUM's eligibility for funding taking into consideration that it had been accused of discrimination against members on the basis of sexual orientation. The review was solely based on formal documents produced by SUM, and MUCF concluded that these did not show any discrimination. The 2016 case concerns SUM's annual application for governmental funding and MUCF's denial with reference to its commission to promote democracy and counteract extremism. The suspicion of internal discrimination runs as a thread through this case also, but the concern with violent extremism is a new element, as is the broadening of the legal material invoked when the case was brought to court. Beside formalities such as SUM's statutes and activity reports also six media articles and editorials along with two non-scientific reports were invoked by MUCF both to analyze SUM in relation to wider societal contexts and to hold SUM, as an entire "environment," responsible for the actions of individual representatives, guest speakers, and associated organizations. Finally, the last two sections offer contextualization and discussion of the external criticism of religion implicitly performed by the state agency MUCF from legal, cultural, and religious studies perspectives.

Review 2010

SUM was established in 1991 and today involves 4,000 members and 22 local associations in various towns across Sweden (SUM 2016, 2018). The organization is a heterogeneous community of young people with various ethnic and social backgrounds. Although it is dominated by Sunni Islam, it claims to be open to young Muslims of all denominations:

> Sweden's Young Muslims is an organization that gathers local associations from all over the country and is run by and for Muslim youth. We work for boys and girls of Muslim background to get to know Islam and become strengthened in their Muslim identity. We also promote our members' positive participation and engagement in society and its institutions, as Muslims constitute a self-evident part of Sweden. By disseminating knowledge and broad collaborations we also counteract prejudice and mistakes about Islam and Muslims. (SUM 2018)[4]

MUCF has been evaluating the operation of SUM as well as other youth organizations in connection with their annual applications for governmental funding, which are decided on in December every year. In June 2010, MUCF decided to make an extra review of SUM's eligibility. The main catalysts for this were two particular media events during the spring of 2010.

The first occurred in March when, less than a month before the opening of SUM's national conference, an invited guest speaker was questioned in a public debate in both formal and new social media. The debate was prompted by an article published at Newsmill.se, a Swedish website for news commentary and debate, written by Philip Wendahl, LGBTQ activist and then secretary of the association Liberal Mångfald (Liberal Diversity). The guest speaker in question was the North American imam Abdullah Hakim Quick, who had previously been accused of hate speech by the British LGBTQ rights group OutRage!. Wendahl consequentially called for the withdrawal of governmental funding to SUM (Wendahl 2010).

After a crisis summit, SUM issued a press release explaining that to SUM, both Wendahl and Outrage! were known to use anti-Muslim and Islamophobic rhetoric (see also Puar 2007; Sörberg 2017), and that Quick was invited on the basis of being an inspiring preacher on topics such as co-existence and openness for Muslims to the societies in which they live. Although the organization shared Quick's view that "Islam does not allow same-sex sexual relations," they argued that a pluralistic society should allow multiple choices of lifestyle and referred to their common discussions on LGBTQ questions with other youth organizations:

> We live in an open society where anyone who wants to promote a heterosexual marriage-relation building on an Islamic lifestyle is fully entitled to do so, and anyone who chooses another lifestyle than the Islamic one should of course be free to do so. (SUM 2010)

The negative public attention continued, among other things, based on the claim that SUM does not represent the correct/only interpretation of Islam. A new press release was issued by SUM announcing the decision, in agreement with Quick, to cancel his participation in the conference.

After the conference, the Swedish Radio Channel 1 program Kaliber reported about the approach to LGBTQ people in all the religious youth associations entitled to governmental funding via MUCF (Gahnertz 2010). The investigation claimed that homosexual members in five of these organizations had been subjected to discrimination; they had been pressed to "heal" or "restrain" from homosexuality and denied access to crucial positions within the organizations. The five organizations in question were Sweden's Young Muslims, Sweden's Young Catholics, the youth sections of the Pentecostal and Evangelist Free Churches, and the Youth Initiative in the Syrian Orthodox Church.

Following the radio program, MUCF decided to make an extended review of these five religious youth organizations. It was carried out with reference to the ordinance on central government grants for child and youth organizations (SFS 2001:1060, articles 6–9), which stipulates that, in order to be eligible, organizations need to have a democratic structure with an operation that does not contravene the ideas of democracy (MUCF 2010). The review was solely based on formal documents produced by SUM, such as its annual activity reports, financial statements, membership statistics, statutes, policies, and guidelines, along with its homepage, which included a selection of educational material and documents from camps and conferences (MUCF 2010; Wikström, in Zetterman 2010). With reference to the constitutional law of freedom of association and of speech, MUCF did at the time apply a wide interpretation of its democracy criterion, contending that as long as an organization in its formal documents keeps within the limits for what could be expressed with regard to the constitutional rights or other legislations, its operation is compatible with democracy. The evaluation did not include single activities or statements from representatives or members, as these "are not necessarily representative for the organization" (MUCF 2017: 12). Within these frames, MUCF concluded that there were no indications that SUM was discriminating against members on the basis of sexual orientation and rejected the suggestion to withdraw governmental funding.

Review 2016

In 2016, on the contrary, MUCF actually decided to reject SUM's application for governmental funding (MUCF 2016). The decision was made with reference to the earlier-mentioned ordinance on central government grants for child and youth organizations, which stated that funding can only be rewarded to organizations that "in their operating activities respect the ideas of democracy including equality and prohibition against discrimination" (article 8). MUCF confirmed that the interpretation of "respecting the ideas of democracy" is complicated, and that it had previously considered an organization as living up to this standard as long as it operated within the limits of constitutional rights, such as the freedom of association and freedom of speech. However, now MUCF had come to see it as necessary to weigh these rights against yet another of its commissions, that is, "to counteract extremism." Specific reference was given to the ordinance on central government grants for activities to safeguard democracy (SFS 2011:1508, article 3) and its aim to "reduce the number of active persons within violent extremist environments". Therefore, MUCF found itself obliged to sharpen its interpretation of the democracy criterion and identified the following central circumstances for declining SUM's proposal:

> Sweden's Young Muslims (SUM) and its local affiliated associations have, at various occasions and in various contexts, been pointed out as an environment where there are individuals who do not respect the ideas of the democracy, including the principle of equality and prohibition against discrimination. It has been a matter of individuals who have expressed themselves in ways not compatible with the aim of the ordinance on central government grants, but also about connections to other organizations that can be regarded as not compatible with the ideas of democracy, for instance the Muslim Brotherhood. (MUCF 2016)

New to this decision in 2016, in contrast to that of 2010, is the association of SUM with extremism and the very defining of the organization as an entire "environment," which is held responsible for the actions of individual representatives, guests, and assumedly related organizations. New also is the widened scope of material used by MUCF to substantiate its decision. This time it was based not only on SUM's formal documents, but also on six media articles and editorials. MUCF also invoked knowledge received in collaboration (*samverkan*) with other agencies, none of which however was shared publicly. Hence, the only sources made explicit are the six listed media articles and editorials.

One of the texts stands out in the sense that it was authored by the current president of SUM, Rashid Musa (2014). The remaining three articles (Eriksson 2014; Lundberg 2016; Van Den Brink 2016) and two editorials (Kronqvist 2015; Gudmundsson 2016) were written by non-Muslim journalists. In these texts, SUM is in various argumentative formations associated with movements such as the Muslim Brotherhood, the Islamic State, and Salafism. Moreover, the texts contend that SUM constitutes a platform for non-democratic extremism with regard to religion, gender oppression, antisemitism, homophobia, and violence.[5] The next section demonstrates how SUM used such criticism when composing an appeal to the Administrative Court.

Insufficient Communication—An Infringement of the Administrative Law

In January 2017, SUM appealed MUCF's dismissal at the Administrative Court in Stockholm (SUM 2017). The appeal was made with reference to the Administrative Procedure Act (SFS 1986: 223, article 17), which states that in matters where state authorities exercise public power, no matter may be determined without the applicant having been informed about anything brought into the matter by someone other than herself or himself and having been given an opportunity to respond to it. The allegation of deficient communication is chiefly based on the argument that the material used by MUCF to ground its verdict had not been fully communicated to SUM. When MUCF states that the six media articles and editorials used are but examples, this means that SUM has been denied the opportunity to respond to other possible sources.

Deficient communication is furthermore described in terms of a perceived misinterpretation of the organization and its activities. SUM agrees with MUCF about the need to control organizations that are granted governmental funding and that such funding is not a right in itself. However, SUM does not share MUCF's conclusion that the organization has failed to respect democracy. SUM lists its formal memberships in and collaboration with other organizations, such as The National Council of Swedish Youth Organizations and the Discrimination Ombudsman, and further examples of its efforts in support of democracy and equality are offered. These include a lecture about the Swedish Police Authority's work against hate crimes held by a police representative who is also a founder of the Gay Police Association in Sweden, and data showing that women constitute 40 percent of its regular members and 60 percent of the board.

The Administrative Court found in favor of SUM in its criticism of insufficient communication. With reference to the Swedish constitution (chapter 1, article 9) on equality before the law and right to due process, the court confirms that "it is a given premise for trials made by administrative authorities and courts of law that the circumstances constituting the basis for a decision should be concrete and possible to respond to and verify" (Administrative Court 2017). The court furthermore states that "the fact that an organization has been criticized in media for its operation cannot in the administrative court's opinion form the basis for a rejection of an application for governmental funding" (Administrative Court 2017). Lastly, the court comments on a source that MUCF had retrospectively acknowledged to have been influential on its decision. The source is a report published on the homepage of the Swedish Civil Contingencies Agency (Myndigheten för Samhällsskydd och Beredskap, MSB), which is organized under the Ministry of Defense and is responsible for public safety, risk management, and civil defense. The report, titled Muslimska Brödraskapet i Sverige (The Muslim Brotherhood in Sweden) (Norell, Carlbom, and Durrani 2017a), was also published in English (Norell, Carlbom, and Durrani 2017b) by the Clarion Project, which is a Washington, DC-based organization that has been studied as an anti-Muslim think tank (see for instance Hafez 2017). The report received criticism from renowned Swedish researchers for containing errors and lacking scientific quality and evidence (Ackfeldt et al. 2017), and the Administrative Court ruled it out for having "very limited evidence value." In sum, the Administrative Court dismissed MUCF´s decision to reject SUM's proposal and referred it back to MUCF for reconsideration.

Evoking a Radical Religious Other in Discussions on Societal Dilemmas

When MUCF processed a new decision, it was supported by a report on SUM, commissioned from journalist Magnus Sandelin (2017), which contained more specific examples of non-democratic activities. Again, the decision was to reject SUM's application (MUCF 2018c). In so doing, MUCF chose to apply one of its strongest sanctions against a youth organization: the denial of governmental funding. SUM has long been seen as worthy of state support, but this view is now weighed against the threat of it as a potential platform for non-democratic activity and violent extremism. This shift of mindset can be compared to the tension identified by ethnologist Kim Silow Kallenberg (2016), in her analysis of the relation between youth and state institutions. Here, she argues that "teenagers are alternately being constructed as children in need and as manipulative criminals: articulations that are made part of either a logic of care or a logic of punishment" (Silow Kallenberg 2016, abstract). The balancing between such logics has consequences for institutional work, like when MUCF interprets SUM as irresponsible at best, or with a hidden agenda of violence and oppression at worst. The latter logic was eventually expressed by the director of MUCF in a media comment on the withdrawn support to SUM: "Citizens must feel safe that the taxpayers' money will not at any occasion be exploited by *mischievous interests* [author's emphasis]" (Nyberg 2017).

The material substantiating MUCF's rejection of SUM's application for funding was not produced in a vacuum. For instance, MUCF has claimed to be targeted by a campaign promoted by the market liberal think tank Timbro, with the aim to get rid of the system of tax-based governmental funding to organizations altogether (De Vivo 2017). Public debates are intertextually taking place in several forms of media and become integrated into the workings of other institutions, including state agencies (Brubaker 2012; Jensdotter and Lövheim, chapter 12). In fact, MUCF's analysis of SUM's formal documents was intimately intertwined with its analysis of a number of media articles and editorials that reflect particular social events and opinions which were used for a broader external analysis, a so-called "environmental scanning" (*omvärldsanalys*) (MUCF 2017). Therefore, although the invoked media articles and reports in the SUM case constitute a rather limited basis for decisions, it may be argued that this material reflects broader developments in Swedish society which motivate MUCF's new restrictive policy. I will now continue to look into how religion is approached in this material, and furthermore what ways of religious criticism and dialogue this may (dis)enable. The analysis will be carried out with help from three different strategies of critical engagement on religious issues: a secularist, a restrictionist, and an open strategy as described in Stenmark (chapter 1 in this volume).

The first one, the *secularist strategy*, aims at minimizing the influence of religion on society, since religion is thought to undermine liberal democracy. In Jensdotter and Lövheim's chapter 12, we can see how a large part of the so-called handshaking debate in a Swedish context has focused on secularity as an essential part of Swedish or broader Western values. Also, the sources invoked by MUCF demonstrate a polarized normative distancing from religious attitudes, like for example in the report by Norell et al.:

> All systems of government based on a particular interpretation of a religious (or political) ideology are incompatible with the liberal democratic structure we have created in the West, where the separation between religion and politics is fundamental. However, this does not only apply to Islam; regardless of dominant religious tradition, a conflict between secular and religious values arises. (Norell, Carlbom, and Durrani 2017b: 5)

Another example points to criticism against SUM president Rashid Musa's representation of religion in a secular society:

> Many people were provoked exactly because he, as representative for a religious organization, makes himself a spokesperson for all Sweden's young Muslims, of whom a large part is secular or see religion as a private matter. Musa [. . .] thinks that his members are deprived of their rights when they for example do not have a calm place for prayer at school. (Van Den Brink 2016)

Like in Jensdotter and Lövheim's study (chapter 12), secularism is predominantly expressed in dichotomous terms, not only between a "Swedish we" and a "Muslim other," but between a "secular we" and a "Muslim extremist other." Such distinctive positioning is relevant to the second *restrictionist strategy* of critical engagement on religious matters, where religion as such is not seen as a problem, but instead the forms of religion designated as religious fundamentalism or extremism are. One way of interpreting this strategy is to say that it invites dialogue, but under certain restrictions: moderate religious representatives are invited, but not those deemed as fundamentalists, extremists, or radical religious others. Sociologist Shirin Amir-Moazami (2011) underlines the importance for European democracies to reflect over their part in such polarization, not least in the selective process where some actors are identified and invited as the genuine Muslim representatives in state-initiated dialogue, while other voices are excluded.

In its decision, MUCF explicitly associates SUM with "extremism" when claiming that the youth organization has not convincingly lived up to the ordinance of reducing the number of persons active within violent extremist environments. Moreover, SUM is associated with other organizations explicitly claimed to be religious extremist, such as the Muslim Brotherhood. In fact, the authors of the invoked articles and reports point to SUM and its alleged associative movements as the very initiators of the breakdown of any legitimate dialogue:

> Basically, Islamists are building a parallel societal structure that competes with the rest of society over Swedish citizens' value systems. In this way, the Muslim

Brotherhood's activists constitute a long-term challenge in terms of the country's social cohesion. (Norell, Carlbom, and Durrani 2017b: 26)

Such a claim can be interpreted according to Robert Putnam's concept of bridging and bonding social capital (2000). Before 2016, SUM was identified as a platform that provided *bonding* activities that reinforce the identity of a single community (e.g., a religiously devoted Muslim organization) but also *bridging* activities that strengthen social cohesion across social boundaries (both within and beyond the minority group). However, the authors of MUCF's invoked sources in the 2016 case found it important to emphasize SUM as failing to perform bridging activities for the unity of broader society, while promoting an essentialist identity position for Muslims only. As social anthropologist Aje Carlbom explains (in a revised report commissioned by the Swedish Civil Contingencies Agency [MSB] after the first one by Norell, Carlbom, and Durrani 2017a was withdrawn from its homepage due to lack of scientific quality):

> A problem with organizations associated with the Muslim Brotherhood is that they contribute to creating political and social polarization by pitting an imagined "we" (Muslims) against an imagined "them" (non-Muslims). This is an identity politics strategy that pits groups against each other and thereby has a negative impact on democratic rules regarding the debate of factual issues. (2018: 2)

The term "identity politics," which is applied in this quotation and in several other of MUCF's invoked sources, is highly ambiguous. According to professor of psychosocial studies Ann Phoenix, it can be defined as "an intersection of *group* identity and politics, which can lead to social change. Identity politics arises when oppression becomes the focus of a strong separate group identity around which support, political analysis, and action are developed" (Phoenix 2000: 1097). For a youth organization with a religious profile, as is SUM, it may seem unproblematic to say that it is working for its members' maintenance of their religious faith and practice, while the maintenance of their religious identity becomes problematic in the case of a politicized and securitized minority. SUM has sought recognition for *Muslims*, while challenging discriminating appellations such as "immigrants," "blacks," and now "terrorists." In this sense, SUM's identity political mobilization is not necessarily different from that of other movements grown out of the experience of discrimination, for instance "women," "homosexuals," or "laborers." However, authors of the sources invoked by MUCF (Gudmundsson 2016; Lundberg 2016; Norell, Carlbom, and Durrani 2017a; Carlbom 2018) emphasize what professor of political science and communication Amy Gutmann highlights as a "bad" side of identity politics, which "entails putting considerations of group identity above considerations of justice" and leads to hatred and violence against others (Gutmann 2003: 16).

Viewed through the lens of this side of identity politics, SUM's engagement against racism and social injustice is then interpreted as a "polemic rhetoric" (Norell, Carlbom, and Durrani 2017b: 18). SUM's presentation of statistics that demonstrate women constituting the majority of its members are then criticized as a form of tokenism without substantial female participation, and SUM's agenda for education and political participation is scrutinized as built on premises alien to democracy. Altogether, the suspicion of "doublespeak" is triggered in the sense that the young activists of SUM are thought to follow a radical Islamist agenda internally before a Muslim public, while presenting themselves as good democrats before the general public and those governmental agencies that ignorantly grant them state support (Eriksson 2014; Gudmundsson 2016; Lundberg 2016; Van Den Brink 2016; Norell, Carlbom, and Durrani 2017b; Sandelin 2017).

MUCF is required to take decisions on state funding amidst various burning societal issues, such as equality and security. As highlighted by researchers like Cesari (2018), Puar (2007), and Beaman and Lefebvre (chapter 12 in this volume), the use of categories such as gender, sexuality, race, and ethnicity to infuse ideologies of nationalism and securitization constitute an important driver of the contemporary critique of religion. In this intricate context for decision-making, MUCF applies sources that are bordering on the thin line of constructing SUM as an unambiguous "radical religious other."

Continuing Communication and Constructive Religious Criticism?

Political scientist Farid Hafez (2017) warns against uncritically applying such sources that evoke an unambigous radical religious other and highlights how prominent a part think tanks play in the production of negative knowledge on Muslim civil society actors, in order to influence policymaking at the governmental level as well as in the European Union. In a study on the European Foundation for Democracy (EFD), which is a Brussels-based think tank with transatlantic relations, Hafez demonstrates how it

> [s]ystematically produces knowledge about Muslims that follows a strategy of defamation and delegitimization. It especially draws on the allegation of a connection between visible Muslim civil society actors and the Muslim Brotherhood. The conspiracy lies not only in the construction of a connection, but rather in the accusation of a unified agenda of social destructiveness and world domination, a planned Islamization of Europe. [. . .] The discourse on terrorism and extremism/radicalism is used against vocal Muslims and organizations to dismantle, disable, and discharge from the civic and political activism. (Hafez 2017: 131)

Drawing on empirical cases from Sweden and Austria, Hafez explores how the Muslim space of action is consequently reduced when Muslim actors are not only rejected for funding but also forced into a defensive position. Having to invest resources to challenge allegations in court, media, and political circles, they are further interrupted in their civil society activism. This motivates the question as to whether SUM's disqualification for governmental funding also means that it is disqualified as a continuous partner in dialogue, in line with the second *restrictionist strategy* of critical engagement on religious matters, which invites moderate religious representatives to dialogue, but not alleged fundamentalists/extremists/radical religious others.

The third *open strategy* would instead favor dialogue even with those who are deemed as radical religious people engaged in non-democratic behavior. This open strategy would include the acceptance of radical religious others' viewpoints being openly expressed and accessible within the framework of a democratic society. For the time being, MUCF seems to find this too high a price to pay, at least through tax-based governmental funding. Nevertheless, this reasoning is in line with Stenmark's argument (chapter 1) that permitting or even encouraging religious reason-giving is important for understanding why deeply devoted religious believers think and act like they do. This form of open communication is expected to lead to insights that would yield a more constructive external as well as internal religious criticism.

MUCF has long granted governmental funding to SUM in line with the Swedish model for subsidies to civil society organizations, based on the principle that they constitute arenas for dialogue and the strengthening of democracy. In this chapter, I have found that MUCF has shifted its view on SUM by emphasizing its failure to handle discrimination and violent extremism within its own ranks and associating it with Islamic radicalization. As a consequence, MUCF has applied its strongest sanction and disqualified SUM as eligible for state support.

A critical reading of this act is that it may silence any evidence of SUM's positive contribution to democracy. Much research on Muslim youth organizations in diaspora emphasizes complexity in their composition and outcomes, and their role as sites where different trends within contemporary Islam are expressed and tried out by their young members, spanning from Salafism to feminism and covering the full political spectrum (Frisina 2010; Karlsson Minganti 2007, 2012, 2016; Schmidt 2017; Nyhagen 2019). Such heterogeneous debate, including immanent critique of religion (see for instance chapter 3 in this volume), is disregarded when polarizing against a definite "radical religious other." MUCF itself points out that fear within the public sector of being associated with certain actors, activities, and attitudes can be a consequence of such polarization (MUCF 2018d). A similar worry is detected among Muslim civil society actors. Research shows how both individuals and organizations hesitate to use explicit references to Islam and Muslim identity since they fear being categorized as extremists and associated with anti-democratic behavior (Berglund 2012; Karlsson Minganti 2017; Beydoun 2018). Such a situation seems to shrink the freedom of religion and the scope for constructive religious criticism.

Given MUCF's new restrictive policy, a subsequent question is whether governmental funding is necessary for constructive religious criticism to happen. The answer might be no. Both MUCF and SUM agree that state support is not a right in itself. Civil society builds on freedom of association and voluntary work. One could even argue that for a social movement, to stay free from state grants would mean to create an autonomous space for developing societal critique, religious viewpoints, and identities independently from imposed structural prerequisites and monitoring (see for instance Karan 2008). For example, SUM's Italian counterpart Giovani Musulmani d'Italia [Young Muslims of Italy, GMI] manages to maintain its operation without access to direct financial support from the state (Frisina 2010; Coglievina 2013: 353). However, this makes GMI dependent on occasional project funding with predetermined agendas and the borrowing of premises from others, such as more established religious and cultural organizations and political parties. Thus, governmental funding might be necessary in order not to push youth organizations in the direction of underground activism or dependency on other, possibly even undemocratic, actors.

One more crucial question is the context in which religious constructive criticism can take place. In a climate of distrust between the state and some youth organizations, as described in this chapter, there is no obvious site for dialogue. The development of such distrust is intertwined with the ongoing dismantling of the Swedish model for the relation between state and civil society organizations, in which state support was seen as a way of acknowledging religious freedom as a cornerstone for democracy (SOU 2018). Spaces for dialogue and religious criticism will be lost or changed into new ones. This chapter has looked into the legal system as a growing space for such communication to take place. All around Europe, there is an increase in the solving of conflicts concerning religion by or with reference to the judicialization of religion (Foblets et al. 2014; Fokas chapter 6). The court is a means for bringing structural order and safeguarding fair trials. A few days before the finalization of this chapter, the Administrative Court for a second time dismissed MUCF's decision, after SUM had mobilized a renewed appeal (case no. 9821-18). The court points to the lack of evidence that SUM is connected with the Muslim Brotherhood and to the disregarding of SUM's pro-democracy and anti-extremist activities. Thus, it demonstrates that criticism cannot be delivered in any manner of means. Yet, a question for further discussion is whether the court is the right place to develop constructive religious criticism or, as indicated in this chapter, it rather emerges as a site where antagonism is expressed and communication is drawn to a close.

Studies on contemporary programs against violent extremism remind us that the hazardous relationship between Islamophobic knowledge production and Islamic radicalization can be likened to "a medicine causing another sickness while intending to cure it" (Iner 2017: 1). Even though MUCF's dismissal of funding to SUM may not be meant to undermine Islam as religion, but rather to improve the way of life of these young Muslims and of all Swedish citizens, it does not establish interactions for transformative learning. In that sense, MUCF's rejection of SUM entails a breaking with the view on constructive critique of religion suggested in this book. Invoking SUM as a religious "radical other" turns out a stance which loses sight of the organization's heterogenous knowledge production, including immanent religious criticism, while disqualifying it as a partner in dialog on vital societal issues, such as democracy, equality, and security. Ultimately, this stance jeopardizes young peoples' chances of being recognized and heard and runs the risk that they interiorize and elaborate on a polarized identity and worldview.

8

Critique of Religion in Public Commissions on Cultural and Religious Diversity

Lori G. Beaman and Solange Lefebvre

In their introduction, Lövheim and Stenmark define critique of religion as an assessment or evaluation of religion that is differentiated from a simple understanding of religion. Critique may involve rejection, questioning, or pointing out areas within religion where change is needed. Lövheim and Stenmark also call for a more comprehensive and methodical examination of resources for critique located within religious worldviews themselves. This chapter takes up that challenge through an examination of three public commissions, how they provide a structured format for critique of religion, and the links between this critique and the social and cultural contexts of the commissions. Both internal and external criticism stimulated the critical questions addressed by the commissions established in the three countries under study. Ultimately, the entanglement of religion with its cultural and social contexts poses a challenge to any strict division between critique from within and from without.

The following sections examine the ways critique of religion has been expressed in three contexts, namely, Belgium, France, and Quebec (Canada), since the year 2000, and how governments have established and used public commissions as a strategy to structure and channel the highly polarized debates in which these criticisms are elaborated.[1] We chose to compare these three contexts not only because their commissions have confronted similar challenges and concerns, but also because of the relationships between the three. For example, the province of Quebec maintains close ties with France, because most people in Quebec can trace their ethnic origins back to the colonial period. Belgium also has a connection with France, as well as with Quebec, based on its tradition of civil law and its large French minority. All three are historically Catholic societies in which anticlericalism and secularism exist in varying degrees; they share Francophone intellectual points of reference; and they have maintained academic, cultural, and political relationships among themselves. Belgium and Canada are both multinational and multilingual states. An analysis of the commissions in these three societies allows us not only to compare their similarities, but also to identify their unique aspects.

Ultimately, this text reflects on the way that highly mediatized events have shaped the critique of religion over the last few years, using analyses conducted by our research team.² The first section describes four sociocultural and historical drivers that contextualize religious critique within the commissions. The second section presents the commissions and the main public debates that occurred, focusing especially on two issues related to the aforementioned drivers: gender equality in relation to religious symbols, and how cultural Catholicism tends to translate into religious power.

Critique of Religion

Four drivers of critique of religion are important in our areas of study: non-religion as a generator of criticism; a matrix of critical intellectual forces; Catholic critical theologies; and lastly, concerns about security, human rights, extremism, and gender equality. Each of these drivers constituted part of the social context in which the commissions conducted their inquiries, and they formed part of the public discussions and submissions to the commissions. During the past twenty years, in each of the contexts under consideration, these drivers have converged in an intense public discussion about gender equality, sexuality, culture, and religion in the public sphere.

Non-religion

In many Western countries, the number of people who identify as non-religious is rising rapidly. In Canada, Australia, the United States, Sweden, and France, for example, the proportion of non-religious people represents over one quarter of the respective total populations (Statistics Canada 2011; Deseret News 2018; Pew-Templeton 2015a, 2015c). In Britain, nearly half of the population identify as non-religious (Woodhead 2016). Twenty-nine percent of the French population identify as a "convinced atheist" (WIN-Gallup 2012). In Belgium, 29 percent of the population is "unaffiliated" (Pew-Templeton 2015b). While definitions of non-religion and approaches to measurement vary, the trend, in many Western countries, toward disaffiliation or never having had a religion is clear.

What has yet to be adequately explained is why people have left and are leaving organized religion. We speculate that non-religion is both an expression of religious criticism, such as the recent case of Rahaf Mohammed al-Qunun (Alexander 2019; Zuckerman 2012), as well as a cause of religious criticism (e.g., people like Richard Dawkins). There is likely no single cause of the departure from religion as an expression of criticism, but an amalgam of causes that range from discontent with church doctrine, clergy behavior (including sexual abuse), and a disconnect between everyday life and systems of religious meaning (Marks 2017).³ Generational differences—there is a higher percentage of young people who are non-religious—occur because many in newer generations have had no religious socialization (Pew Research Center 2018: 8–9). Pew concludes that "adults under 40 are less likely to be religiously affiliated," in

41 countries inclusive of North America, 22 out of 35 countries in Europe, and 14 out of 19 countries in Latin America (Pew 2018: 33).

It remains to be seen whether non-religion will continue to grow; certainly there is a budding scholarship suggesting that it will (including for example that of Clarke and MacDonald (2017)). At least some proportion of those who join these ranks take a critical stance toward organized religion, although a number of people who self-identify as "nones" are simply indifferent (Quack and Schuh 2017). The Pew Research Center (2015a) estimated that the world population included 1.17 billion "religiously unaffiliated people" (atheists, agnostics, and those who do not identify with any religion). This segment of "nones" represents 16 percent of the global population (Lipka and McClendon 2017). In the three societies under study, 62 percent of Belgians (under age 40, 54 percent), 67 percent of Canadians (under age 40, 49 percent), and 72 percent of France's population (under age 40, 63 percent) claim a religious affiliation (Pew Research Center 2018: 64–5). Of course, numbers do not tell the story of the relationship between the affiliated and the "nones," and the context of the debates is also important in determining the extent to which religious critique is linked to either the religious or the non-religious. As we will discuss below, there are some elements that may help to shed light on that relationship, namely, some intellectual influences and the history of conflict between *laïcité* and Roman Catholicism.

The non-religious hold a variety of worldviews: some consider themselves spiritual but not religious (Ammerman 2013: 258–78); some identify as humanists; and a portion identify as atheists (Brown 2017: 439–56), some of which are specifically anti-religious. Many non-religious suffer discrimination as a result of their choice to disengage from organized religion (Cragun et al. 2012; Edgell et al. 2016).

A consideration of non-religion is relevant to our discussion not only because it represents a form of religious criticism (as discussed also by LeDrew in this volume), but also because it impacts the social contexts in which the commissions we studied conducted their work. In these contexts, tensions between the highly religious and the non-religious are likely to increase unless there is a more sophisticated understanding of similarities, differences, and the ways in which criticism can be respectfully constructed. In part, non-religious criticism of religion draws on a matrix of critical intellectual forces, and it is to these that we now turn.

Critical Intellectual Forces and Suspicion of Religion

A second driver of critique of religion involves a broader history that is too complex to detail here, but is important to mention as a cultural backdrop and part of the global influential European intellectual tradition. French philosopher Paul Ricœur identified three "masters of suspicion" in a "school of suspicion," an expression that would become quite famous (also known as the "hermeneutics of suspicion"): Marx, Nietzsche, and Freud (Ricœur 1965; Scott-Bauman 2009). Though divergent in approach, their main point is that the human mind must carefully interpret the meaning of life and things by dispelling "illusions" (Marx), detecting "lies of the conscience" (Freud), and unmasking "false values" (Nietzsche), thus opening the way for a solid critique of ideology and religion. Their common intention, observed

Ricœur, was to consider human consciousness as a "false consciousness" that should be questioned and transformed. Ricœur proposed a new interpretation of meaning and symbolism, a "phenomenology of the sacred," by considering the approaches adopted by these three influential thinkers. It is important to remember that these thinkers link their criticism particularly to religion, using metaphors that became famous: religion as the opium of the people (Marx 1844), the great psychological illusion (Freud 1955), and the death of God (Nietzsche 1982). The three had a major influence on numerous academics and intellectuals, who would base their reflections on these visions of religion. Several of them, like Ricœur, elaborated a critique of religion from within, and others would adopt the thinkers' radical critical and antireligious views, such as the French existentialists Albert Camus, Jean-Paul Sartre, and Simone de Beauvoir.

More precisely, and in relation to the context of the commissions under study, these thinkers had a deep influence on Francophone thinkers (Aron 1955; Simard 1998). Particularly through the mandatory teaching of philosophy and literature to adolescents and young adults at the secondary and college level, this influence went beyond the circles of specialists, and had a lasting effect on general culture. After the 1950s, and at least until the 1980s, professors celebrated Marx, Camus, Sartre, Lenin, Freud, Marcuse, and Lacan in their classrooms. Feminists were inspired by the existentialist Simone de Beauvoir and the psychoanalyst Luce Irigaray (Simard 1998: 83–5). We propose that the contemporary public criticism of religion is still partly based on the diffuse and vast influence of this complex intellectual network of scholars or on the three masters and their heirs. This occurs through what Simard calls a French paradigm, emphasizing how religions controlled and perverted sexuality (Freud); how religion subjected humankind to false transcendent values (Nietzsche); and how religion has functioned simultaneously as a compensation for and a source of oppression (Marx). Even today, these viewpoints are common themes in public debates.

Catholic Critical Theologies and Their Conservative Counterpart

The three commission reports we analyzed in our study were generated in nations that have historically been Catholic majoritarian societies, and therefore we must recognize the important role that internal voices play in the overall critical engagement with religion, our third driver under consideration here. Attracted by the masters of suspicion and their followers, left-wing Catholicism was influential during the twentieth century, as seen with Emmanuel Mounier and Catholic social movements (Simard 1998; Meunier and Warren 2002). Especially after the 1950s, critical theologies emerged as dynamic religious leaders, theologians, and others actively engaged in current social issues. This opened paths to new theologies such as critical moral theology, liberation theology, and feminist theology, partly inspired by Marx, Freud, Nietzsche, and other critical thinkers. These approaches plead for a more flexible and deeper understanding of sexual diversity (Curran and McCormick 1982, 1988; Ratzinger 1986; Schermer 2017), gender equality (Daly 1985, 1973; Schüssler Fiorenza 1984; Schüssler Fiorenza, Collins and Lefébure 1985; Ross 2001), and power and wealth redistribution (Baum 1999), inside the church as well as in society.

However, with the development of critical theologies, there also emerged a strong resistance from conservative Catholics. Some highly influential Catholic religious leaders and groups vigorously resisted these progressive efforts, leading to a polarization inside Catholicism which continues today as the theological debates intensify. So, for example, since the 1970s, popes, bishops, and cardinals have harshly condemned abortion, divorce, contraception, homosexuality, gender equality, and also progressive theologies (Pope Francis 2013; Conseil Famille et Société 2012; Béraud and Portier 2015). Such was the case in Spain (Burns 1981; Blofield 2006), in France, in Canada, and in Belgium (Boffey 2018; Herinckx 2018). They have put pressure on national legislators to criminalize abortion (Gendron 2018), keep marriage as an exclusively heterosexual institution (Béraud and Portier 2015; Rayside and Wilcox 2011), and limit access to divorce, and in some cases they have actively campaigned against condoms in countries where HIV is spreading (Molligan 2010). While moralizing about personal sexual conduct and family matters, within their own ranks, sexual abuse of children by priests has been a pervasive problem that was being systematically covered up by many levels of Church hierarchy (Keenan 2012).

Some of the conservative representatives in the Church attribute internal sexual problems and scandals to the influence of critical theologies, and of social, cultural, and sexual revolutions:

> Particularly among conservatives, however, there is a growing feeling that . . . it is not only the priests and bishops who must examine their consciences, but lay believers who have grown used to flouting the church's teaching on, for example, artificial contraception. We have fallen into the traps of the sexual revolution . . . We need to take seriously our sins and realize our faults rather than just be angry at our bishops. (*Economist* 2018)

The current pope of the Catholic Church, Francis, seems to be more liberal, but he is not fundamentally changing discourse and doctrine on these matters, except regarding inequalities between the rich and the poor, and a more flexible approach to divorce (Pope Francis 2016). Pope Francis engages in a less moralistic speech than some of his predecessors, notably on homosexuality, insisting on mercy, but without questioning elements of doctrine. His position regarding women in the priesthood illustrates this paradox:

> Demands that the legitimate rights of women be respected, based on the firm conviction that men and women are equal in dignity, present the Church with profound and challenging questions which cannot be lightly evaded. The reservation of the priesthood to males, as a sign of Christ the Spouse who gives himself in the Eucharist, is not a question open to discussion, but it can prove especially divisive if sacramental power is too closely identified with power in general. (Pope Francis 2013: para. 104)

The fact that he is not bringing about fundamental change may be because conservative factions inside the Church have been attacking him very aggressively on any front concerning change (Nemo 2018). The tenuous hold of critical theologies is rendered even more so by another development that has potentially significant consequences: the gradual disappearance of public places in which critical theology has traditionally developed and been nurtured. As some public universities loosen their ties with religion in response to the increasingly diverse social contexts in which they operate, they are letting go of their faculties and schools of theology. Meanwhile, the Church is creating or reinforcing conformist training institutions (Lefebvre 2016). We now turn to the fourth driver of religious criticism, which has emerged from both religious and non-religious social actors in the wake of terrorist attacks around the world.

Security, Human Rights, Extremism, and Gender Equality

Public discourse about religion has changed following the September 11, 2001 terrorist attacks in the United States (Mamdani 2004; Birt 2006; Nagra 2011). Anxiety about religion in general rose considerably, since religion was clearly referred to as a source of violent ideologies, both by terrorist organizations themselves and by politicians, particularly in the United States. The years that followed saw the emergence of new forms of racialization of Muslims in Western countries, and negative attitudes against Muslim immigrants (Razack 2004, 2008; Guénif-Souilamas and Macé 2005; Selby, Barras, and Beaman 2018). Anxiety around Islam and variations of Islamophobia increased dramatically after subsequent terrorist attacks in London (2005), Madrid (2004), and elsewhere, even though terrorism within Muslim countries against Muslims was also prevalent (Razack 2008; Shazad 2014). There was an amplification of criticism of religion more generally, as an irrational ideological threat (Dawkins 2006; Hitchens 2007) and also as a root cause of gender equality (Thistlethwaite 2014).

A second topic around which criticism of religion has emerged has to do with human rights and gender equality and, specifically, with the sustained attack on reproductive and same-sex rights by Catholic leaders. This attack has been orchestrated by Catholic leaders, especially in countries where the Catholic Church was majoritarian (Belgium, Canada, France, Ireland, Italy, and Latin America). In the United States, where roughly 20% of the population is Catholic, the Catholic Church allied itself with Evangelicals to push forward the agenda against abortion and homosexuality (Béraud and Portier 2015; Rayside and Wilcox 2011). In addition, the combined ongoing effects of large-scale sexual abuse committed by members of Catholic clergy and Catholic religious communities, especially those involved in school settings, has also yielded religious criticism. Other forms of religious extremism have also given rise to criticism of religion. These include expressions of Christian extremism against USA abortion clinics, and racist and violent acts by Christian white supremacists (Juergensmeyer 2017). All of the above has led to a particular type of criticism of religion which depicts the latter as backward, conservative, and toxic for individuals and groups, especially for women and for gender equality. In the three country contexts we studied, this form of critique emerged in the submissions to the commissions and in public statements and discussions.

With these drivers and contextual factors in mind, we turn to the specifics of the three commissions, including the ways they framed religious criticism and how religious criticism, in turn, shaped their outcome.

Public Debates and Commissions

Our team began a multidisciplinary research project in 2008 in which we studied national public commissions that had addressed the challenges of managing cultural and religious diversity (Lefebvre and Brodeur 2017). We examined the issues and controversies each commission focused on and explored their framing of the issues; the contexts in which they were established; their results, recommendations, and impact on their respective societies; media debates surrounding them; and how they were received by the public. While there were many similar commissions held in different countries, this chapter focuses on those organized in Belgium (2010), Canada (2008), and France (2003). All focused on the ideas of coexistence and living together. They addressed major identity shifts and demographic changes within their individual societies, such as integrating religious minorities and dealing with discrimination against minorities (particularly Muslims). Their broad mandate was to encourage citizens to respect equality and the human rights of others. They shared contextual similarities in that they were conducted in Francophone areas that were historically majoritarian Catholic.

None of these commissions explicitly reference religion in their general mandates. This presents an interesting paradox for researchers: despite the fact that religion is at the heart of many controversies, it is addressed in many different ways and with varying levels of visibility. The reports of each public commission focused on methods of handling diversity in each society: application of the concept of laïcité in France (Stasi 2003); racism and discrimination in Belgium (Foblets and Kulakowski 2010: 10); and social cohesion and reasonable accommodation in Quebec (Bouchard and Taylor 2008: 17). Nevertheless, religion was at the core of each commission, and in their discussions we see traces of the drivers of religious criticism we have identified above. The tension between religious and non-religious identities and worldviews, the intellectual legacy of suspicion of religion, a weakening critical theology, and a fear of extremism all played a role in the public discussions and reports produced by the commission. These coalesced around two themes in particular: a growing anxiety about Muslim women's head coverings and the related perceptions of erosion of gender equality; and increased focus on the importance of protecting majoritarian religion, often associated with "our culture and heritage."[4]

When we examined the content of the reports, including their numerous recommendations, and the massive media coverage of the commissions and their final reports (France, Quebec, and Belgium), it was obvious that almost all recommendations were either ignored by the public or given only fleeting attention (Lefebvre et al. 2017). The recommendations that attracted attention had something in common: they provoked an upsurge of concern about national identity and gender equality. This concern was mostly reduced to questions of symbolic significance.

In Quebec, a less reported but equally pervasive theme in the submissions and in the reports was a desire to create ways to live *well* together in a diverse society. Beaman distinguishes this from the concept of *"vivre ensemble,"* which is more suggestive of a model based on tolerance and accommodation. These expressions of "deep equality," the everyday interactions essential to living well together, came from a wide range of social actors, both religious and non-religious (Beaman 2017). Here equality is not something prescribed by law, but a blending of respect, caring, and inclusion. We see these expressions as a version of immanent critique, in that they subverted seemingly prohibitive differences that might be created by religion, with pragmatic acknowledgments of similarities. If the ultimate goal of religious critique is to facilitate living well together in societies that are characterized by diversity—which includes differences that are actually or potentially divisive—models for living well together can be gleaned from the complex narratives that emerged during the Bouchard-Taylor Commission hearings. These are not academic critiques but lived differences that can be interpreted as such and yet navigated in such a way as to facilitate peaceful coexistence. In some cases, they represent the resolution of critique. With this important nuance in mind, we will now focus on the dominant issues discussed in public discourses.

Gender Equality and Religious Symbols

The issue of equality between men and women takes center stage in the three commissions, reflecting a growing anxiety about Muslims which is expressed through discussions about the hijab and the niqab. The French report explicitly mentions previous work from 1989 on the subject of the veil that makes no mention, however, of the male-female issue: "The evolution of the terms of the debate over the past fifteen years allows us to measure the growing power of the problem" (Stasi 2003: 28). The Stasi Report proposes linking the principle of *laïcité* to the principle of equality between the sexes (2003: 52). It describes at length the type of family pressures to which migrant women are subjected, including specifically forced marriage, as well as limits on interactions with men, particularly in the area of health care.

The Belgian report also alludes to this issue, recalling that most contemporary work conducted on diversity management is based on three major principles: "equality between citizens, the fight against racism and xenophobia, and equality between men and women. In reality, however, things are not so simple. These principles are indeed not absolute, they coexist with other principles, which sometimes leads to the need for rebalancing" (Foblets and Kulakowski 2010: 9). In the section on media and business, the report raises the issue of tensions between traditional family cultures and society at large, suggesting the encouragement of daily civic interactions in order to mitigate such tensions (Foblets and Kulakowski 2010: 103). Nevertheless, the report demonstrates France's influence by recommending a partial ban of the hijab in schools.

The Bouchard-Taylor report also addresses the challenge of creating a hierarchy of rights, rejecting the hypothesis that yielding to such a hierarchy would compromise the freedom of the courts to balance between them, depending on the case and the context. However, it endorses the introduction of an interpretive clause into the Quebec Charter of Human Rights and Freedoms that "establishes gender equality as a core value of our society" (2008: 267). Unlike the Stasi Report, it did not endorse a ban on the hijab and other religious symbols, except for certain very specific state functions like "judges, Crown prosecutors, police officers, prison guards and the president and vice-president of the National Assembly of Québec" (2008: 271). Thus, while gender equality was highlighted as core to Quebec values, the importance of religious expression was also acknowledged.

Since the reports of the commissions were released, the issue of the hijab and the burka continues to dominate. In France, despite the variety of recommendations included in the Stasi Report, the most visible and widely recognized effect is the prohibition of hijabs in public schools. Since then, legislation regarding the banning of the burka has occupied political and public discussions in France, Quebec, and Belgium (Beaman 2016). In Quebec, since 2008, successive governments have tried to follow up on the Bouchard-Taylor recommendations, focusing their bill of laws on religious symbols, without being able to reach a large consensus (Lefebvre and St-Laurent 2018). In February 2019, a new Quebec minister for women's affairs declared that a woman should not be required by a religion to wear a symbol, presenting it as a sign of oppression (CBC News 2019).

In our analysis of the submissions made by the public and women's groups to the 2008 Bouchard-Taylor Commission, a recurring theme was the oppression of women in the specific historical context of the Roman Catholic Church in Quebec, which can in part be linked to the weakening of critical religious feminism since the beginning of the twenty-first century.[5] The argument was that "we" did not want to return to the days of women's oppression caused by religion, which was in turn linked to the contemporary presence of hijab-wearing women in Quebec society.

In the wake of the Stasi Report, French sociologist Nicholas Dot-Pouillard (2007) notes that the veil controversy has torn apart French feminism and resulted in three disparate strands that are also present in Quebec. As has always been the case with feminism, each type imagines or endorses a particular social order. For republican feminism, the model is assimilationist, homogeneous, and based on a formal notion of equality that does not account for difference. Most importantly for the purposes of our discussion, in France, it is closely aligned with the state, which is something new. Historical feminism, which might be understood as most closely aligned with traditional liberal feminism, challenges the actions of the state as being repressive. Thus, it does not "approve" of the veil, but seeks non-forceful ways to end its use by Muslim women. Here we can see the theme of false consciousness arising (see previous section on masters of suspicion). Embedded in both approaches is a refusal to acknowledge the complex reasons for the wearing of the hijab. Finally, a hybrid feminism identified by Dot-Pouillard challenges the colonial approach to Islam, and offers the possibility of collaboration between occidental feminism and Muslim feminism. We can see each of these types of feminism in the submissions to the Bouchard-Taylor Commission, in the report itself, and in Quebec society, as did Dot-Pouillard in French society. The Belgian context presents similar trends, being strongly influenced by French feminists.

Cultural Catholicism and Religious Ower

In the context of this volume, which draws special attention to immanent criticism of religion, it seems helpful to reflect on the stance of the Catholic churches that participated in the public conversations around the commissions. In Belgium, the Catholic Church maintained a distance in the debates about diversity. However, in the following remarks by Guy Harpigny, the Bishop of Tournai, we find an indication of the Church's reticence when confronted with various trends that could weaken its influence and status in Belgian society. In doing so, it makes strategic alliances with other world religions, such as Islam:

> The Belgian situation is quickly changing. *Les Assises*, led by the federal government, desire that henceforth cultural, religious, and philosophical plurality be recognized by all, on the basis of the principle of non-discrimination. Some would like to start over and invent a new society whose prime quality would be a type of neutrality toward all beliefs. Such people are colliding with advocates for a slower transformation that has its roots in religious and philosophical traditions. Among these advocates are the Catholic Church and Islam. (Harpigny 2009)

After the Belgian report was released, it was the subject of very harsh criticism by several social actors for its promotion of diversity. If we focus on the Christian religious aspect (which is not dominant, as the ethnic factor is emphasized more), the outcry was caused particularly by the report's suggestion to replace two Christian holidays with optional celebrations. The government's openness to it was very limited, a fact that was perhaps exacerbated by the divisive political context in Belgium.

In France, the Stasi Report attaches special importance to religions by way of historical remarks about the evolution of their status and an analysis of how *laïcité* is applied in the country. Moreover, representatives of major world religions in France were invited to present their viewpoints to the commission, as evidenced by the list of hearings. The report describes the religious context in this way:

> Our country . . . has become spiritually pluralistic. Previously called the "oldest daughter of the Church," France began to welcome a diversified Protestant tradition, and brought together the first Western European Jewish community. Over the last few decades, new religions have developed . . . Consequently, the France of today is one of the most diversified European countries. This significant break with its history also allows it to be enriched by free dialogue between these diverse elements. (2003: 17)

Another section addresses the empiricism with which the legal framework of *laïcité* is applied, pointing out that "*laïcité* does not take the same form in Paris, Strasbourg, Cayenne or Mayotte" (2003: 19). Stasi also mentions that the European Court of Human Rights recognizes some degree of latitude in each country in the management of relationships between church and state (2003: 20). The report further proposes to strengthen the management of Islam particularly, in terms of both negative and positive aspects. However, it reinforces the importance of maintaining existing arrangements with religious groups, notably the Concordat in Alsace-Moselle, which favors Christianity and Judaism.

The reactions and opinions of Christian churches consisted of suggestions that this *laïcité* of compromise, which was fully developed by Cardinal Lustiger (2003) during a hearing, be retained. Churches were cautious about the issue of religious symbols, not necessarily proposing that they be banned, but not opposing such a recommendation. Not surprisingly, they were pleased with the continuation of the Concordat in Alsace-Moselle and expressed that they were open to greater respect for pluralism, for example by extending some support and recognition to Islam and to non-religious people.

The Quebec report takes a different direction and has its own unique context. On one hand, the commission welcomed submissions from several religious groups (900 organizations and individuals deposited their briefs). On the other hand, in the report, Christianity gets a certain public legitimacy from the standpoint of respect for historical heritage. Broadly speaking, the report recognizes religions as a resource of general moral value. The report deals with individual rights and the religious dimension of their expressions and endorses the progressive but effective secularization of the Quebec state. It contests the relationship of religion with political power by suggesting the removal of a crucifix affixed to the wall of the National Assembly in Quebec City. The response of the elected representatives was pointed: the same day the report was released, they voted to retain this crucifix, citing historic and cultural justifications. At the same time, a majority of Catholic bishops endorsed religious diversity and the protection of religious heritage.

Although they have lost their historic and strong influence on public policies, churches are attempting to retain symbolic power over societies by defending a kind of cultural religion. Cultural religion is found in Christian holidays, religious symbols, certain types of religious education, and other traces of religions in the public arena.[6] In this way, we must admit that from within the Church, there is an absence of critique. After decades of dynamic theological critique, it seems that the critical voices have faded away to give place to debates reducing religion to history, heritage, and a rite of passage.

Conclusion

In this chapter, we have reflected on the notion of critique of religion in the context of three public commissions that were mandated to address diversity and the challenge of living together in pluralistic societies. In the end, religion played a key role in the commissions' processes and reports, despite this broader "diversity" framing. We have considered four drivers of religious critique that informed the social contexts in which these commissions conducted their work, including non-religion, important intellectual traditions, the presence of internal critique, and contemporary developments including gender equality and terrorist attacks. We have identified gender equality and the defense of majoritarian religion as "culture" as two galvanizing themes in the commissions' approaches to religion and their engagement with critique of religion.

The defense of gender equality is an important hub of critical debate around religion. Religion has certainly facilitated patriarchy; for example, in our Quebec research, there were many personal narratives of women's oppression referring to the hardships suffered by "my aunt" or "my grandmother" that were caused by the Church. These narratives were juxtaposed with stories of women who wear a niqab or hijab, to create a somewhat monolithic picture of women who identify with and practice either Catholicism or Islam. The narratives often excluded, refused, or minimized the agency of women and the meaningfulness to them of their religious traditions. They also ignored social scientific evidence about women who choose to wear a niqab or hijab. This was the case in the three contexts of Quebec, Belgium, and France.

Valid criticism of religion—women's exclusion from church leadership, the control of women's reproductive choices, and the more general limitation of women's roles—was subsumed by a complete rejection of religion in the way that secularist voices were louder and more influential. This had the effect of contributing to the marginalization of theological critical voices, as religious feminists were caught between the conservative views of theisssswr religious leaders and external critiques of religion. Paradoxically, religion as "culture" retained an exalted place: the linking of religious symbols in public places to oppression or an entanglement of political processes and religion was very muted.

We might describe the positioning of the majoritarian religion as culture as a defensive stance in response to the critique of religion. However, it can also be seen as an offensive stance, because it can be interpreted as a move to sidestep religious criticism by simply removing majoritarian religion from the very category of religion and reconfiguring it as culture (Lefebvre 2014). For instance, arguing that keeping a crucifix on a wall in the political arena (Quebec) or favoring Christianity in diverse kinds of policies (France, Belgium) is a matter of history and culture. Beyond significant contextual differences, the analysis of the commissions and their contexts reveals that the stance of churches is to a great extent determined by questions of national belonging and the pressures that increasing diversity put on social institutions such as schools. In other words, increasing diversity has created pressure to be more inclusive, which in turn is perceived as a loss of power and a shift in the majoritarian status of Catholicism in all the contexts we studied. There is a great deal of tension around how to maintain this cultural privilege, which is linked to issues of national identity and perceptions of belonging. Even some of those who identify as non-religious are still attached to its cultural dimension, for political and cultural reasons. Moreover, the weakening of critical theology, the increased power of ecclesiastical authorities over Catholicism, and the critique of minority religions through the debate about Muslim women and the hijab are creating a certain retreat on the cultural dimensions of the majority religion.

9

The Crocodile and the Gardener: Swedish Radical Nationalism and Critique of Religion

Per-Erik Nilsson

"Be more Islamophobic! I wish Swedes were more Islamophobic; that we could openly show that we don't want Islam in our country and that we could have a government that forbids all public practice of this totalitarian ideology of violence" (Carlqvist 2018a: 15). This quote is from the journalist, author, and self-acclaimed ethno-nationalist activist Ingrid Carlqvist. While she clearly states that she wishes Swedes were more Islamophobic, one notable keyword in Carlqvist's statement is *could*. It signals that, according to her, Swedes *cannot* currently openly criticize Islam negatively or express their Islamophobia in what is often argued to be legitimate critique of religion, without running the risk of being stigmatized as racists or convicted for hate speech.

Conspicuous anti-Muslim statements of this kind have become commonplace in Swedish and European radical nationalist milieus and resound along the political mainstream (Fekete 2018; Gardell 2010; Nilsson 2019). Islam and Muslims are commonly articulated as a millennial threat that is currently colonizing Europe and as the new totalitarian threat akin to Nazi Germany. They are moreover thought to be backed up by the European political elite, who are allowing Europe to turn into Eurabia (Carr 2006; Larsson 2012). However, a less-studied aspect of anti-Muslim statements is their relation to anti-Jewish ones,[1] and in particular how they converge in what Reza Zia-Ebrahimi refers to as "conspirational racialization" (Zia-Ebrahimi 2018; cf. Murji and Solomos 2005).

For example, Carlqvist considers the following question in her writings: "If your garden is full of crocodiles (Muslims) is it not better to take care of them before you start pondering who (Jews) let them in? Not if he still stands there letting the crocodiles in" (Carlqvist 2018a: loc. 2001). How can this articulated link between Islam and Judaism, Muslims and Jews, possibly be understood through the wider lens of a critique of religion? Moreover, can this type of external critique be understood as constructive?

Carlqvist has been a leading anti-Muslim voice in Sweden and, since 2017, the cofounder of the radical nationalist and culturally conservative social movement *Det fria Sverige* (DFS), with its associated news portal *Svegot*, containing editorial and news articles and the web-based radio channel *Radio Svegot*. DFS has brought together the loosely connected alternative news media *Motgift,* the podcast *Ingrid & Conrad,* and leading actors and intellectuals from the Swedish white supremacist, race revolutionary, and counter-jihadist scene with ties to the Swedish alt-right movement. At the time of writing, DFS had a thousand or so paying members (Carlqvist 2018f). During the period under discussion, the chairperson of the DFS was Carlqvist's co-founder Dan Eriksson, previously a prominent member in the now-dissolved ethno-nationalist party *Svenskarnas parti* (The Swedes' Party), with Carlqvist as vice-chairperson.[2] Other prominent members and cofounders of DFS, whom I collectively refer to as DFS spokespeople, are Magnus Söderman, Björn Björkqvist, and Daniel Frändelöv.

The material analyzed in this chapter was published between 2014 and 2018. It consists of thirty radio broadcasts, today gathered under the *Svegot* web portal. They come from the shows *Ingrid & Conrad, Gomorron med Magnus, Den här Dan, Kväll med Svegot,* and *Nyhetssvepet*. Fifty or so articles from *Svegot* are also analyzed, most of them signed by the editorial board, i.e., Carlqvist, Frändelöv, Björkqvist, and Söderman. The material has been selected based on search words ("Islam," "Judaism," "Christianity," "critique," and "religion") in a digital archive containing the majority of the publications from *Svegot* and its forerunners.[3] The material represents but a small fraction of the heterogeneous Swedish radical nationalist milieu, but it nonetheless serves as an instructive example of how critique of religion is articulated in this world, in Sweden as in Europe (cf. Zackariason, Chapter 4).[4] Drawing on anti-essentialist and anti-foundationalist approaches to nationhood, populism, racialization, and religion, I have employed discourse analysis and digital ethnographic methodology to analyze the material (Pink et al. 2016; Torfing 2005). This means that I explore how critique is articulated in *Svegot* in relation to the category of religion, and in particular Islam and Judaism. While DFS is not fully representative of the heterogeneous Swedish radical nationalist milieu, their self-acclaimed radical view of society and politics is an analytically useful prism through which to consider the critique of religion in this milieu in Sweden, since it brings to the fore how radical nationalist actors convey anti-Muslim and anti-Jewish speech in terms of alleged rational arguments.

In the following section, I introduce the reader to the Swedish radical nationalist milieu and discuss the emergence of web-based citizen journalism within this milieu. Section 3 discusses how I approach the category of critique in order to analyze the social and political background against which DFS spokespeople articulate their critique of religion. The fourth section is dedicated to the analysis of how DFS spokespeople articulate the category of religion and the related categories of Islam and Judaism, and how they relate these categories to one another. In the fifth section, I conclude the analysis. Throughout the chapter, the analysis will be discussed in relation to previous research on Swedish and European radical nationalism.

Swedish Radical Nationalism and Citizen Journalism

Swedish populist radical nationalism has become a force to reckon with in the political arena (Rydgren and der Meiden 2018). Just like other radical nationalisms in Europe, it has become adept at making use of citizen-based journalism and Internet-based communication (Krämer 2017). Swedish radical nationalist and anti-democratic groups and movements were early to recognize the potential of the of the emerging Internet in the 1990s in terms of communication (Ekman 2016; Lööw 2016). Web-based communication provided new means of communication and ways to reach out for purposes of propaganda, organization, commercialization, and recruitment (Wieder 2013). However, during the last decade, the increased use of social media (Web 2.0) has changed the landscape of political and social mobilization as well as citizen journalism and activism (Tuten and Solomon 2014). Although web-based citizen journalism and activism is in itself nothing new for radical nationalist and populist actors (Aday et al. 2010), self-acclaimed alternative news media, such as *Svegot*, and citizen journalism based on various types of social media platforms and classical websites have become the go-to tools for Swedish and European radical nationalists to convey their message (Bartlett, Birdwell, and Littler 2011), often employing a sarcastic tone and satirical imagery and memes (Hawley 2017; Weaver 2013). By using the type of direct communication with its audience that web-based channels provide, radical nationalist and populist actors can, as pointed out by Sven Engesser et al., "circumvent the journalistic gatekeepers" and thus "[relatively] uncontestedly articulate their ideology and spread their messages" (Engesser et al. 2017: 1110). In terms of web-based citizen journalism and activism, the Internet should not be considered solely as a relatively new means of communication; it is also a site for a social and political meaning-making struggle as well as for the construction and negotiation of individual and collective identities (Kavada 2015).

While the political party *Sverigedemokraterna* (The Sweden Democrats, SD) is the most conspicuous representative of contemporary radical nationalism in Sweden,[5] it is important to stress that Swedish radical nationalism is not a monolithic bloc.[6] In terms of nationhood, radical nationalists stress the importance of national homogeneity and hold that national identity is determined beyond citizenship; and a useful distinction is to be made between cultural monists, ethnomonists, and ethnopluralists.[7] Cultural monists, e.g., *Sverigedemokraterna*'s official line, hold that one's national essence is determined less by blood, i.e., race, than by culture. Ethnomonists, e.g., race revolutionaries and white supremacists, differ with their assertion that blood and race are the determining factors in distinguishing one people from another, and seek to create a racially pure and homogenous nation through (violent) revolution (Teitelbaum 2017: 5). Ethnopluralists, e.g., identitarians, are more complex since they are more eclectic in their view of national identity (Zúquete 2019); although they see ethnicity or race as a quintessential defining feature of a given people, they are against racial hierarchies and do not limit ethnic or racial classifications to any nation per se (Zúquete 2019). This represents a transnational understanding of ethnic and cultural homogeneity, often leading them to use identity markers such as the West and the European (Christian) civilization (Lundström and Lundström 2011: 52–53).

While these groupings differ in their strategies for societal change, they all follow two logics: an anthropoemic and populist logic. Anthropoemic logic is one by which a given society or nation conceives of strangers. It is a strategy of exclusion with the goal of excluding the stranger from the national body by such strategies as segregation, confinement, or destruction (Bauman 1997). The populist logic refers to how these groups tend to conceive of society along two axes of inclusion and exclusion into the national "we" (Brubaker 2017). Along the first axis, the horizontal, they articulate a distinction between a culturally, religiously, and/or ethnically/racially pure people, versus culturally, religiously, and/or ethnically/racially impure others, e.g., the Jew and the Muslim. Along the second axis, the vertical, they articulate a distinction in social and political terms between the true people and the traitors to the cause of the people, e.g., the political elite, the news media, and feminism.

In the analyzed material, the statements by DFS spokespeople can be classified as ethnomonist working along an anthropoemic and populist logic, with a mixture of race revolutionary and identitarian influences from Sweden, Europe, and the US. They should be seen in the light of the Swedish and European post-fascist movements' metapolitical turn in the 1960s and 1970s (Bernsand 2013; Lindquist 2010), as well as rising white supremacism in the 1980s and 1990s (Lööw 2015). They locate themselves in the tradition of Swedish National Socialism and align themselves with the writings of Swedish fascist intellectual Per Engdahl (1909–1994) (Berggren 2014b). They hold race and ethnicity to be essential attributes in terms of nationhood, use ethno-nationalism and cultural conservatism as self-identificatory markers, and stress the importance of sharing a common heritage, culture, and faith. While ethnicity and race are continuously referred to as quintessential features of a people, so is loyalty: "We, the tribe *Det fria sverige*, we take care of one another" (Söderman 2018a). They criticize the Sweden Democrats for being cultural nationalists, thus not realizing the importance of ethnicity and race. Carlqvist (2018e), for example, in a sardonic and ironic tone, states that for the Sweden Democrats, being "a cultural Swede is enough." However, DFS spokespeople see the benefits of articulating national enmity in terms of culture and religion instead of race tout court (what is often referred to as cultural racism) (cf. Deland 1997). It is a strategic way of "playing one's cards correctly," as Söderman (2018b) argues (cf. Lööw 2015; Bjørgo 1997). Moreover, while DFS spokespeople encourage Swedish people to act and make their voice heard through the ballot box to express support for the recently established political party *Alternativ för Sverige* (AFS, Alternative for Sweden) (e.g., Söderman 2018b), they do not exclude violent anti-democratic revolutionary measures (e.g., Eriksson 2018c). One of their recurring slogans of how to deal with enemies of and traitors to the people is "detain, deport, repatriate (*internera, deportera, repatriera*)" (Eriksson 2017), which captures DFS's anthropoemic logic and its preoccupation with racial and/or cultural national homogeneity (cf. Berggren 2014a).

Placing Critique into Context

How should the type of critique of religion found in these milieus be approached? Is there not a risk of inadvertently legitimizing what to some readers will surely be a question of conspicuously overt Islamophobia and antisemitism? It depends on how critique is conceived (cf. Stenmark chapter 1). First of all, and with the risk of generalizing, I argue that there is no neutral or objective critique. Critique and associated practices have their own contingent histories. This is not the place to discuss the genealogy of critique in modern Europe but, as Wendy Brown (2009) states, it appears as if the category of critique has been associated with the "tacit presumption of reason's capacity to unveil error" (9). Through the course of Enlightenment thought and by the emergence of scientific thought, critique has been, to paraphrase Talal Asad (2009), a marker for the standards of universal reason, between that which can be upheld as a scientific fact and that which is based on faith. Unveiling the errors in religious and theological thought was based on the premise that the criticizing agent was practicing critique from an objective and rational standpoint, which was seen as the path to freedom and reason.

Secondly, a particularly articulated critique, for example self-acclaimed secular notions of critique, must be understood in relation to the construed objects that the critiquing agent takes. A secular critique of religion not only brings with it tacit notions of what religion is but also engages in an identificatory process by which the construed object turns into a skewed mirror reifying the criticizing agent's identity. For example, as Brown (2009) explains, today the very notion of secular "derives much of its meaning from an imagined opposite in Islam, and, as such, veils the religious shape and content of Western public life and its imperial designs," while simultaneously, Christian conservatives decry what is labeled "secular humanism" and hold it responsible for "destroying the fabrics of the family, the moral individual, and patriotism" (10).

Finally, by taking analytical cues from anti-essentialist ontology and anti-foundationalist epistemology, my interest with critique thus relies on how the analyzed actors negotiate and navigate around the notion of criticizing what is being conceived of as religion (cf. Fitzgerald, Stack, and Goldenberg 2015). My aim is to understand how they construe an object (or objects) of alterity for critical scrutiny (i.e., Islam/Muslims and Judaism/Jews); the specific language used to do this; the logic and premises they uphold to legitimate their critique as reason or truth (i.e., how they rationalize the critique), and how this object (or objects) reifies their self-identification (an ethno-national "we"); and whether this critique can be conceived of as constructive, i.e., if the aim is to change the object of critique or to dismiss it entirely.

In *Svegot*'s publications, critique of religion and society at large is articulated in relation to truth and censorship. Just like other Swedish and European radical and nationalist alternative media forums, DFS spokespeople present themselves as educative conveyers of a hard truth. Eriksson (2018d), for example, starts one radio show by stating, "I would like to declare a *trigger warning* for those of you who are offended by reality, to those of you who are snowflakes, and to those of you who can't cope with hearing hard truths." The expression "snowflake" is commonly used in radical nationalist milieus to name anyone they allege is easily offended, commonly people from the political left, whom they also refer to as "leftards" (e.g., Söderman 2018c)" or "ego-humanists" (e.g., Carlqvist 2018b).

According to DFS, the major and overwhelming truth is that the true Swedish people, just as other European people, are suffering from what in these circles is commonly referred to as the Great Replacement and the Islamization of Europe, i.e., theories maintaining that the native white people of Europe are being strategically replaced by immigrants, most notably by Muslims, and are forced to live in multicultural societies where, in the near future, the whites will be the minority (e.g., Camus 2012). These theories have gained widespread traction in radical nationalist milieus in Europe and form, according to DFS spokespeople, an undeniable truth. The problem according to them is that the alleged political elite, the politically correct mainstream media, and academics strategically and systematically hide the truth from the people. In lengthy discussions, they ask: "Has truth become illegal in Sweden" (Eriksson, Söderman, and Björkqvist 2017)? In several publications and radio shows, they deplore this situation, discuss strategies to avoid being accused of hate speech, and ironize over the alleged current state of the media. Carlqvist and Daniel Frändelöv (2017), for example, discuss if certain statements would make Carlqvist an anti-Semite, causing Frändelöv to retort: "Oh, the horrible anti-Semite Ingrid Carlqvist… There are certain things that you cannot talk about." According to DFS spokespeople, the concepts of "antisemitism" and "Islamophobia" are shared "stupidities" (Eriksson, Söderman, and Björkqvist 2017). The word "racism" was supposedly "created and spread by the left to silence their opponents" (Björkqvist 2017). By quoting Danish author Kristian Tørning, Carlqvist (2018b) explains that "ego-humanists" and "totalitarian humanists" are using "quasi-religious terminology" to expel their "hate," and to "guilt-blame" their contradictors as being "impure infidels—racists, xenophobes, Islamophobes, Nazis, or indecent."

DFS spokespeople express concern about the "left's guilt-blaming," and also express a hopeful joy in what is explained as normalization of their worldview, as if the people are slowly awakening from their slumber (Det Fria Sverige 2017: 57). In one news report, Frändelöv reads an article from "mainstream media" claiming that Islamophobia in Sweden is being normalized. His response: "Fantastic news!" (Eriksson, Söderman, and Björkqvist 2017). Instead of shrinking from identifying with categories like i

Islamophobia and antisemitism, DFS spokespeople seek to neutralize their meaning by adopting some of them, or by creating neologisms from others.[8] For example, when someone calls them Nazis (*nazist*), they retort that they are "Nice-is" (from the English adjective "nice"), and, similarly, nationalists turn into "nice-onalists" (Söderman 2018c). In one article, Carlqvist (2018b) discusses the national daily *Svenska Dagbladet*'s tweet in 2018 that referred to *Svegot* as "nazi" and retorts: "This is the same old lame attempt to prohibit Swedes from awakening. But it is no longer enough to call someone xenophobic, racist, or Islamophobic. These words have already lost their appeal and are merely met with a yawn." In a podcast with Eriksson, Söderman, and Björkqvist (2017), the former ponders whether or not he is an Islamophobe and concludes: "I actually have a quite developed phobia against Islamism, but wait, phobia is referring to the irrational, right?" This last quote captures how DFS spokespeople understand critique: they see the truth hidden from the general public; their critique of Islam and Judaism or Muslims and Jews is not based on irrational hate but, rather, on rational reason and hard facts. This type of articulated factual approach is typical for radical nationalist and populist communication in Europe.[9]

Religion and Racialization

How do DFS spokespeople articulate a critique of religion and how is this critique rationalized? In terms of Islam, DFS spokespeople echo central tropes in European and American counter-jihadism (cf. Asprem 2011). First of all, Islam is articulated as a millennia-old threat. According to Söderman (2014), "a war is raging between Islam and the Western world, as it always has." Björkqvist describes Islam as an "expansive religion" that, "since its foundation has never avoided confrontation to gain new territory" (2017a). Adopting a factual voice, he declares: "To claim the opposite would be as anachronistic as it would be untruthful" (2017a). Söderman (2014) similarly states that Islam "is an expansive religion whose goal, according to the Koran, is to make the world Muslim." Jihad is described as a foundational aspect of the religion and of any practitioner: "Jihad applies as soon as a Muslim sets his or her foot in a foreign land to expand its Kalifate" (2014). Taken to belong to a religion that is described as "expansive" and "confrontational," it follows that migrants and refugees from Islamic countries are not in Europe "to escape war" (Eriksson 2018b). Eriksson (2018b) explains that Muslims "are not here to become a part of Sweden and of that which has made Sweden so successful; they are here as colonizers to spread Islam and to Islamize the world." Björkqvist (2017a) quotes white supremacist author Arthur Kemp: "Today Europe faces a renewed Muslim invasion. This time the weapons are no longer the steel blade or the cannon: they are the passport, the visa stamp, corrupt liberal and Western regimes who have allowed mass Third World immigration, and the baby's crib."[10] The reference to a baby's crib is particularly important, since it alludes to the alleged demographic replacement of the Swedish people. Islam's supposed conquest is carried out through women's wombs: "Somali women are like hens hatching eggs" (Söderman 2018c).

DFS spokespeople discuss to what degree Islam is an ethnic or racial feature and whether "moderate Muslims" really exist (cf. Kundnani 2008). Although Muslims are not, in this material, explicitly described as an ethnic or racial group, it is inferred. According to Carlqvist, "a moderate Muslim can suddenly, at any given point, through fear of hell, turn. Even the kindest and most moderate Muslim can suddenly become a jihadist" (Carlqvist and Frändelöv 2017). Frändelöv similarly imagines a Muslim Londoner who, during his youth has not paid Islam that much attention; he "has smoked pot, slept with white women" but, on becoming middle-aged, "meets an imam and starts to panic and thinks: 'Fuck, I'm going to hell, if I don't randomly stab some Christians because then everything will work out for me, then Allah will give me my 72 virgins.' And again, these people really believe in this!" (Carlqvist and Frändelöv 2017)! This imagined potential violence that inhabits Muslims is not only thought of as turning any Muslim into a suicide bomber but points to a supposed disturbing fact about Islam: it is not merely a religion; it is a totalitarian societal and political system. Carlqvist states that "Islam is not a religion, nor a sect. In its full form it is a complete, total, 100-percent system for life. Islam carries with it religious, juridical, political, economic, social, and military aspects. The religious aspect is merely a cover-up for the other aspects" (Carlqvist 2018g). Söderman (2016) makes similar statements and argues that this is what distinguishes Islam from Christianity: "When one thinks of Christianity, one thinks of someone who goes to church. Islam is something else." Christianity is here articulated as a true religion, one that distinguishes between private and public, religion and politics, while Islam is presented as a false religion universally and essentially incompatible with Sweden and Europe. This logic makes Carlqvist reach the conclusion that "[w]e cannot allow people acting like they're in the stone-age to live here believing that the only safe ticket to paradise is to kill unbelievers" (Carlqvist and Frändelöv 2017).

Now, not all is bad with Islam and Muslims within this narrative: for one thing, there are some Muslims with whom Swedish nationalists could potentially cooperate. One radio broadcast discussed statements by the British alt-right figure Nick Griffin on convergences of interests between white nationalist and certain Islamic organizations (Motgift 2016). During the broadcast, Söderman takes his cue from Griffin and states that not all Muslims can be held accountable for jihadi attacks in Europe and ponders whether or not there are some Muslim "natural allies." The answers of DFS spokespeople vary. Eriksson replies hesitantly by recounting his meetings with the Syrian National Socialist Party: "They don't really understand the ethnic or the racial aspect that is so important to us," but "you don't have to agree on everything if you can find common interests for cooperation." This type of reasoning resonates with earlier Swedish and European radical nationalist debates, in which Islam and Muslims had been discussed as potential allies in the fight against liberalism, globalization, and Jewish influence. However, Björkqvist weighs in on the debate and states, "we should not be giving any form of legitimacy to Muslim groups," and in another article adds, "I hold that non-ethnic strangers do not have a place in the national opposition, although we can take advantage of them in various ways (Björkqvist 2018)." Hence, while common social and political interests might, to a certain degree, open potential for cooperation, the ethnic and racial aspect trumps all others. This is also where the distinction between cultural and ethnic nationalism becomes clear. While culture and religion are, as shown, held as a key explicatory feature in articulating alterity, ethnicity and race are more important. Björkqvist (2017c) states for example that "it is doubtful if religion can be tied to crimes such as murder and rape" and concludes:

> One cannot simplify the problems of multiculturalism by pointing at one religion. Christian Swedes do not have much in common with Christian Ethiopians. The similarities between Christian and Muslim Palestinians are bigger. Islam is a conquering and expansive religion and does not fit in Sweden, but it is not the only problem we have with migration to Sweden.

What about Judaism? Given the background of DFS spokespeople, i.e., racial revolutionary and National Socialist, it is not surprising that they draw on centuries-old anti-Jewish myths and rearticulate them for their diagnosis of contemporary society. However, my interest here resides in how anti-Jewish speech of this kind is tied together with their conspicuously anti-Muslim speech. Recall Carlqvist's riddle of the crocodile and the gardener; while crocodiles (i.e., Muslims) are taking over the garden, it is the gardener that lets it happen (i.e., Jews). Söderman (2016) makes a similar statement and urges his listeners not to "be blinded by Islam" and forget to question "who's letting the predators in?" Söderman (2016) goes on to describe the chain of events that lies behind migration and the smuggling of refugees into Sweden, which is all orchestrated by the Jewish financier, author, and human rights activist George Soros: "The migration smugglers are selling an image of Sweden that it is a country for fortune seekers… Who are these smugglers? Well, it is George Soros, that's where the money comes from to finance this invasion of refugees, we know this." In radical nationalist milieus in Europe and the US, George Soros has become emblematic of the Jewish international financier who seeks world domination.[11]

Following this logic, if Jews or "globalists" are behind the refugee crisis, one wonders why. Carlqvist (2018d) states that it "appears as an unsolvable mystery." But she goes on to claim that "it all makes sense considering the strong Jewish forces that for long have tried to turn Sweden into a multicultural state." For one thing, it is argued, in a multicultural state Jews would not be the only minority and could hide themselves and preserve their people in a plethora of ethnic, racial, and religious groups (e.g., Björkqvist 2018). Secondly, to undermine the majority population, Carlqvist (2018d) suggests that they could impose "a minority dictatorship" where "minorities who originally hate one another can join to punish the Swedish majority" and "take away what belongs to us." Soros is not the only one in this imagined devious plan to control the Swedish nation. Soros is, according to Eriksson, but a "tree that hides the forest" (Eriksson, Söderman, and Björkqvist 2017); behind him hide "multinational and nationless banks" (Eriksson 2018e). According to Söderman, this does not apply to "all Jews, not everywhere; most of the Jews probably haven't got that much power," but "there are Jews with a lot of power, surprisingly many considering how few there are" (Eriksson, Söderman, and Björkqvist 2017). Thirdly, by replacing the Swedish people with minorities and notably cheap labor, Jewish global capital would have a lot to gain. Similar to how anti-Muslim speech is articulated as a rational apprehension of the order of things, anti-Jewish speech is presented as a sound critique; i.e., DFS spokespeople are not targeting "all Jews" but only those with "a lot of power." Still, several statements infer that Jews are devious and greedy, where the term "Jew" itself is being used as a derogatory marker for greed. For example, Eriksson (2018a) deplores the fact that the Swedish state finances cultural initiatives by the Sami people, stating that "there are those who call the Sami for 'Mountain Jews'" but adds, "I wouldn't go so far," before summing up with a sardonic imitation of the Sami: "Money, money, money—I want money."[12] Inferences of this kind are used on purpose to avoid using hate speech (*hets mot folkgrupp*), which, to them is a Jewish invention. Björkqvist (2018), for example, holds that the Swedish 1962 law against hate speech was the result of "global Jewish organizations' pressure on Sweden" in order, as Eriksson puts it, to prevent people from saying that "Jews are cockroaches and should be gassed to death" (Eriksson, Söderman, and Björkqvist 2017).

As shown in this section, the DFS spokespeople's critique against Islam is rationalized and Muslims are racialized, based on a mixture of historical (the millennia-old threat), theological (Islamic scripture is inherently violent and Islam is not a true religion), social (Islamic customs are incompatible with modern life), political (Islam is a totalitarian, all-encompassing political system), and ethnic and racial (all Muslims are potential jihadists and an Islamic identity is incompatible with Swedish whiteness) arguments. The critique of Islam is tied together with the conspiracy theories of the Great Replacement and the Islamization of Europe, which is supposedly orchestrated by Jews in an attempt to rule Sweden, Europe, and the world. The critique against Judaism and Jews differs from that of Islam. Judaism is rarely discussed in terms of religion (false or not), and theological readings of scripture are rarely done, nor is their customary or social incompatibility with Swedes discussed in a broader sense. Instead,

Jews are conceived of as an ethnic or racial group, and the main object of critique is their particular weight in politics, economics, and culture. This form of anti-Jewish speech and conspirational racialization is nothing new. It echoes the myth of the Jewish world conspiracy that gained widespread traction with *The Protocols of the Elders of Zion* in the early twentieth century and that is still prevalent in certain radical nationalist milieus (Wodak 2018). In the myth, Jews are described as planning the construction of an international supra-government by infiltrating national governmental institutions with the aid of Jewish capital and controlling national and global media to shape the minds and the will of the people (Cohn 2005). However, while both Jews and Muslims are racialized as foreign threats to an imagined pure, white Swedish homogeneity, the merging of these conspiratorial theories is noteworthy, since it ties together the Jew and Muslim as an omnipotent threat, holding the future of European nation-states, Europe, and the supposed white race in their hands (Zia-Ebrahimi 2018).

If, in the logic described in the analysis, Islam is merely a religion in disguise, as it is often portrayed, and Judaism less of a concern than Jewish financial, political, and cultural power, does it make sense to talk about critique of religion? First of all, my approach has been to understand the articulations of how anti-Muslim and anti-Jewish speech are understood in terms of critique as well as to understand the extent of this critique. In relation to Islam, DFS spokespeople employ categories such as rationality and truth to articulate what in their eyes is a legitimate critique against Islam and Muslims. Their critique of religion should be understood as a strategy following the lines of post-fascist theorizing in terms of normalizing racist speech and as a strategy to navigate around the constraints on free speech introduced in order to curb hate speech. Moreover, the critique does not define Muslims in terms of national belonging but the opposite, that they, in their very essence, are inclined to state their allegiance to the supposed supra-national entity Islam and not a specific nation. Regarding Jews, the critique focuses on how Jews are supposedly attempting to extrapolate the Israeli state to a global level in a drive for a supra-national global government controlled by themselves.[13]

I want to stress here that the category of religion and associated categories, like Islam and Judaism, should be analytically conceived of as contingent; their attributed meanings and relations to one another change over time, as do the categories of ethnicity and race. While the Jew in nineteenth- and twentieth-century Europe was increasingly articulated in terms of biology, race, and along the lines of *The Protocols of the Elders of Zion*, earlier theological anti-Jewish speech was expressed in terms of pure Christian blood versus impure Jewish blood coupled with other somatic essentializations (Carr 2017; Meer 2013). In a broader perspective, this shows the importance of treating religion not as a sui generis category related only to theological thought, faith, and practice but as a category that lends itself to various types of identificatory practices, such as racialization, where the categories of religion, race, and ethnicity are conflated.

Conclusion

In this chapter, I have sought in particular to understand how critique is employed by the ethnomonist, populist, and anthropoemic DFS as a strategy to convey anti-Muslim and anti-Jewish speech. Islam and Muslims are articulated as millennia-old foes, and their presence in Europe as the emblematic image of the alleged decline of European nation-states and therefore of European civilization. In this logic, a detrimental multicultural politics is described as a strategy by national and global political and Jewish financial elites to replace Sweden's essentially white population with Muslims, who are perceived as being incompatible with the values and lifestyles of Swedes. I have moreover sought to understand if this type of external critique can be classified as constructive. Given DFS's complete dismissal of Islam, Muslims, Judaism, and Jews, the answer is no. There is in DFS's logic no possible cohabitation between the Swedish people and these supposed foreign elements, regardless of any adaptation to the wishes and desires of the Swedish people, since the distinguishing line between them is drawn in blood.

Swedish radical nationalism and the ethnomonist statements analyzed in this chapter are not self-contained spheres. Several studies on European radical nationalism and populism have noted that Islam and Muslims have come to replace Judaism and the Jews as the emblematic enemy and symbol of a society gone wrong and led by a mischievous political elite and politically correct mainstream media. However, as this analysis shows, now-commonplace exoteric and racializing anti-Muslim statements within radical nationalist milieus may harbor a more complex dynamic regarding the interplay of the conspirational racialization of Jews and Muslims than simple replacement of one national scapegoat by another. This calls for an analytical sensitivity of the contingency of the relation between how the categories of religion and race are employed as identificatory markers (we/them) in order to assess the continuities and discontinuities in radical nationalist milieus.

10

Tolerance and Criticism within Religious Education

Malin Löfstedt and Anders Sjöborg

There is a growing awareness in many Western countries concerning religious and cultural diversity. In this situation, expectations are often raised that public education should provide pupils with knowledge and competences to prepare them for a society characterized by a variety of worldviews. Also, in the non-confessional Swedish school subject of Religious Education (RE), central aims of the subject include the fostering of tolerance and literacy of citizens. Another principal task is to promote critique of religion (National Agency for Education 2011). This makes the Swedish case especially interesting for exploring if and how these timely but also demanding tasks may be combined, and to what degree public education can contribute to a more sensible and nuanced public discussion on religion. The role of RE teachers in this respect is however understudied, which is notable since the teachers are pivotal. They can be caught between demanding, multiple, and sometimes diverging aims regarding the subject. This chapter will investigate how RE teachers describe critique of religion in relation to their teaching, and what didactical strategies they use to handle critique of religion.

The Swedish Case: Teaching Religion in a Secular Context

As one of the Nordic countries, Sweden has in recent decades experienced an augmented debate regarding the public presence of religion. This debate is set against a historic background often read as a religious monoculture (Furseth 2018; see also the introductory chapter, p. 10). Sweden is often considered one of the most secularized countries in the world, while at the same time rapidly growing more religiously and culturally diverse, partly due to migration. Membership in the former state church remains relatively high, 59 percent (Church of Sweden 2018), at the same time as the number of people who take active part in religious services are low. Because of the low rates of church attendance, social institutions such as mass media and school have become significant in providing people in general with information about religion (Klingenberg and Sjöborg 2015; Sjöborg 2012).

RE is a subject for which there are a number of different models, among which is it possible to identify three main ones (Schreiner 2013): the confessional model teaching into a specific religious tradition (e.g., Italy, Spain); the confessional model teaching the tradition of the pupils but also teaching about some other traditions (e.g., Finland, most states in Germany); and the non-confessional model, teaching about a range of major religious traditions (e.g., England, Sweden). A fourth model may be found in for instance France and the US, where RE is kept out of the public school system and rather relegated to the family and the private domain. In Sweden, RE has been a non-confessional subject since 1962, when the government stated that RE should be taught in an objective way and that world religions other than Christianity should also be brought up in the classroom. Prior to this change, the subject of Christianity was central already from the establishment of general education (*Folkskolan*) in the Swedish Public School Regulation of 1842. At this point, the confessional subject Christianity was regarded as the most important subject in providing the pupils with knowledge about the Bible and nurturing them to become good, Christian citizens. Today's RE subject includes the major world religions but also non-religious worldviews, ethics, and existential issues.

School: Criticism of Religion on Many Levels

Moving closer to the theme of the book, constructive critique of religion, and in our case to how this is handled in school and RE, we first have to reflect on the school as an institution within a specific setting. Institutions as we understand them here are entities consisting of "socially constructed, historical patterns of material practice, assumptions, values, beliefs, and rules by which individuals produce and reproduce their material subsistence, organize time and space, and provide meaning to their social reality" (see also the introduction to this book). This volume explores how particular contexts of social interaction shape the content and form of criticism of religion. When approaching the educational context, it becomes evident that criticism of religion appears on several levels. It is also obvious that the criticism of religion comes with many qualitative differences. For one, teachers face the general societal tendency to treat religion as a contested issue (Lundby and Repstad 2018). In the Nordic public square, such as politics and media, religion is often connected with immigration problems or terrorism (Hjelm 2014; Lövheim et al. 2018). Since news media has become an important source of information about religion (Lundby et al. 2018), these negative pictures and understandings of religion also find their way into the classrooms (Toft and Broberg 2018). This means that teachers, against a background of a general critique of religion on a societal level, need to handle pupils' negative attitudes toward religion.

When it comes to the national school level, all schools in Sweden are regulated by the School Act. Education is compulsory between the ages of 6 and 16, with a formally voluntary but practically mandatory upper secondary level (ages 16-19). About 82 percent of all pupils attend state schools, and all schools (state or private) are governed by the same national syllabus and curricula. In these steering documents, the concept of "fundamental values" is central. This entails respect, equity, gender equality, tolerance, and solidarity, and in the general curricula every member of staff is required to promote these values in teaching as well as in the school environment. There are also formulations promoting critical thinking. For example, the general curricula states that "it is the responsibility of the school that all individual students can use their knowledge as a tool to: formulate, analyze, test assumptions, and solve problems; reflect over their experiences and their individual ways of learning; critically examine and assess statements and relationships; and solve practical problems and tasks" (National Agency for Education 2011, Gy11). Furthermore, all students need to "have the ability to critically examine and assess what they see, hear and read in order to be able to discuss and take a view on different issues concerning life and values" (National Agency for Education 2011, Gy11). This demonstrates how, on a general level, Swedish schools have the task of training critical skills, in relation to both the learning process and matters that are more personal. It also illustrates how the educational context is especially suited for studying how a certain context influences how criticism of religion is shaped.

If we look closer to the RE subject, the national syllabuses for both secondary and upper secondary school contain formulations aiming at developing critical skills among pupils. In Lgr11 (for secondary school, pupils aged 13–16), it is for instance prescribed that "pupils should be given the preconditions to be able to interpret cultural expressions related to religious traditions. Pupils should also be given the opportunities to develop knowledge about how sources and societal questions related to religions and other outlooks on life can be critically examined" (National Agency for Education 2011, Lgr11). Furthermore, the teacher is required to make pupils reflect on their own identity related to existential issues. According to the syllabus, instruction shall prepare students "for understanding and living in a society characterized by diversity." Meanwhile, in the syllabus for upper secondary school (upper secondary school, pupils aged 16–19), it is stated that the subject rests on the academic discipline of religious studies, and that "teaching should give students the opportunity to analyse texts and concepts, critically examine sources, discuss and argue" (National Agency for Education 2011, Gy11). Pupils should also learn to understand different religions and worldviews, especially questions concerning science and religion.

It can be noted that around the RE subject there is a multitude of lofty aims concerning factual knowledge but also regarding abilities to think critically about religion. At the same time, recent studies suggest that teachers are not always able to realize the challenging goals set out in the steering documents. Explanations include a shortage of time, a lack of proper training, or a fear of facing controversial topics in the classroom, all frequently in the light of a secularistic discourse in society (Kittelmann Flensner 2015; Löfstedt and Sjöborg 2018). A recent Norwegian study indicates that even when teachers see it as urgent to handle bigotry or negative attitudes toward religion in their teaching, they often find themselves lacking adequate tools and training concerning how to deal with controversial situations in class (Hammer and Schanke 2018). Hammer and Schanke also point out that teachers seldom give the pupils the opportunity to view their own beliefs from an outside perspective—i.e., to be critically self-reflective.

Furthermore, on the local level, the social and demographic composition of the school makes a difference. Whether the specific school is located in a small town with mainly ethnic Swedes and a low degree of religious diversity or instead in a religiously and culturally diverse suburb will likely have an impact, as will socioeconomic factors such as unemployment rate, education level, and income level among parents in the district. In addition, factors directly related to education, such as whether teachers have a certificate for teaching in the subject or not, or if teachers have stable positions or frequently change jobs, will also likely be relevant. Any teacher would need to consider the composition of the student body at hand. These aspects on a local level would also serve as an example of factors likely to affect the conditions for developing constructive criticism of religion in school.

The school and its teachers are to train pupils to make critical evaluations and deal with critical perspectives in relation to a range of topics in school, including religion and worldviews. At the same time, the school as an institution exists within a wider societal context. We argue that both in the wider societal context and in the educational setting, there are a number of ambiguities regarding religion. Thus, the RE teacher appears to face a challenging task. Against this background, the purpose of this text is to analyze how teachers describe critique of religion in relation to their teaching, and what didactical strategies they use to handle different levels of critique of religion. When discussing whether the didactical strategies used in the classroom are constructive or not, we will employ the theory of "critical religious literacy."

Theoretical Perspectives: Religious Literacy

Writers on both side of the Atlantic have brought forward the concept of religious literacy to underline the serious consequences of religious illiteracy in contemporary societies (Brömssen 2012; Dinham and Francis 2015; Goldburg 2010; Moore 2007, 2015; Prothero 2007; Wright 2003). British sociologist Grace Davie notes two concurrent trends in Britain: a decline in religious knowledge as well as in religious belief on one hand, and on the other increased visibility of religion in the public realm, where religious pluralism is contested (Davie 2015: ix). Lack of knowledge about religion, Davie argues, contributes to ill-informed debates and misunderstandings.

Originating from pedagogical research, literacy refers to the ability to read and make use of texts. Diane Moore proposes the following definition of religious literacy, which also is endorsed by the American Academy of Religion:

> Religious literacy entails the ability to discern and analyze the fundamental intersections of religion and social/political/cultural life through multiple lenses. Specifically, a religiously literate person will possess 1) a basic understanding of history, central texts (where applicable), beliefs, practices and contemporary manifestations of several of the world's religious traditions as they arose out of and continue to be shaped by particular social, historical and cultural contexts; and 2) the ability to discern and explore the religious dimensions of political, social and cultural expressions across time and place. (Moore 2015)

Worth noting here is the implication that religions and religious influences are understood as part of a context and "as inextricably woven into all dimensions of human experience." In other words, religious traditions are shaped in a social, political, and cultural setting. In Moore's perspective, it becomes inadequate to approach religions through merely ritual or textual studies. Studying ritual practices or trying to discern "what scriptures say" about a certain issue is flawed, as it may lead to simplistic and even inaccurate representations of the roles religions play in human agency and understanding.

Moore underlines the ability of a student or teacher not merely to address facts but rather to engage with an analysis of social, political, and cultural dimensions of religion. This includes an analysis regarding gender, ethnicity, and class in relation to religion. Peta Goldburg argues that too little attention has so far been paid to the critical and liberative aspects of (religious) literacy. She advocates a critical religious literacy, one which challenges a view of religious identity as something singular, autonomous, and uniform and which contributes to literacies that enable communication across lines of religious difference. For Goldburg it is important to employ a problem-based way of working where language, preunderstanding, and critical capacity of the pupils are actively put to use. By critical, Goldburg means not only one's own attitude to specific content but also and foremost "ways of thinking" which can help us identify our underlying assumptions and preconceptions. Thus, critical religious literacy also includes an aspect of self-reflection. The communicative aspect is key for all mentioned theorists of religious literacy, as is the ability to evaluate one's own presuppositions. We argue that in order to contribute to a fuller understanding of religious literacy and critical religious literacy, research needs to be more informed by empirical studies of actual RE, rather than relying on conceptual and political discussions. By applying the concept of critical religious literacy to our material, we intend to illuminate how RE teachers contribute to raising critical awareness among pupils. We also intend to demonstrate how constructive criticism of religion can be realized in an educational context.

Methods and Material

The study on which we build this chapter was carried out among RE teachers in compulsory and upper secondary schools in Sweden and was part of a larger project, *Teaching Religion in Late Modern Sweden* (TRILS).[1] The project included a nationally representative survey among teachers and classroom observations and interviews with 22 teachers. The main project aimed to investigate how teachers deal with controversial issues and tensions in the teaching of RE, and if so, how they deal with such challenges. In this chapter, we concentrate on using the main material in our research project, which are the interviews, but we will also use some classroom observations to highlight the issues discussed here. The interviews have been analyzed with help of the NVivo software for qualitative analysis. We undertook text-based content analysis in order to analyze the data and will in this chapter present themes that enable us to discern how teachers reflect on critique of religion in Swedish RE. Observation notes and interviews containing names, which include data that may reveal personal identities, have been masked for reasons of individual integrity of respondents and pupils.

Main Goals According to Teachers: Tolerance and Critique

A striking impression from a vast majority of the interviewed teachers is the emphasis on tolerance as the major aim of teaching RE. This complies with key formulations in the steering documents and it can also be related to the communicative aspect of religious literacy. Inez, for example, teaches RE and Swedish at a suburban upper secondary school, close to a major city, and explains the aim of the subject in one word: tolerance.

> For me the aim of RE is tolerance. It's the word tolerance. To learn so much that you get familiar with a . . . general knowledge. I tell them that it is a course of general knowledge. To give them knowledge so they can understand what is happening in the world. It becomes a bit cutified, but enough to make them start thinking.

In contrast, only a couple of the interviewed teachers stress critical skills as the most important aim of RE as they see it. For Tariq, who works at an upper secondary school in a suburb of a city, the most central aim of the RE subject is that the pupils learn to see things from different perspectives and think critically. Since quite a few of his pupils are religious, he is sometimes concerned when they show "too much respect for religions." Erik, working at a culturally and religiously diverse secondary school in a major city, also thinks the main goal with RE is to make pupils think critically. More precisely, he wants

> to make them think, to embrace democracy, to expose them to thoughts they never have met. To have the courage to stand up for equal value of all human beings. To consent with the progress due to the French Revolution and that religion and democracy can exist side by side.

In our analysis, we have identified different aspects of criticism of religion and didactical strategies used by the teachers in relation to such criticism.

Working with Secularistic Attitudes

One form of critique that RE teachers feel obliged to handle is a general, secularistic critique present in society that also slips into the classroom. This kind of reasoning, which we have chosen to call "secularistic attitudes," is similar to what Stenmark in his chapter in this volume calls a "secularistic strategy." According to Stenmark's characteristic of this critique, in modern society it is not necessary to deal with issues related to religion because the modernization of a society results in the decline and eventually the disappearance of religion. A popular way of stating these ideas would be that religion is something outdated and not of relevance to contemporary society.

For instance, Katarina, teaching RE and Swedish at an upper secondary school in a small town in the middle of Sweden, compares RE teaching to climbing uphill because of all the prejudices among the pupils. She finds it necessary to work with her pupils to motivate them to understand why they should even learn about religions and other topics in RE. The pupils have prejudicial attitudes toward religion in general, and as a teacher she feels compelled to strive to help the pupils see that religion is more than what their preconceptions suggest. This is especially obvious at the vocational programs, she says, and imitates the pupils:

> Why should we learn about religion? This is just fabrications. This is just nonsense, fairy tales—why should we learn about that? It leads to wars. Just negative.

Katarina states that these prejudicial attitudes are stronger toward Islam and Muslims, and she thinks this reflects the climate in society in general. She is, however, careful to add that this often changes during the RE course, and that pupils get more interested and engaged as they learn more about religions.

Sanna, who is a teacher in civics and RE at a large upper secondary school in a middle-sized town, has had similar experiences concerning negative attitudes toward religion:

> In the beginning, the first weeks, much is about working with the negative approach that can be quite permeating. And this has a lot to do with the pupils who are the leaders of the pupils in the classroom. If they have a negative attitude everything gets harder.

According to Sanna, these kinds of attitudes are more common in the vocational programs. The status of the subject is very low at these programs, among students as well as other teachers. Moreover, the pupils are more outspoken about their attitudes, since they seldom strive for good grades to the same extent as pupils at academic programs.

Similar negative attitudes toward religion on the part of the pupils also arose in the observations. During one observation, in a lesson focusing on the relation between science and religion, we heard one of the pupils exclaiming that believing in a god is the same as believing in Father Christmas, in a patronizing way. The teacher didn't hear his comment, but his friends laughed and nodded confirmatively.

Didactical Strategies

We have identified different didactical strategies that teachers use to meet these kinds of critical attitudes and prejudices. Johan, for instance, is quite direct in his strategy. He talks to the pupils about their attitudes, advising them to be open-minded in order to be able to understand what the subject is all about. "I told them, you can't do that talk, it won't work next year. If you continue like this in RE, you won't get any further." In this way, Johan strives to model the reactions and behavior from the pupils by questioning them when unwanted behavior comes up.

Katarina works a lot with media materials in her teaching, instructing pupils to be source-critical. She uses ordinary daily newspapers, but also more controversial websites and social media. Methodologically, she combines RE with Swedish language, more specifically rhetoric, to analyze how the language is used to convince the reader about different perspectives. Through development of the pupils' critical religious literacy, pupils are stimulated to discern different arguments and sources and are able to have a more informed discussion on religion.

Another teacher, Sanna, uses sociological perspectives. She tries to make the pupils understand that they are embedded in a certain context, where other people influence their views and values. She uses this to make pupils reflect, in a critical way, upon their own context and understanding:

> I think it is rewarding to discuss, to talk about socialization and that you inherit your parents' views and that first time voters usually vote like their parents. And they start thinking a bit about themselves. I try to place them in a context, so that this is not something that occurs on the other side of the earth, but rather here and now, here with you. And you too have a relation with religion.

Another way of tackling these kinds of attitudes is to start up the course in a strategically inclusive way. Regina, for instance, starts from the standpoint that everybody has a worldview and lets the pupils reflect on this in relation to their own beliefs and values. Normally, she also shows a clip from an educational TV program on religion, pointing to the similarities between religious and non-religious behavior, as for instance religious ceremonies contra the behavior of football supporters. By applying a functional and critical perspective on religion, she strives to make them self-aware also of their own worldviews and values.

To sum up, negative attitudes, resulting in stereotyped, one-dimensional ways of understanding different religions, are present in society in general as well as in school. These types of attitudes could be said to mirror a form of religious illiteracy. To overcome this kind of illiteracy, the interviewed teachers strive to give their pupils a more critical religious literacy which takes into account the social, cultural, and economic context of religious traditions and emphasizes internal pluralism and nuances within religious traditions. Some of the teachers strive to make pupils more self-reflective concerning both their own personal context (family, values etc.) and the wider sociological context (secularism, Sweden).

Bringing up Problematic Sides of Religions

Another form of critique of religion that the teachers encounter concerns the problematic sides of religions. Examples mentioned include gender equality, sexual equality, or human rights. While critique founded in secularistic attitudes are critical of religions in general, this kind of critique is directed at certain aspects of religions that are not seen as compatible with democratic values and the fundamental values promulgated in schools. This can be compared with what Stenmark calls a restrictionist strategy for critique of religion (see chapter 2), which is a kind of critique directed to fundamentalist and exclusive forms of religions. How do the teachers manage teaching about these aspects, then?

Lisa, working at a secondary school in a culturally and religiously diverse school in a major city, finds it difficult to raise problems related to religion. The difficulty is not the issues in themselves; it is the risk of stepping on someone's toes. If, for instance, she knows that the parents of some of the pupils are religiously very strict and critical toward the school's teaching about sex and relationships, this becomes more difficult:

> You have to weigh the words, and at the same time my role as a teacher is to stand up for freedom of choice, for democracy. Sometimes there is a conflict between freedom and religion [. . .] And it is difficult if you know that . . . I mean, we have had parents here, mothers that refused to shake hands with a male teacher. I really have a difficulty to understand that. It is deeply rooted . . . It is in one's fundamental values that "you shouldn't be able to do that."

Lisa tells us how some girls that joined the schools' sports profile came to school wearing headscarves but took them off when arriving at school. Lisa says it illustrates something that is difficult and that it runs counter to her own values.

Erik believes in highlighting the "problematic sides" of religions, though he does note that teachers in general are afraid of bringing up controversial topics in the classroom. Erik is convinced that pupils need to reflect on these kinds of issues, not the least in relation to human rights and more specifically freedom of religion. To illustrate what he means, Erik tells about a classroom discussion concerning some controversial images of the prophet Muhammad[2]. Some of his Muslim pupils wanted to show him pictures from the Internet and to discuss them. In this situation, Erik chose to address the discussion in the classroom even though he knew it could be sensitive to some pupils. On another occasion, he used a cartoon of the Pope, which had to do with the crisis of child abuse in the Catholic Church. Erik used this to make the pupils direct their critical analysis not only toward Islam but also Christianity.

Like Erik, Tariq believes in explicitly bringing up controversial topics related to religion in the classroom. He sees it as a problem that the textbooks seldom address these sides of the religions: "Textbooks are more like 'this is Christianity, this is Islam.'" Thus, to further the critical thinking of the pupils is an important part of his role as a teacher of RE. He sometimes meets with the confusion of pupils with a more fundamentalist take on religion when they experience his critical, philosophical approach to the subject:

> Some religious pupils and religious people in general have an attitude of overstated respect for religious issues. So that no one gets annoyed. And I don't like that. I can't stand it. In that case I would have quit working as a teacher of religious education. (Interviewer: You mean some pupils, who are more fundamentalist?). Yes, exactly. Unreflected fundamentalist . . . that only have one position which they haven't . . . which is very easy to make . . . as soon as you start questioning it, it starts to tremble.

For Tariq, who was born and raised in a Muslim country and who has struggled for years to come to terms with religions and worldviews, meeting pupils with an immigrant background—especially with a Muslim identity—introduces dilemmas. While he strives to help the pupils reflect critically also about the beliefs and traditions they themselves are part of, he is cautious about the pupils being in a vulnerable position: as he pointed out, the ground under them can sometimes "tremble." It is clear in the interview that it is the encounter with the more conservative or fundamentalist pupils with Muslim backgrounds like his own that challenges him most.

The difficulties around bringing up problematic sides of religion also arose during our observations of a class with pupils from various backgrounds: some of them obviously religious (wearing headscarves) and others more secular. The lesson, about the relationship between science and religion, had the form of an examination seminar in which students were expected to take part actively. The teacher led the seminar by posing different kinds of questions, some of them of a more fact-based character and some of them more open and reflective. As observers, we experienced the atmosphere as quite open, and most of the pupils were actively participating in the conversation. However, something happened in the last quarter of the lesson. One of the girls, who seemed both well informed about and interested in the topic, tried to raise some critical questions and reflections directed at religious arguments within the debate. Some of the religious pupils argued against her, and the teacher seemed to lose control of the situation. This led the girl to approach the teacher after the lesson. She was upset and explained that she felt that it wasn't okay to be critical to religion during the lessons of RE. In our interview afterwards with the teacher, she reflected on the need to be even more explicit in stressing that RE is a subject where students should be able to raise critical questions concerning other pupils' stances, as well as handling this kind of critique. She says: "You must be able to do this in the RE classroom, because you do it in real life... Sometimes it can be difficult when people are critical to what one finds is important, but this is how it is. It is sometimes hard to live [with difference], and if you can practice it here [in the RE classroom] you should do that."

Didactical Strategies

We have identified different strategies for handling critique concerning problematic sides of religions. Lisa, for instance, underlines the importance of being reflective when it comes to problematic sides of religion. She doesn't want to get into discussions without being well prepared. When her pupils bring up issues that she doesn't know how to handle, she prefers to step back for a moment, to have the time to reflect.

Erik believes in open discussions to increase the pupils' understanding. Besides addressing sensitive issues in discussions (as in the case of the images of Muhammad), he also uses panel debates about controversial topics to make the pupils think outside their own beliefs and values and where pupils have to take positions with which they normally do not sympathize. He argues that teachers have the responsibility to stand up for democratic values, even though it can be difficult. Erik says that it can be really challenging but that he has the courage to do this thanks to his good relationship with the pupils. His own opinion is that it may take "a measure of secularism" to make the pupils understand that freedom of religion also can be freedom from religion. He believes pupils need to hear this, not least in relation to their parents, who in many cases have stricter religious values.

Tariq uses an active presence in the classroom in order to attain his ambition. He challenges the pupils in discussions by using humor, provocations, and sarcastic comments, which sometimes leads to further discussions. Central to his approach is an aim to get the pupils to think critically about their own beliefs. Nevertheless, he finds that his role mainly becomes to present alternatives and to teach the pupils to think from several perspectives, rather than to prescribe one certain way to think as the only right one. Tariq also brings up positive examples from the pupils' own religions to give them alternative ways of thinking about certain issues:

> Sometimes I wonder: Should I do this? What is the point? But critical awareness can sometimes be a nuisance but I think this is the way I am as a person . . . my job as a teacher is not only to criticize but also to offer an alternative. Maybe not a meaning, but an alternative. There is not only deconstruction but also the positive side. But this other side (the positive side) can become problematic in my role, because that is maybe not my task. Maybe as a teacher my task is just to get them to question and think critically. [. . .] Lately I have strived hard to also offer alternatives, like, "so you are a Muslim; did you know there are also homosexual Muslims or LGBT-friendly mosques?" So instead of talking about atheistic hedonism it can be a number of alternatives. "So, you are a Muslim; there are a number of ways of being Muslim," and so on.

In seeking to offer alternatives rather than merely to criticize, Tariq is taking a constructive approach to the critique of religion: his critique of religion has an underlying aim of training his more conservative religious pupils to see an internal diversity in the religion in question. By referring to theological voices within the Islamic tradition on such issues as homosexual Muslims and LGBT-friendly mosques, he struggles to reach those of his pupils who express more conservative Muslim beliefs.

To sum up, critique of religion in the form of highlighting the problematic sides of religions seems to be present in the Swedish RE classrooms we studied. The interviewed teachers display an awareness regarding the importance of addressing these issues in RE, but they also express reservations regarding how challenging this can be. In contrast to previous studies (Hammer and Schanke 2018), which pointed to teachers lacking adequate tools and training concerning how to deal with this kind of critical perspective, we found that some of the interviewed teachers demonstrated more reflection and experience in using didactical strategies in this regard.

Concluding Discussion

Being an RE teacher in a secularized and plural society is challenging. This is confirmed by this study, in which RE teachers describe critique of religion in relation to their teaching and the didactical strategies they use to handle different kinds of critique of religion. Already, the framework of the educational context provided tensions: according to the steering documents, RE is meant on the one hand to stimulate critical abilities among the pupils, but on the other hand also to contribute to increased understanding of and tolerance for different kinds of worldviews. There are, in other words, different aims with the subject, which at times go in different directions.

Through thematic content analysis of the teacher interviews, two tracks of critique of religion were identified. Both are clearly connected to the curricula as well as the syllabus (as for fundamental values) and are thus sanctioned in the steering documents. The first strand of critique was labeled "secularistic," as it is based on a secular attitude whereby the role of religion in society should be as limited as possible and where the view of religion is negative and harsh in discussions. The second kind of critique, regarding the "problematic sides of religion," entails a constructive critique of religion, insofar as it applied a restrictionist approach to religious traditions and customs in relation to, e.g., human rights, gender equality, and other fundamental values. The first kind of critique is not a new finding; rather, it is partly in line with previous research on contemporary RE, such as that of Kittelmann Flensner (2015) and Hammer and Schanke (2018), and is compatible with what Mikael Stenmark calls a secularistic strategy for criticizing religion. The second kind of critique, raising problematic sides of religion, has been less developed in previous research, and therefore further discussions of it are important. In Stenmark's terms, this is a form of restrictionist strategy, since it is a critique which pinpoints specific parts of religion as incompatible with democratic and fundamental values.

Another novelty of the present study is that we identified *didactical strategies* that RE teachers use. In the light of Peta Goldburg's understanding of critical religious literacy, we suggest that by applying active didactical strategies, the interviewed teachers strive to realize Goldburg's critical religious literacy. For instance, Goldburg talks about a critical religious literacy that works in a problem-based way, where language, preunderstanding, and critical capacity of the pupils are actively put to use. Our interviewees achieve this by raising problematic topics in order to give the pupils the possibility to and discuss sensitive issues. The critical capacities of the pupils are also promoted by discussing alternative ways of interpreting and "living" different religions, in order to make them discover new perspectives and reconsider their own presuppositions. Goldburg further talks about ways of thinking that can help to identify our underlying assumptions and outsets as an important part of a critical religious literacy. In our study, teachers strive to make pupils think about their own context and preconceptions by using sociological perspectives and by making them aware of their own worldviews even if they are not religious. Overall, the strategies mainly involve increasing the pupils' ability to reflect on and communicate about religion, which also concerns self-reflection in that it involves making the pupils reflect critically on their own values and worldviews. In this way, pupils may develop a critical religious literacy in line with Goldburg's understanding of the concept. Against this background, we argue that teaching RE by training pupils' communicative and self-reflective ability in relation to religion is likely to contribute to a constructive criticism of religion. Achieving such an aim is congruent with both general and specific curricula and syllabuses in Swedish schools.

The present study has also illuminated that teachers find these topics difficult, both in terms of fear of annoying pupils who are strongly religious and in terms of a genuine ambiguity as how to deal with this type of criticism of religion. Further research into how pupils with different religious profiles receive the proposed didactical strategies would be worthwhile. Furthermore, we find increased training of methods and continued education in the field of cultural and religious diversity to be important areas for professional development. Based on the present study, it is especially important that such endeavors pay particular attention not only to pupils of different religious belongings but also to self-defined non-religious youth, who at least in many places in Sweden constitute a vast majority. Taught with more emphasis on critique of religion, RE may have a better possibility to contribute to a constructive criticism of religion.

Part Three

Civil Society, Media, and Family

Illusive Religion in the Public Sphere: The Debate on Confessional Independent Schools in Sweden

Johan von Essen

Introduction

A common point of departure for this edited volume is a discussion of how interactions across diverse commitments and a constructive critique of religion can be developed in contemporary society. Dialogues, discussions, and debates are studied to unfold patterns that may nurture or perhaps threaten constructive criticism of religion. Moreover, the societal contexts wherein these interactions are enacted are also studied to understand how contexts enable or constrain criticism. The present chapter contributes to this endeavor by exploring criticism of religion in the public sphere, here mediated in debate articles in Swedish newspapers. The focus is primarily on how the societal context of the public sphere conditions interaction between opposing worldviews, and the subject matter addressed is the conflictual debate between critics and proponents of confessional independent schools.

As stated in the introductory chapter, the public dimension and conflictual character of religion have increased in contemporary European societies, and this applies as well for Swedish society. One reason for this is that Swedish society has become more religiously diverse during the last thirty years (SCB 2015), which means that religion potentially has become more conflictual (Göndör 2017). Religion has become a topic in public discussions and political conflicts and is no longer considered a private matter, not to be discussed, maybe ignored but certainly not criticized in public. Instead, religion and religiosity have become societal phenomena among others and objects of public debate and open for critique (see also Jensdotter and Lövheim's chapter in this volume).

The fact that religion is becoming a public phenomenon in contemporary Swedish society may have the consequence that religious individuals are bereft of free spaces where they can worship and practice their religiosity with others: instead, they run the risk of becoming prey to hostile opinions and to the secular society's ignorance. However, becoming a public and conflictual societal phenomenon may also make religion an object of discussion and productive criticism, which may revitalize and refine religious convictions and contribute to reasonable and communicative relations between groups with diverging worldviews. Since the public and conflictual position of religion can be described as a communicative situation that can lead to both oppression and productive debate, it is essential to explore and discuss in what contexts constructive criticism of religion may be developed.

Civil society is a societal sphere where citizens can interact in lateral and public debates to resolve common problems and critically assess convictions and ideologies (e.g., Calhoun 2011). Civil society is a context where citizens ought to be able to interact across diverse commitments to develop a productive criticism of religion. Civil society fulfils external functions such as mediating between state power and citizens, but what is of interest here is its internal function of offering public spaces where citizens may interact in discussions without the interference of the state or the business sphere in order to examine and challenge, but also to refine and renew, prevalent political or religious convictions.

The public sphere is considered to be such a space, as it comes into existence wherever citizens affected by general social and political norms of action engage in a practical discourse, evaluating their validity (Benhabib 1992: 87). Therefore, a public sphere used by civil society actors will be studied as a possible context where constructive criticism of religion may be developed.

The Open and Public Character of Religion

Interactions in civil society are precarious, as they may offer a necessary and vitalizing dialogue on norms and convictions affecting society, in this case religion, but there are also sad examples of threats and hatred obstructing public debate and excluding the religious "other" (Ouis 2009; see also Karlsson Minganti; Jensdotter and Lövheim in this volume). Already, the term "public" implies an exclusion of private matters (Benhabib 2000: 206), and in liberal political theory, religion has been treated as a private matter and excluded from the public sphere (Calhoun 2008). For this reason, arguments aiming at constructing religion as a private matter will exclude it from public debate. However, arguments aiming at putting religious practices outside of the legal system will also hamper a constructive criticism of religion, since prohibited matters are not meaningful to debate (cf Sigurdson 2009: 174f).

Therefore, a constructive criticism of religion demands a willingness to participate in the various forms of ideological and social interactions that constitute civil society, including when they imply critique of one's own religious conviction. But it also demands arguments that maintain the open and public character of religion. Therefore, we need to treat religion as a public matter open for debate beyond the legal-illegal binary to make use of spaces for interactions in civil society.

The aim of this chapter is to determine under which contextual conditions interactions in civil society enable a constructive criticism of religion. The conclusions could be used to indicate conditions for communication that preserve the public and open character of disputed questions that make productive interactions in civil society meaningful and possible.

Confessional Independent Schools in Swedish Society

To meet this aim, the public debate concerning confessional independent schools in Sweden, founded and managed by religious communities in civil society, will serve as an empirical case. The deregulation of welfare in Swedish society in the early 1990s, initiated by the non-socialist government, opened up possibilities for confessional independent schools. The schools were massively criticized even from the beginning, as they challenge both the welfare state tradition and the secular character of Swedish society (Qvarsebo 2013). Hence, they have been perceived as both profit seeking and God seeking and have caused a lively debate in media.

Arguments of critics and defenders of confessional independent schools are studied in order to establish whether this debate comprised a constructive critique of religion. The criticism of confessional independent schools coming from politicians and organizations critical of religion, as well as how interest organizations representing the confessional independent schools and other actors have defended these schools, are studied. As the investigation will serve as an empirical case in order to explore how the public sphere enables or constrains interactions in civil society, the chapter will not offer a thorough empirical investigation of this debate. The empirical case will rather serve as a point of departure for analyzing how the context of this particular public sphere conditions the debate.

Civil Society and the Public Sphere

The role of religion in society is most often discussed in relation to the state, public authorities, and legislation (e.g., Laborde 2017). Religious freedom is expected to be guaranteed by the neutrality of the state in liberal societies, implying a two-way protection, as the state both protects the freedom of religion and abstains from establishing, endorsing, or promoting any religion. More seldom, however, is the integrity of religion discussed as a public phenomenon in civil society, which is by contrast not characterized by neutrality toward religion or any other worldview.

Civil society is often used as a catchword referring to a benevolent but vague societal realm where individuals and organizations may appear as public actors, preferably cooperating for the good of democratic society. Organizations in civil society, adapted to democracy, are therefore often financially supported by the state (see the chapter of Karlsson Minganti in this volume). However, organizations in civil society fulfill several different contradictory functions, and the concept of civil society is therefore ambiguous and normative (Alexander 1998; von Essen 2012: 27f). Scholars and politicians have above all been interested in the external function of civil society as a welfare producer (Salamon and Anheier 1998) or by advocacy and formation of public opinions to influence institutionalized politics (e.g., McCarthy 1992). Therefore, civil society as an arena of conflict that encompasses a normative pluralism is rarely taken into consideration, and interactions internal in civil society discussing, challenging, and opposing political standpoints or religious beliefs have attracted less attention.

In contrast to the private sphere, civil society is public, where groups and organizations argue and make propaganda for their particular beliefs or convictions. And in contrast to public institutions, organizations in civil society are neither universal nor neutral: it is a societal sphere where political and religious organizations may compete or stand in opposition to each other, sometimes representing provocative ideologies.

There is no given privileged normative position where we can assign a definite and objective value to competing ideologies and societal visions in civil society. However, the fact that there is no privileged normative position does not mean that civil society is amoral or apolitical; on the contrary, it is shaped by ideological positions and political conflicts because of its normative pluralism. Such a Hegelian perspective on civil society makes conflicts and struggles an inherent aspect of civil society (Hegel 1820/1991). Thus, to be recognized as an actor among others in civil society and appear in the public sphere implies exposure to criticism and conflicts.

It is not only the pluralistic character of civil society that constitutes a context of potential change and growth for religion. This opportunity is also due to the fact that civil society is a societal arena that offers an alternative to the binary view of society, in which the only relevant aspects of society are the state and private life. Such a binary view makes dialogue, conflicts, and tolerance superfluous, since deviant opinions and practices are categorized as either illegal or private issues. A society without a public and pluralistic realm may not attach any significance to discussions between groups and individuals, nor recognize the political impacts that these discussions may have (Mouffe 2006: 320; Walzer 1997: 89).

Civil society may have the capability to provide scope for discussions that are neither trivial nor private, and scholars have argued that such discussions have the potential to change society and those involved in the interactions. David Tracy (1987) has argued that discussions with "the other," an individual person or a text, have the potential to change convictions because discussions imply opportunities to reinterpret taken-for-granted aspects of society and ourselves. With the help of the "other's" criticism, visions of the good life may be reconsidered (Ricœur 1992), but conflictual debates may also reveal the importance of defending ideas and sharpening arguments (Tännsjö 2013). Discussion is also the form of communication between citizens in which they may talk sensibly so that everyone's voice may be heard in decision-making (Dryzek 1990). Finally, it is in conflictual discussions that views can be charged with political importance beyond private opinions (Alexander 2006).

The public sphere will be understood here as a space where citizens are able to communicate in public with others. As the notion of the public sphere occurs in normative political theory, it may not come as a surprise that there are several models of the public sphere reflecting different philosophical outlooks on society (e.g., Benhabib 1992), and there are different ideas of who should participate in interactions in the public sphere and in the expected outcomes of such interactions (Ferree et al. 2002). Some of the models of the public sphere are grounded in abstract theories of political participation, whereas others are shaped by sociological or historical prerequisites (Hohendahl 1992). To be productive, studies of the public sphere should combine these two approaches, so that it is considered as a concrete venue where questions of the common good can be negotiated and discussed in a practical discourse and where some are included and others excluded, implying particular communicative rules and involving a particular audience.

Habermas has suggested that the public sphere emerged historically in concrete venues such as coffeehouses and freemasonry lodges but also in networks of public communication (Habermas 1962/1984, 1992: 423f). Scholars have discussed whether the interaction will be distorted when new and more abstract public spaces are used, including not only the present audience of the debate but also a broader public to follow and consume the interaction (Alexander 2006: 72; Meyer and Moors 2006: 7f; see also Jensdotter and Lövheim in this volume).

Presenting the Empirical Material

The debate between critics and supporters of confessional independent schools has been going on for several years in Swedish newspapers. This chapter focuses on a particularly intense debate which took place in the spring and early summer of 2017 which was provoked by media reports of a religious free school with a Muslim principal treating girls and boys differently, and by the fact that the Swedish Social Democratic Party (Socialdemokraterna) and the Liberal Party (Liberalerna) were about to discuss a potential ban on religious free schools at their annual conferences in 2017. To study this debate, I searched for an intense period with several debate articles published in a short period of time so that the articles related and referred to one another. Specifically, the empirical material consists of thirty-two debate articles published in 2017. Twenty-six articles were published during the four months from March to June, one article in February, three articles in August, and two in November.

To trace this debate in public media, I searched for relevant debate articles on webpages of nationwide Swedish newspapers and found articles on this topic in the following sources: *Svenska Dagbladet* (independent conservative newspaper), *Dagens Nyheter* (independent liberal newspaper), *Dagen* (independent Christian newspaper), *Aftonbladet* (independent social-democratic newspaper), *Expressen* (independent liberal newspaper), and *Altinget* (politically neutral website).[1]

I treat the debate articles as part of the public sphere, following Jeffrey Alexander (2006: 75), who has argued that the media of mass communication, especially when it functions as a forum for debate and deliberation, articulates the public character of civil society (see also the chapter of Jensdotter and Lövheim in this volume for a discussion on media and the public sphere). However, public media is not an unproblematic arena for debates and deliberations, as it is influenced by economic considerations, and the limited space in the debate articles may make arguments too simplistic. Even more importantly, the audience consists of all citizens, as the debate articles are accessible for every potential reader, but since mass media is exposed to and has an influence on institutional politics and power structures, the articles may be addressed to influential actors in society (Garnham 1992: 361; see also Habermas 1992: 454).

By reading the articles, it is not possible to know if voices were excluded or ignored. However, most of the authors participating in the debate represent influential organizations or are politicians holding official positions. Thus, persons with access to organizational or institutional power were dominating the debate. Some authors represent organizations in civil society: an interest organization for confessional independent schools, a religious community, and an atheist organization. Others represent a political party. Formally, political parties are civil society organizations but function as actors in institutionalized politics, and therefore they are part of the state apparatus (for the ambiguous role of political parties, see Evers and von Essen 2019). Finally, some participants represent particular confessional independent schools which are organized as business companies. Four authors present themselves as independent individuals, two priests and two teachers, and they refer to experiences of religion in the context of education to back up their arguments.

Since nearly all authors arguing for a ban on confessional independent schools represent a political party or an atheist organization, they situate themselves outside the religious context they are criticizing. There is, however, one author critical of confessional independent schools who presents himself as part of a religious context. Most authors arguing for the existence of confessional independent schools present themselves as situated inside a religious context, as they are representing the schools, an interest organization, or a religious community. There are also politicians defending the schools, representing the Christian Democratic Party (Kristdemokraterna) or the Liberal Party (Liberalerna); their relation to religion is not defined.

The Debate

As the articles are polemical, they are quite unambiguous, which makes them easy to categorize. Two themes frequently recur in the debate articles, and the debate between critics and defenders is clearly dominated by their dispute over these themes. The first theme concerns the private or public nature of religion and education, and the second theme concerns the diversity of the school system.

Since the debate articles are either critical of or defending confessional independent schools, they can be divided into two groups. By reading the articles in each group, it becomes obvious that the authors above all were discussing the two themes mentioned above. The arguments related to the public-private theme were coded in two categories, one concerning religion and another concerning education. Each category was divided into subcategories, depending on whether the author argued for *religion* being a private or a public matter, and depending on whether the author argued for *education* being a private or a public matter. Arguments related to the second theme, that concerning the diversity of the school system, were coded in two categories: one with arguments for diversity in schools by a common public school system, and another with arguments for diversity among schools by a school system allowing for separatist schools.

When arguments were coded in these categories, some arguments remained, as they were not covered by these categories. Among the remaining arguments, there were meta-arguments used to give the positions concerning confessional independent schools authority, and these arguments were coded in two categories: legal arguments and societal arguments.

My aim is not to take all nuances in consideration and depict the different positions in much detail. Instead, the arguments for and against confessional independent schools are refined according to the categories briefly outlined above. I will refer to debate articles I deem as relevant to exemplify the arguments.

Public or Private

The public or private character of religion and education is a recurrent and dominant theme in the debate on confessional independent schools. Several of the debaters arguing for a ban on confessional independent schools maintain that religion is a private matter, to be practiced within the family or in leisure time, and that parents are entitled to give their children a religious upbringing since it is a private matter (e.g., Avci, Nilsson and Elvin 2017; Ericson et al. 2017b). A group of social-democratic politicians maintaining the private character of religion argue that consequently there should be a ban on confessional schools in Swedish society, since schools are to be considered public institutions (e.g., Bengtsson et al. 2017b).

However, the group of social-democratic politicians arguing for a ban also assure that Bible schools, Koran schools, or atheist organizations should be allowed to pursue education among young people, but on evenings, weekends, and holidays (Bengtsson et al. 2017a). Thus, according to these debaters, religion is not only a matter for the nuclear family and the household, as they also recognize organizations in civil society as legitimate venues for religious practice. Another politician representing the Social Democrat Party even encourages a closer cooperation between public schools and actors in the business sphere and in civil society (Burell 2017). However, it is not the pluralism of civil society with openness for differences and possible conflicts he is asking for. Instead he appeals to the willingness of churches and religious parishes to cooperate with the public secular schools to enhance safety and welfare for children and youths. Other debaters arguing for a ban also mention religious communities and organizations in civil society as proper venues for religious groups and for practicing religion. However, this is due to the fact that these organizations separate different religious groups from each other so that different groups may have their own religious contexts. Thus, they express a communitarian ideal of civil society organizations protecting identities and convictions rather than a pluralistic perspective on civil society where beliefs may be challenged (cf. Moyn 2015). According to authors arguing for a ban, it is their separatist character and not their ability to offer pluralism and interchange that gives religious organizations a productive role in civil society.

Education, on the other hand, is considered a public matter, according to authors arguing for a ban. They contend that public authorities have the privilege to design courses of study and teachers and parents should not be allowed to choose between secular and religious schools. The reason for this is their conviction that if parents have the right to choose confessional independent schools for their children, they will prevent children from choosing religious beliefs or secular worldviews themselves (Ericson et al. 2017a).

Therefore, debaters arguing for a ban on confessional independent schools call for legislation regulating schooling for children and youths. Some of them admit that the European Convention, which is intended to defend human rights, awards parents the right to choose schooling for their children.[2] However, they maintain that schools and education are for the good of the children and are not meant to protect the religious freedom of the parents. For this reason, debaters representing an atheist organization and arguing for a ban maintained that children's right to choose their religion or worldview trumps the parents' right to choose schooling for their children (Ericson et al. 2017a). In sum, according to those arguing for a ban on confessional independent schools, religion is a private matter that should be restricted to the family and religious organizations in civil society. Education, on the other hand, is a public matter that should be regulated by public authorities and the legal framework.

As expected, authors arguing for the existence of confessional independent schools maintained the opposite opinion. According to them, religion is a public matter. Some of the authors call attention to the fact that the idea that society is characterized by a binary opposition between religious beliefs and neutral secularity is false. Instead, society is characterized by a plurality of different religious beliefs and secular worldviews, since public life always has been structured by the presence of different worldviews and religions (e.g., Douid and Westergård 2017). One priest argues that there are no neutral zones or venues free from influences or beliefs. Instead of defending an imagined neutrality, he suggests that the real issue is to ask ourselves which influence we prefer for our children (Burén 2017). Two politicians representing the Liberal Party argue that religion may be an important resource in society, not least for young people. Religion, it is maintained, may enhance integration of immigrants and strengthen a civilized society by conveying and defending sound values (Olofsgård and Ekström 2017).

Education is on the other hand conceived as a private matter by debaters defending confessional independent schools, as they argue that it is the parents' privilege to choose schooling for their children. Recurrently, these debaters refer to the aforementioned European Convention on Human Rights and its assurance that parents have the right to determine the choice of school for their children. Besides this legalistic argument, authors representing an interest organization maintain that parents generally have a better judgment than public authorities concerning issues that affect their children (Westergård and Douib 2017). Moreover, it is argued that the family should be treated as a unit and as the fundamental constituent of society. A ban on confessional independent schools constructs a conflict between parents and their children which may be destructive of the children's safety and development. In sum, according to authors arguing for the existence of confessional independent schools, religion is a public matter since it is an integral part of public life in society. Education, on the other hand, is a private matter as it is the privilege of the parents to decide about their children's education.

Common or Separate

The other main theme in the debate on confessional independent schools concerns their common or separatist character. A consequence of allowing confessional independent schools is that some compulsory schools in Swedish society are not included in the common public school system. Such an exception from the public school system is at odds not only with the social democratic welfare regime, where welfare is a universal right (Esping-Andersen 1990), but also with the Swedish model implying that public institutions are expected to be ideological and religiously neutral (Sigurdson 2000). For these reasons, it is no surprise that confessional independent schools are provocative phenomena in Swedish society.

Authors arguing for a ban on confessional independent schools are referring to the fact that public schools are neutral as to children's religious beliefs. Another recurrent argument is that public schools offer a common meeting place, where children from varying backgrounds can meet and interact, irrespective of their own or their parents' religious beliefs. This is considered important, as such common venues are expected to counteract segregation by making it easier for divergent opinions or convictions to be exposed to each other and challenged in discussions (e.g., Avci, Nilsson and Elvin 2017; Burell 2017). Besides the idea of the common neutral school as a pluralistic meeting place, it is also argued that public schools may function as free zones where children may form their own worldviews and beliefs regardless of their parents' traditions and demands. In contrast to confessional independent schools, in public schools parents cannot exercise their power over their children. Thus, it is argued that public schools both protect a desirable pluralism and imply free zones that limit parents' influence over their children (e.g., Bengtsson et al. 2017b).

What is interesting, though, is that although the proponents of a ban on confessional independent schools are referring to heterogeneity as an important argument for common schools, some of them do so by reference to the school law, the juridical framework regulating schools, which simply makes confessional independent schools illegal (Avci, Nilsson and Elvin 2017) or to international conventions which oblige the Swedish government to protect the rights of minorities (Burell 2017). The fact that arguments for a ban on confessional independent schools may imply a limited plurality becomes evident when politicians representing the Liberal Party argue that schools are supposed to teach children about human rights (Avci, Nilsson and Elvin 2017).

This contradiction between a desirable plurality on the one hand and the legal framework or secular norm in Swedish society on the other is used as an argument by debaters in support of the existence of confessional independent schools. They are objecting to the idea of common schools offering free zones. In reality, they argue, it is not the case that public life is a neutral venue opening up for a pluralism where various worldviews or confessions are accepted and can interact, and this is even less so for common schools. A pedagogue, specialized in democracy and human rights, calls attention to the fact that Swedish society is characterized by a secular norm, which is especially troublesome in public schools, where children and young people from religious, and in particular immigrant, families run the risk of falling prey to bullying and racism as they deviate from the secular norm in Swedish society (Lundgren Aslla 2017a). To avoid a situation where children and young people from religious families have to choose between adapting to the secular norm and being bullied, it is argued that confessional independent schools are needed as free zones in secular Swedish society (e.g., Selander 2017). Thus, the secular norm that is said to offer neutral venues where everyone is welcome is, according to these debaters, in reality excluding children from religious families. The pedagogue, advocating separate schools, also refers to the legal framework when pointing to the fact that constitutional law of Sweden guarantees every citizen participation and equality in society (Lundgren Aslla 2017b). Thus, the legal framework is used by authors from both sides, to both defend and oppose confessional independent schools.

Some debaters supporting confessional independent schools and hence separatist schools also refer to integration. Since children from religious, and not least immigrant, families become marginalized and deviant, certain participants in the debates suggest, separatist schools as confessional independent schools may give them the strength and recognition they need to integrate into Swedish society (Lundgren Aslla 2017a, b, c). As children in separatist schools are more successful and perform better in general, they will have the means they need to counteract segregation and economic deprivation (Douib and Westergård 2017).

In sum, those debaters calling for a ban on confessional independent schools are referring to the need for common schools as pluralistic venues for all children and that public schools may function as free zones where children can be independent from their families. In contrast are those debaters advocating for the existence of confessional independent schools referring to the need for a pluralistic school system that also includes religious schools so that children marginalized by the secular norm may be offered freedom from the secular norm in Swedish society.

Societal Arguments and Legal Arguments

Both critics and defenders of confessional independent schools argued for a pluralistic society and for the freedom of children and young people to express their beliefs, but as they had different views on these schools, they reached different and competing conclusions. To render authority to their views on confessional independent schools, the debaters primarily offered two types of meta-arguments: societal arguments and legal arguments.

Both critics and defenders of confessional independent schools referred to societal problems such as segregation, oppressive traditions, racism, marginalization, etc., but the critics maintained that the schools are the causes of these problems, whereas the defenders argued that they are the solutions to them (e.g., Bengtsson et al. 2017a; Nyberg et al. 2017). By using this societal argument, both defenders and critics of confessional independent schools attached an instrumental value to the schools as causes of or solutions to societal problems. One author, a priest, used a substantive religious argument and argued that it is for the good of society that confessional schools teach the golden rule. However, except for this argument, when the debate concerned society it did not include arguments for or against religion as such; instead, both arguments for and against confessional independent schools derived their political authority from the notion that each entailed the solution to societal problems.

Legal frameworks were even more frequently used to render authority to the arguments for or against confessional independent schools. As indicated above, the authors referred to laws, international conventions, and human rights to justify both the proposed ban on and the existence of confessional independent schools. As both sides heavily relied on legal frameworks and international conventions, the debate became preoccupied with questions on the proper interpretation of such frameworks or conventions. Thus, the interpretation of the European Convention on Human Rights and the Convention on the Rights of Children, and more importantly the perspectives on how they relate to each other, were heavily debated and contested. Authors supporting the existence of confessional independent schools often argued that the European Convention was superior to the Convention on the Rights of Children (e.g., Olofsgård and Ekström 2017), whereas the authors arguing for a ban offered the opposite interpretation (e.g., Bengtsson et al. 2017a). Also, when the legal framework was used to give the different views on confessional independent schools authority, the arguments did not concern religion as such; instead, they concerned the proper interpretation of legal frameworks.

Societal arguments and legal arguments supplied the authors with the authority they needed for their positions. No author referred to, or argued against, God, a religious tradition, a community, or sacred texts in order to vest authority in his or her position. In this respect, the public debate on confessional independent schools concerned religion to a very little extent (see Axner 2013; Köhrsen 2012 for similar result). Since religion as such was hardly discussed, its presence was illusive and the debate did not lead to a constructive criticism of religion. Instead, the debate consisted of efforts to construct religion as a private or public matter and to render confessional independent schools either banned or allowed within the legal framework. By discussing societal problems and legal frameworks instead of religion, it seems as if both sides in the debate avoided a discussion about religion and hence a criticism of religion.

The Fragility of the Public Sphere

Since religion was avoided in the debate on confessional independent schools, the public sphere constituted by debate articles was not a social context that promoted a constructive criticism of religion. This may suggest that civil society is not an institutional context capable of offering public spaces for interaction. However, I argue that the dominance of arguments aiming at making confessional independent schools illegal and religion a private matter, and consequently not leading to a discussion on religion, can be explained by the debate's exposure to institutional politics and the influence of the legal framework.

Most authors presented themselves as politicians, some of whom were holding public office, or as representatives of influential interest organizations, which in the Swedish corporatist tradition are often linked to institutionalized politics. Moreover, the debate articles are abstract public spaces used as a means to influence power structures, since the addressed audience comprises politicians and policymakers. For this reason, the debate is an example of civil society's external function, as the articles offered an arena for will formation to influence institutionalized politics, although it was enacted as an interaction between actors in civil society. Thus, the debate was strictly speaking not between defenders and critics of confessional independent schools. Instead, by debating, the participants tried to influence the state apparatus in order to make the schools illegal or protected by the legal system, which in both cases would make discussion on religion unnecessary. Thus, after all, there was no dialogue or conflict over religion, since the debate in reality was about the legal status of confessional independent schools.

The idea of the public sphere is associated with Jürgen Habermas and theoretically understood as an arena for deliberation and political legitimacy. Although Habermas was deeply influenced by Hanna Arendt when forming the concept of "the public sphere," there is a crucial difference between the Arendtian and the Habermasian concepts (Benhabib 2000: 199f). Arendt used the term "public space," whereas Habermas used "public sphere." The importance of this difference becomes more evident in the German language: Arendt used the spatial concept of *der öffentliche Raum* and Habermas the more abstract notion of *Öffentlichkeit*. Thus, the Habermasian notion of the public sphere comprises already from the beginning the abstract relation between an audience and the voice of the absent author; this implies a shift from the model of an ocular to an auditory public, and the public sphere is expected to fulfill external functions as will formation and legitimizing democracy (Benhabib 2000: 199f).

If the analysis of the debate studied here is sound, it seems as if a public sphere, or rather a public space, that allows for interactions across diverse commitments and a constructive critique of religion presuppose contextual conditions that allow the actual presence of individuals involved in the interaction. Further, ideally, such a public space allows no exposure to power structures. Thus, Arendt's spatial concept seems to meet these demands better than Habermas' more abstract public sphere, as it implies the presence of those involved in the interaction and that it is sheltered from institutionalized politics. In such a social context, discussions on and criticism of religion would not run the risk of being used as a means to influence the institutionalized politics or the legal system.

Both contemporary Swedish society and religious traditions would benefit from vital and ongoing interactions across diverse commitments to develop constructive criticism of religion. To achieve such interactions, pluralistic and normative environments are needed where the public and open character of religion can be preserved. What the debate over the confessional independent schools demonstrates is that public spheres are fragile, and that when exposed to state power, they may be used for external will formation instead of for internal interactions to develop constructive criticism of religion.

Appendix

Table A.1 Debate articles in 2017 on confessional independent schools

Date	Newspaper	For/against	Authors representing
02/14	Dagen	For	The Christian Values Party[a]
03/17	Svenska Dagbladet	Against	The Liberal Party
03/20	Svenska Dagbladet	For	An interest organization representing confessional independent schools
03/20	Svenska Dagbladet	For	A confessional independent school
03/21	Svenska Dagbladet	For	The Liberal Party
03/24	Dagens Nyheter	Against	Swedish Social Democratic Party
03/25	Dagens Nyheter	Against	Swedish Social Democratic Party
03/27	Dagens Nyheter	For	An interest organization representing confessional independent schools
03/30	Dagens Nyheter	For	A confessional independent school
04/03	Dagens Nyheter	Against	Swedish Social Democratic Party
04/05	Svenska Dagbladet	For	An individual citizen
04/05	Aftonbladet	Against	The Liberal Party
04/11	Dagen	For	An interest organization representing confessional independent schools / A confessional independent school
04/12	Aftonbladet	Against	An atheist organization
04/18	Aftonbladet	For	An interest organization representing confessional independent schools
04/25	Aftonbladet	Against	An atheist organization
04/25	Svenska Dagbladet	For	The Christian Democrats
04/27	Svenska Dagbladet	Against	Swedish Social Democratic Party
04/28	Dagen	Against	An individual citizen
05/01	Svenska Dagbladet	For	The Christian Democrats
05/04	Svenska Dagbladet	For	A confessional independent school
05/07	Svenska Dagbladet	For	An individual citizen
05/10	Dagen	For	A religious community
05/10	Dagen	For	A confessional independent school
06/01	Dagen	For	The Liberal Party
06/30	Dagen	For	An interest organization representing confessional independent schools
08/17	Altinget	For	An individual citizen
08/21	Altinget	Against	The Centre Party
08/24	Altinget	For	An individual citizen
11/17	Aftonbladet	Against	The Liberal Party
11/17	Expressen	For	The Liberal Party

[a]Kristna Värdepartiet, which is a small Christian conservative political party.

12

Criticizing Religion in Mediatized Debates

Linnea Jensdotter and Mia Lövheim

The media saturation of highly modernized societies means that the spaces as well as conditions for public debate are increasingly becoming shaped by the dynamics of various media.

The aim of this chapter is to discuss what this situation, which we will refer to as mediatization, means for the possibility of a constructive critique of religion. Our focal point will be a debate concerning the place of religion in politics that took place in Swedish media in 2016. We will present how critique of religion in this debate was expressed in two different forms of media: editorials in the daily press and comments to news articles posted on Facebook. We will then discuss whether and how the affordances of these media enable a constructive critique of religion. In other words, to what extent do these media enable forms of critique that aim at reforming rather than debunking a religious worldview, and that promote enhanced understanding and dialogue rather than increasing hostility and polarization?

The analysis in this chapter is situated within a broader discussion about the implications for democratic deliberation of the current shift from conventional forms of mass media to digital media technology. This debate has been ongoing since the introduction, by the turn of the millennium, of new software allowing for the inclusion of user-generated content and new forms of user interaction on Internet applications and platforms. One key issue in this area of research has been whether this development can contribute to a larger plurality of voices in public debate, in particular with regard to groups that have traditionally been excluded or marginalized in the mass-media public sphere. Another is whether digital media can enable forms of communication that encourage understanding and collective action across social groups. This chapter aims to contribute to this discussion by comparing the possibilities of developing constructive critique of religion in two forms of contemporary mediatized debate. In assessing the potential for constructive forms of critique of religion, we will use the models for deliberative democracy in a pluralistic society presented by Sheila Benhabib (1992, 2002) and Chantal Mouffe (2013). In order to discuss whether the ideals of democratic deliberation proposed in these models can be applied to an actual case of mediatized critique of religion, we will refer to the framework proposed by John Downey and Natalie Fenton (2003) for analyzing the implications of new media technologies for alternative forms of democratic deliberation.

Shaking Hands—Shaking Values?

In April 2016, the so-called handshaking debate dominated Swedish media. The actual event concerned a local Green Party politician, Yasri Khan, who during an interview with Swedish Channel 4 refrained to shake hands with the female reporter with references to his values and Muslim upbringing. Instead, he greeted her by placing his hand on his heart. The event, however, was connected to an earlier news report in the tabloid paper *Expressen* about how the then Minister of Housing Mehmet Kaplan, representing the Green Party and a practicing Muslim, had participated in a dinner with representatives from a neo-fascist Turkish organization. Yasri Khan defended Kaplan in the television interview, and at that time he himself was shortlisted for the board of the Green Party and was also chairperson for the organization Swedish Muslims for Peace and Justice. The debate about these events continued for approximately one month and involved conventional media such as news articles and editorials in the daily press, television news, and radio as well as digital media such as Facebook, various websites, and Twitter. As will be discussed further below, a range of critical arguments were raised against the conduct of both Kaplan and Khan. The focal point of the debate became, however, the place of religion in Swedish politics and society at large, as made clear by the Swedish Prime Minister Stefan Löfven's comment: "In Sweden, you greet one another. You shake hands with both women and men" (SvD 2016).[1] In the wake of the debate, both Kaplan and Khan resigned from their political assignments.

Mediatization and Public Debate about Religion

Mediatization refers to "the long-term interrelation processes between media change on the one hand and social and cultural change on the other" (Hepp, Hjarvard, and Lundby 2010: 223). The processes of media change involved in mediatization concern the increased use of technical media for social interaction as well as the dominant role of the media vis-à-vis other institutions in society; both these processes have developed over the twentieth century. Mediatization, then, has consequences for several aspects of the form as well as function of public debate in a democracy. As argued by media scholar Simon Cottle, increased mediatization of conflicts plays a significant part in defining, challenging, and defending values in public debate (Cottle 2006: 3–9). Thus, mediatization can be seen as an integrated part of the social process through which societal conflicts are recognized, defined, and sometimes solved by social actors (Hjarvard and Lundby 2018; Hjarvard, Mortensen, and Eskjær 2015: 2–3).

The changes in conditions for public debate brought about by mediatization also relate to critique of religion. Sociologist James Beckford argues that in highly modernized societies, religion has "come adrift from its former points of anchorage"; nevertheless it "remains a potent cultural resource or form which may act as the vehicle of change, challenge, or conservation" (Beckford 1989: 170). With mediatization, the meaning of religious beliefs and practices is shifting from religious individuals and organizations to the media. As the media debate about Yasir Khan's refusal to shake hands with a female reporter shows, the meaning of personal faith and conviction becomes interpreted according to wider political tensions and changes in social values focused on by the media (Hjelm 2014).

Concerns about how increased mediatization will impact the possibilities of democratic deliberation have been raised by Jürgen Habermas (1992), who argues that the vertical communication of modern mass media, dominated by a few global multimedia conglomerates, erodes the horizontal communication between citizens that is crucial for the public sphere to function as an arena for deliberation and democratic decision-making. Through digital media technology, these processes become enhanced but also more complex. Norwegian media scholar Terje Rasmussen (2008) argues that digital media technology changes the role of the media as "translator of" issues and demands raised by citizens in the civil society and the established political system. Digital media extends the "representational dimension," meaning the diversity of subjects, styles, and participants that take part in public communication. This process can contribute to democratization through the inclusion of previously marginalized voices (Rasmussen 2008: 78–79). However, the same process also complicates the "presentational dimension" of public communication, meaning the coordination of various opinions and needs into common issues and collective action, which have resonance for political decision-making. Enhanced pluralism or heterogeneity of the actors and issues taking part in public communication can, however, also mean new opportunities for a critical discussion of dominant norms and social hierarchies.

British media scholars John Downey and Natalie Fenton (2003: 189) discuss the significance of digital media for deliberative democracy through the concept of "counter-public spheres." These spaces are the result of tensions in the public resulting from the exclusion of some actors and concerns from the dominant public sphere. Thus, they are shaped by a relation of opposition toward the dominant public sphere. The "counter-public" offers a space for a reciprocity based on shared experience of marginalization. Downey and Fenton argue that the key factor for countering fragmentation and polarization between various interests is whether actors in counter-public spheres are able to formulate shared societal concerns. In order to successfully promote social change, they need to develop a discourse that is both rational–critical and promotes solidarity, for example through creating alliances with other groups (Downey and Fenton 2003: 191). However, due to the character of digital media, the forms of solidarity and alliances that emerge are always subject to, and therefore need to encompass, conflict and negotiation (Downey and Fenton 2003: 193).

This understanding of how increased mediatization and the merging of various communicative forms in contemporary society affect conditions for constructive criticism and how dialogue between actors with different opinions and concerns connects to the models for deliberative democracy in a pluralistic society is presented by Sheila Benhabib (1992, 2002) and Chantal Mouffe (2013). Benhabib's model for deliberative democracy follows the tradition of Jürgen Habermas. Benhabib proposes three criteria to make a democracy based on universal respect possible: egalitarian reciprocity, a voluntary self-ascription, and freedom of exit and association (Benhabib 2002: 106). Dialogue and conflict in the civic public sphere are crucial elements for engaging citizens in a process where "good public reasons" can emerge, in order to legitimize established norms and strengthen citizenship (Benhabib 2002: 114–15).

As deliberative debate takes place in the public, it is problematic that questions regarding the meaning of life, the ultimate good, and moral principles have been seen as private and not possible to solve rationally: in other words, as something for the individual to decide on in accordance with his or her worldview (Benhabib 1992: 89–91). To construct a public and constructive critique of religion, religion will need to be discharged from the private sphere in which it has been located. This corresponds with Habermas' (2006) call for "complementary learning processes" as key for democratic deliberation in a post-secular society. Like Habermas, Benhabib argues that for citizens to publicly partake in dialogue and conflicts over important societal issues; it is crucial that all arguments are understandable for all the actors involved, whether secular, religious, or other. However, a democratic process based in universal respect is hard to achieve if religion is critiqued without reciprocity, and without the openness for every participant to self-definition and to change position and opinion.

Chantal Mouffe's theory of political deliberation is based on the understanding that all identities are relational and based on the embrace of difference. From this position, she is critical of theories of deliberative democracy that do not acknowledge that collective identities aiming to create a "we" always involve an "other" as a necessary delimitation. The question at heart is then how to combine openness to pluralism with a recognition of the difference between "us" and "them." The answer given by Mouffe is to find a way to see "them" not as enemies to destroy but as opponents with ideas to defeat, without questioning "their" right to keep or vindicate these ideas. Crucial in this conception of deliberative democracy is that a conflict should not transform to an antagonism, a battle between enemies where the presence of the "other" becomes a threat toward "our" identity and existence. Instead, conflicts should take the form of an agonism, a struggle between opponents. Disagreement around the interpretation of ethical-political principles is, in other words, both necessary and legitimate in the pluralistic democracy, as are the political forms of identification formed around them. Mouffe sees passions as the driving force of the political, and when passions are not mobilized in the democratic process, they will become a hotbed for politics grounded in essential identities of a nationalist, religious, or ethnic sort. This leads to an increase of confrontations between non-negotiable values, with antagonism as a consequence (Mouffe 2013: 4–8). Whether as imposed by other or voluntary, religious identity as a form of essentialized identity represents a failure for an agonistic democracy (Mouffe 2013: 141). However, also the idea of translating underlying (religious) motivations into a common language understandable for all citizens risks deflating the desirable conflict in the agonistic model. Critique of religion in an agonistic debate therefore needs to acknowledge opposing opinions between "us" and "them," as well as common goals (Mouffe 2013: 9).

The Handshaking Controversy in the Media

The debate over the handshaking controversy is an example of how different forms of communication become intertwined in highly mediatized societies. In the following section, we focus on two different forms of mediatized debates, which shape the forms of critique against religion that become expressed. One of these represents a conventional form: editorials in four of the largest Swedish daily newspapers. The second form represents a hybrid media space, where the characteristics of digital media and conventional media are mixed (Chadwick 2017).

Debate in the Editorials

Editorials have historically played an important role in Swedish public communication. The Swedish state subsidizes newspapers with different connections to political parties to stimulate and ensure a diversity of political opinions. By expressing the papers' political opinion and mirroring the political debate, editorials differ from other parts of a newspaper. As a genre, the editorial is rooted in an idea of media as an arena for democratic participation, characterized by freedom of opinion, rational reason, and a balanced argumentation between various views and interests (Nord 2001: 74). The logic of the editorial is based on evaluation of political opinions rather than news criteria, and the editorial pages can be expected to express a higher degree of continuity of values and opinions than other media genres (Lövheim and Linderman 2015: 35). Editorials still hold a strong position in Sweden, partly as an effect of high levels of readership in the population. The levels of confidence in the daily press as an institution have been stable during the last two decades, with ratings that are in line with those of the Swedish parliament (Andersson and Weibull 2018: 75).

This chapter focuses on debates concerning the event described in the introduction, where Yasri Khan, Green Party politician and chairperson of Swedish Muslims for Peace and Justice, refrained from shaking hands with a female reporter during an interview. This event was part of a larger debate, referred to as the "Green Party crisis," that focused on critical issues and discussions with reference to the future of the Green Party. The material has been collected during a period of one month, which coincides with the most intense debate around the handshaking controversy. The analyzed editorials are collected from four of the largest newspapers in Sweden: two daily papers, *Dagens Nyheter* and *Svenska Dagbladet*, and two tabloids, *Aftonbladet* and *Expressen*.[2]

In total, 127 editorials bring up various issues related to the "Green Party crisis," and among these, 19 editorials in particular concern the handshaking controversy.[3] Handshaking is the main theme in five of these texts, while six texts explicitly refer to this event as an example of broader debates concerning the Green Party, women's rights, welfare policy, etc. The remaining eight texts implicitly discuss the question through making references to Khan, Islam, or diversity in Swedish society.

When analyzing the arguments, it becomes clear how opinions about the handshaking event are closely connected to value-oriented issues in current political debates, such as diversity, integration, and the rights of women. The left-oriented tabloid *Aftonbladet* writes that Yasri Khan, as a representative of a party that claims to be feminist,[4] should be expected to shake hands with women (Pettersson 2016). Even so, the editorial argues that questions of equal distribution of, for example, welfare are more significant for political change than value-oriented issues:

> The left cannot avoid talking about the value conflicts that emerge in a diverse society, the chaos after the missing handshake makes this clear. But the welfare state is in itself our main integration project, just because it is color blind. The answer is increased equality. Then the rest settles over time. (Lindberg 2016)

In the largest liberal-independent daily newspaper *Dagens Nyheter*, the focus is on the consequences of liberalism in a pluralistic society. A core issue is whether liberal values such as individual freedom of thought and lifestyle can be compatible with the choices of those who, on the basis of religious worldviews, seem to go against for example the value of gender equality. Erik Helmerson (2016) argues that freedom is of greater value than political regulations of some preferred values:

> Regarding the handshake, my starting point is this. Many individuals with religious beliefs, among them Orthodox Jews, are unwilling to shake hands with persons of the opposite sex. Is this to disqualify them from political engagement? I have difficulties combining a liberal conception of life with a wish to regulate other people's preferred way of greeting. Yasri Khan has now been accused of having an attitude to greetings that is not just a problem in itself, but also mirrors an almost Islamistic view. If so, that will show. I will never accept that he or any other fundamentalist with references to God limits my freedom. However, my line is not the handshake. (Helmerson 2016)

The second-largest tabloid, *Expressen*, also liberal, criticizes the Green Party for embracing "identity politics," as "[i]nstead of promoting politicians based on opinions, the focus has been on ethnicity and religious background" (Madon 2016). Thus, religious motivations can be used to promote ideas located outside a party's core ideology, but when politicians such as Yasri Khan reach influential positions, this might, the editorial argues, open the door for actors and ideas with potentially destructive political consequences.

Finally, the handshaking debate is used in several of the editorials to call for a more complex and nuanced public debate about norms and value-oriented questions, not least in relation to freedom of religion. This is expressed in this citation from the conservative daily newspaper *Svenska Dagbladet*:

> The discussion about the handshaking illustrates, unfortunately, something that soon seems to be a Swedish norm: the inability to separate between different dimensions of issues, the unwillingness to problematize, the intellectual shortcuts. So many now exclaim in hindsight of the handshaking question: "in Sweden we treat men and women equally!" But that is not true. Not at all occasions. (Lifvendahl 2016)

Previous research has found that religion in editorials from the year 2000 to a larger extent have become a focal point for discussions about societal core values (cf. Lövheim 2017: 153–54). As the examples show, the handshaking event in a similar way becomes a springboard for discussing deeper political questions concerning tensions between different values and positions in a pluralistic democracy. The core issue concerns if and to what degree religious faith can influence the actions of a political representative. On this issue, the editorials present a wide range of opinions, which vary with regard to the ideological position of the paper (i.e., left-oriented, liberal, conservative). Contradicting standpoints can, however, also be found within the same newspaper.

In sum, the majority of the editorials are critical to Khan's refusal to shake hands with a woman on the grounds of religious belief. They also share the view that the handshaking controversy is an example of the value-oriented conflicts a pluralist society will generate. In most cases, it is not the religious practice in itself that is articulated as the main problem; instead, the critique is directed toward the societal implications of prohibiting, tolerating, or welcoming certain kinds of religious practices as part of Swedish society. Thus, the editorials show a trend toward differentiation of what religious practices and values should be criticized when they appear in various public spheres, but also what reactions toward religion are more or less welcome in a pluralistic, democratic society. Thus, the religious practice becomes not just a question of an individual's choice of action, but something that—through our reactions—concerns us all.

Debate in the Hybrid Media Space

The second part of the material analyzed in this article is from a new form of hybrid media space, where different types of communications and media logics are mixed (see Chadwick 2017). We analyze comments posted to articles published on the Facebook pages of the four largest Swedish newspapers—*Aftonbladet*, *Dagens Nyheter*, *Expressen*, and *Svenska Dagbladet*—and the television program *SVT Nyheter*.[5] As the majority of Swedish Internet users use Facebook every day, and more than half of these read news on Facebook,[6] these comments are a significant form of mediated public communication characterized by the logic of social media. Furthermore, these comments interact with established news media such as the daily press analyzed in the previous section.

As in our analysis of the editorials, the focus here is on comments regarding the handshaking controversy. We have analyzed 1,756 comments that explicitly mention the event where the Green Party politician Yasri Khan refrained from shaking hands with a female reporter during an interview.[7] A majority of the comments express the opinion that Khan should have shaken the female reporter's hand,[8] as exemplified below:

> We have shaken hands with our fellow humans, women as men, for a long time. We shake hands now. We will shake hands as greeting tomorrow. And tomorrow. And tomorrow... It is time to unite all, regardless of religion (We are secular here, don't forget that!) in that it is NOT acceptable to treat 50% of the population as

"dangerous," "dirty," "less valuable," "sex trigger" or what personal (read religious) reasons there can be for not greeting someone through handshaking. I see an alarming compliance when it comes to standing up for Sweden as a secular state. Religion is private. No religious agendas shall rule if you are working for any party in Sweden. We must have politicians who work for equality and democracy, not for separation. (Comment to *Expressen* 2016)

A majority of these comments express a similar set of arguments. One salient argument is that "we," "Swedes," or "Sweden" should not adapt to "other cultures" and/or "other religions." Anyone, Muslims or people of other faiths, who wants to be part of Swedish society must therefore act according to Swedish traditions and norms. The second argument is focused on gender equality, defined as same and equal treatment for men and women. In other words, you cannot choose to shake hands with just one sex and not the other. In this line of argument, gender equality becomes a core feature of "Swedish values," and Khan's behavior is understood as a provocation against such values. This argument thereby links the handshaking case with a discussion of what values and behavior can be accepted in Swedish society in general and in politics in particular. As the comment above shows, religion is defined as belonging to the private sphere, and as such is incompatible with engagement in politics. Thus, Khan becomes a threat to "Swedish values" by acting on the basis of his religious values in politics. This separation of religion and politics as belonging to different spheres affects the evaluation not just of the action, but also of the motivations behind it as presented by Khan himself:

It's OK that he greets women with a hand on the heart, but it should be the same for both sexes—both men and women. His explanation is strained religious mumbo jumbo—so completely unintelligible for the uninitiated. Religion in general and Islam in particular shall not have any place in political life. (Comment to *SVT Nyheter* 2016a)

An additional perspective is expressed in how commentators make a distinction between extremism on the one hand (where Khan's action belongs, for many) and on the other "good Muslims" who have adapted to "Swedish norms and traditions." The latter category repeatedly refers to the Koran, to imams, to Muslim friends or neighbors, etc.

Moreover, the missing handshake is often described as a "symptom" of something "more"; a clash of cultures where religion (Islam) stands in opposition to "Swedish values":

You don't need to shake hands, you can spread infection, have germophobia etc. It's precisely the religious reason that's problematic. Sweden is secular. Those who come here have chosen to establish themselves in a secular society. (Comment to *SVT Nyheter* 2016b)

A smaller group of the commenters defend Khan's choice. Two categories of arguments are central here. According to the first, people should be allowed to greet each other in different ways, and Khan actually greeted the reporter even if it was not through a handshake. The other argument presents an understanding of gender equality different from the one above. Rather than equal treatment, gender equality is articulated as the right to autonomy over how to act and make use of his/her body:

> If everyone shall have the same rights regardless of gender, age, sexual identity, or religion, then people must be able to choose how to greet one another based on the faith of the individual, right? Is it not most important that you treat men and women as equals, not that you greet them in the same manner? It is not as if Khan has refused to greet women, he just doesn't shake hands with them. That's not really more strange than me not giving you a hug when we meet downtown sometime. It's simply about intimacy. (Comment to *Dagens Nyheter* 2016)

In terms of form, the debate can be described as highly polarized with elements of flaming, shaming, and blaming, similar to other political debates taking place in social media (see for example Abdel-Fadil 2018; Hutchens, Cicchirillo, and Hmielowski 2015; Svensson 2014). However, there are also some nuances. Regardless of position, opinions are often presented together with a motivation and it is possible to find a broad range of opinions. The "tag function" is here used to exchange thoughts with one or a few other commentators, and to include different perspectives in the debate.

As was the case in the editorials, most of the critical arguments expressed in the Facebook comments were formulated by individuals situated outside of religious traditions. However, in this debate, voices from individuals who self-identify as Muslim were also heard. Some, but not all, of these participants defend Khan and argue for Islam as a peaceful religion, but their voices are a minority against the strong and negative critique against Islam as an oppressing, dangerous religion. Such strong anti-Islam sentiments were, however, countered also by participants who do not identify as religious. In this sense, this particular discussion reflects how Islam has become a highly politicized issue in the Swedish political landscape (Demker 2018). Further, the debate analyzed in this chapter has many similarities with expressions of critique against Islam on Twitter during the Brexit referendum in Great Britain. As shown by Guilia Evolvi (2017), Islamophobic expressions under the hashtag #islamexit were closely connected to gender, ethnicity, and politics.

Constructive Critique of Religion in Mediatized Public Debate

In this final section, we return to the question of whether increased mediatization can contribute not only to a larger plurality of participants, experiences, and opinions in public debates about religion but also to forms of critique of religion that aim toward modifying or reforming rather than debunking a religious worldview and that promote dialogue and enhanced understanding rather than increasing hostility and polarization.

The presentation of the critique of religion expressed in two forms of mediatized debates in the previous section shows that the specific media form affects the character of the debates. In the editorials, critique of religion was solely expressed from actors that have an established position in mass media, and expresses secular political values and premises rather than religious beliefs. Editorials comment on recent political events and discuss ideological issues, and both these forms are present in the debate. The handshaking was discussed in relation to "the Green Party crisis," but it also becomes a springboard for discussing deeper political questions concerning tensions between different values and positions in a pluralistic democracy. The hybrid media space of Facebook comments on news articles presents more of an interchange between different types of communication. Further, our analysis seems to confirm Rasmussen's theory about digital media as broadening the representational dimension of public communication and thus the democratization of the public discussions, in terms of the range of participants, opinions, and experiences expressed in mediatized debates where critique of religion constitutes a theme.

This connects to one of the questions asked in the introductory chapter, concerning the interplay between the critics and the receiver of the critique of religion in the two forms of mediatized debate. To what extent is the debate in the two forms of media characterized by egalitarian reciprocity, as advocated by Benhabib? The editorials are limited to a small group of people who can present their opinions on a privileged media platform. Not everyone can write an editorial in a prestigious daily paper, and not everyone will read one. Those who do not recognize the interpretation of a religious norm or practice have limited possibilities to respond to and present another version on equal terms as the newspaper editorials.

In contrast, in the Facebook commentary fields, the debates were held in an open forum with access for everyone (in possession of a Facebook account). Although most of the critique of religion expressed comes from actors who do not identify as religious, there are also participants that argue from a religious worldview or that argue for an understanding of religious motivations as legitimate. However, those taking the chance to present their critical views on the event in this specific arena are many, and the plurality of voices in itself has consequences for whose voice is heard. The person in focus, Yasri Khan, cannot realistically meet all the critical comments given in the commentary fields. In a broader perspective, however, the dynamic in this debate holds a potential for different perspectives on an event such as the handshaking case to be discussed and criticized from a broad range of positions and perspectives. Personal experience was, for example, more frequently used in order to legitimize an argument in social media.

For Rasmussen, one concern regarding the presentational dimension in digital media is the need for rational argumentation in order to be constructive. The aim of our analysis, however, goes beyond the question of changes in the representational and presentational dimension of public debate. Mouffe's concept of agonism and Downey and Fenton's model of "counter-public spheres" share a common concern about the need to develop a way of discussing that is based in democratically formulated and shared societal concerns and promote solidarity, but that also can acknowledge and encompass conflicts between various interests and actors (Mouffe 2013: 8; Downey and Fenton 2003: 194–95). Using the theories of Downey and Fenton in combination with the models for democratic deliberation in pluralistic societies presented by Benhabib and Mouffe, we therefore ask whether a larger plurality of participants also makes a difference in terms of the kind of critique of religion expressed in the Facebook comments versus the editorials.

In the editorials, critique of Khan's religious faith does not seem to be the main point of the debate. Rather, the event was used to articulate various ideological positions in current Swedish political debate, and the argumentation focuses on the potential long-term effects of certain types of religious practices for a wider range of issues such as integration, political representation, and gender equality. This form of critique of religion seems to better fit with Benhabib's model for democratic deliberation, since it enables the "presentational dimension" of coordinating various opinions and needs into common issues and collective action, with clear resonance for political decision-making (Rasmussen 2008). The presentational dimension includes a generalizing function, where a limited number of issues were discussed within recognizable frames. Combined with Mouffe's emphasis on conflict as the driving political force, the editorials can thus function as an important forum for the articulation of political forms of identification. Based on these identifications, the debate can focus on a democratic goal and take a form that avoids the antagonistic conflict. This also meet some of Benhabib's criteria for deliberative debates, as the ideological frame of the debate makes her demands of voluntary self-ascription and freedom of exit and association possible to fulfill. The editorials may therefore have a greater potential to impact the public sphere through being a privileged platform with a close connection to the political compared to the hybrid media space (cf. Pollack 2015).

In the Facebook comments, the arguments expressed are more explicitly critical of religion, as in the case where the absent handshaking was made into an example of Islam as an oppressive religion. In this regard, this form of communication fits the aspect of Mouffe's agonistic model better, which is more open to struggle and disagreement as a necessity for a vital debate about common goals in a pluralistic society. At the same time, there are more voices defending Khan and bringing in other dimensions and perspectives from personal experiences, reflections, and emotions concerning how different values and ways of acting toward others can coexist in a pluralistic society. The expression of opinions in a more personal and emotive way gives the impression that the debates have a lower degree of complexity and self-reflexivity than the editorials (cf. Rasmussen 2008: 78). Along with the frequent practices of accusations (blaming and shaming) and antagonistic portrayals of the other, this makes it difficult for debates in the hybrid media space to meet Benhabib's demands of reciprocity and respect, as well as Downey and Fenton's criteria of formulating shared societal concerns in a rational and critical way. Finally, this characteristic also enhances the likelihood for hybrid media spaces to transform into the antagonistic conflicts Mouffe warns against. However, the higher degree of emotion and accusations might not by necessity constitute a problem. Mouffe emphasizes that collective identities are crucial for constructive political conflicts, and emotions are a central aspect in identity construction. As long as a conflict is described as a confrontation between democratic standpoints, passions are an important democratic force (Mouffe 2013: 6–8).

Benhabib and Mouffe's models point to conflict but also dialogue as crucial elements for bringing out "good public reasons," questioning and legitimizing norms, and clarifying ethical-political principles. Both Benhabib and Mouffe recognize that religiously motivated arguments are or should be part of deliberative or agonistic debates, however not as an essentialist or non-negotiable identification or standpoint. Finally, can we see in the debates examples of discussing religion in more nuanced ways, and of handling divergent opinions about Khan's action in ways that promote further dialogue concerning religion?

Among the opinions expressed in the debate, there are clearly those promoting understanding, dialogue, and nuances, as well as those presenting an essentialist and often negative view of religion. In the editorials, a reoccurring theme relevant for this aspect of the critique is the application of societal norms with regard to different situations (see Lifvendahl 2016; Helmerson 2016). In these cases, the general claim that men and women in Sweden are treated equally is called into question, which opens up a discussion of when freedom of religion as a democratic value can be subordinated to gender equality and when this should not be the case. By highlighting the complexity of criticizing religion in an event such as the handshaking controversy, editorials contribute to a more nuanced understanding and further discussion concerning the role of religion in a pluralistic democratic society.

Looking at the hybrid media, there are other kind of examples to be found, not least comments aiming to question essential understandings of what "Islam is and Islam does." These comments instead put emphasis on the fact that Islam, just as all religious traditions, was interpreted in a myriad of ways by human beings situated in various contexts, and Khan's choice of greeting must be understood in this way. Another example is the conversations taking place within the larger debates, using the "tag-function" to direct a comment to a specific person. These conversations give an opportunity to go deeper into the arguments of the opponent and at the same time to clarify one's own position. This kind of direct conversation often includes carefully formulated arguments and an interest in understanding the standpoint of the other.

Conclusion

The handshaking controversy in April 2016 developed into a debate where a broad range of opinions was expressed. Even though the mediatized debates we have analyzed in this chapter show a great deal of polarization, we have also found instances pointing toward a more constructive critique of religion. In the hybrid media space as well as in the editorials, many comments were clearly based on ideological convictions and rational-critical arguments, and the need to articulate opinions makes it possible to identify allies that support one's own position, which strengthens those striving for societal change. Yasri Khan's hand on his heart generated reactions and emotions and gave people opportunity to reflect on the role of religion in political deliberation, which until recently has often been absent in Swedish public debate. The variation of opinions expressed, both in the editorials and on Facebook, shows that the possible answer is not self-evident. Furthermore, the engagement in the debate indicates an urgency to take part in discussion, to examine different arguments, and to be self-reflective concerning one's own motivations in order to be able to understand and criticize the opinions of others. This is, if nothing else, a good basis for a transformative learning process.

13

Parenting Choices, Religious Faith, and Critical Engagement

Martha Middlemiss Lé Mon and Ninna Edgardh

This chapter focuses on how actively religious Christians in Sweden today negotiate decisions in everyday life based on religious beliefs and how they choose to present such choices in meetings with others from outside their religious group. The analysis is based on a close reading of interviews with four individuals who are active members of a conservative charismatic Christian church in Sweden, who were interviewed as part of a larger qualitative study into values and parenting choices. Its contribution to this volume is, unlike some of the previous chapters, not a study of criticism or critique formulated by members of one religious group against others, but rather an analytical study of strategies of critical engagement with the "religious other" adopted in day-to-day situations, in this case in parenting choices. The "religious other" in question here is not differing religious beliefs from within or outside the given religious group, but rather the secular society.

In this chapter, we identify different strategies of critical engagement with the "religious other" adopted in parenting choices. These strategies are then discussed in a critical analysis of Lori Beaman's concept of "deep equality" with the aim of assessing whether this concept can be useful for analyzing forms of engagement with critique that involve a suspension of criticism or retreat to a "faith bubble." Lori Beaman calls for research on religious diversity to "reformulate the focus from the problem of diversity to an exploration of the ways in which people work out difference in day-to-day life" (2014: 90). Beaman starts her own endeavor, as a reaction to the prevalence of negative stories of difference and religion and tendencies to seek to manage such difference in a top-down manner with a reliance on legal solutions (2014: 89). In contrast to this, Beaman argues, focus should be upon the ways in which people approach not just differences but also similarities between themselves and others. This approach leads her to encourage studies of people striving for deep equality rather than tolerance. She points to the findings of both her own and others' research that highlight the lack of clear boundaries and set identities in the experiences of most people, arguing with Linda Woodhead that "the everyday realities of religion lived by ordinary people are often much more diverse, mixed, and 'confused'—and hence less subject to 'problems' of encounter" (2014: 3). So, Beaman continues,

> The idea of religious diversity as it currently circulates depends on and invokes difference or a rigid conceptualization of religious identity as though it exists in pure form. In this imaginary, difference is "pure" and exists in discrete identity packages that serve to separate and to create potentially conflicting social actors through an adherence to religious identity rigidity. Yet this is not how people live their lives, or, it is not the *only* way people live their lives. Flexibility, fuzzy boundaries, "confusion" and shifting contexts shape the negotiation process, which is often so unremarkable in content that it can be understood as a "non-event." (2014: 92)

It is just such "non-events" experienced by individuals with their own complex histories and "fuzzy" identities that are in focus in this chapter. We wish to pay attention to the way people negotiate differences they perceive in relation to "religious others" in everyday life. By this, we mean here individuals or groups who are perceived to hold a different set of beliefs and worldviews from oneself. In doing so, we test whether it is possible to identify the process of what Lori Beaman terms "deep equality," which she maintains "recognises equality as an achievement of day-to-day interaction, and is traceable through agnostic respect, recognition of similarity and a simultaneous acceptance of difference, creation of community and neighbourliness" (2014: 96). Her notion builds on William Connolly's (2005) concept of "agnostic respect" and is of particular relevance to this exploration of concepts of constructive criticism of religion precisely because, in Beaman's words, "respect is agnostic because it requires an abandonment of 'rightness' and the conviction that one is imbued with the truth through some sort of transcendent authority" (2014: 98).

In the lives of the four interviewees on which we will focus in this chapter, however, the "religious other" is not a Muslim or a fundamentalist Christian, but representatives of the majority of secular Swedes, who may very well keep their relation to the Church of Sweden but who do not immediately associate that connection with being religious, or even with being Christian. Stenmark suggests that we term these "secular people," that is to say they are not necessarily those who actively aim to minimize the influence of religion on society, but who embrace secular worldviews. In this respect, the material we analyze in this chapter represents examples of external criticism in the form of perceived or experienced criticism directed toward members of a minority (Christian) religious group from a secular majority. Also of interest, however, is the criticism of those within the religious group toward the norms of secular society, and the extent to which this criticism is formulated with reference to the religious group's own theologies and practices or, rather, in the terminology of the secular. The forms of critique we are exploring in this latter respect could even be defined as a form of immanent critique of secular Swedish society. Those we have interviewed self-identify as part of mainstream Swedish society as much as they do as members of a small Christian community within that society, and as such their formulations of critique of contemporary Swedish society come from within that larger group and are formulated using a secular language.

"Religious Others" in a Swedish Context

Before introducing the stories of the religious minority that form the core of this chapter, it is important to present the "religious other" of the secular Swede. This may be exemplified by our interviewee Lena. When asked if she belonged to a church or religious denomination, she said no, but when the interviewer continued to ask if she had grown up in any religious tradition, she changed her mind, and admitted that she was a member of the Church of Sweden "as one does belong."

This attitude has been found in earlier studies, such as the work of Ann af Burén, who argues that the majority of Swedes are "semi-secular" and rather than taking an "either/or" approach to religion, tend instead toward "both/and" (2015), or Grace Davie's assertion that Scandinavians "belong without believing" to the majority, at least prior to the disestablishment of the state church in 2000, and that what they really believe in is belonging (2000: 3). It is in other words not uncommon in the Swedish context, where 59% of the population are members of the Church of Sweden and pay an annual fee for this, collected via the tax system, but only 10% of these say they have a strong or fairly strong relation to the Church and over half say they have a weak or fairly weak relationship (Jonsson 2018: 29). The situation in Sweden can thus be said to be one of religious change, rather than textbook secularization, where the historic majority church takes on a new role for many as a personal and cultural resource or an arena for communication (Bäckström, Edgardh, and Pettersson 2004: 25). It also fits well with the Swedish situation as presented in the "cultural map of the world," produced using data from the World Values Survey (WVS). In the most recent version from January 2015, Sweden once again appears as "a different country" compared to most of the world, in embracing a high degree of secular-rational values, rather than traditional ones, and valuing self-expression of the individual, rather than issues of survival (Ingelhart and Welzel 2015). For example, the development of Swedish society and the Swedish welfare state led to a particular focus in Sweden on gender equality, and in an international comparison, Sweden was also early in focusing on individual rights (as opposed to family rights for example) in terms of welfare provision, tax, etc.; meanwhile, in legal terms, Sweden was also early in adopting the rights of the child in the judicial system. Today, therefore, these values of gender equality, individual autonomy, and also human rights are arguably "sacred" in contemporary Sweden, in that they are perceived as values which cannot be questioned and which possess a form of transcendental authority (Pettersson 2009: 234–35).

Traditional values as defined by the WVS emphasize the importance of religion and traditional family values. The WVS findings suggest that populations embracing *secular-rational values* place less emphasis on these values. *Survival values* means an emphasis on economic and physical security. They are often linked with an ethnocentric outlook and low levels of trust and tolerance, while at the other end, *self-expression values* give high priority to environmental protection and tolerance of foreigners. According to WVS data, religion is relatively unimportant for Swedes. Traditional family values, in the sense of traditional and conservative values pertaining to the composition and morals of family life, are attributed low value or rejected entirely, although it must be noted that this does not mean that family is not important in the lives of Swedes. On the contrary, according to the WVS, Swedes place significant importance on the role of family in their lives and also to some extent on tradition, simply less so on conservative definitions of family and family values (Edgardh 2018). Accordingly, attitudes toward gender equality and toward same-sex relations are positive. A typical Swede who is unlikely to see religion as an important factor in her or his life and is likely to reject "traditional family values" with a foundation in a Christian moral tradition is thus a religious other in relation to actively religious groups within Sweden, which constitute a minority (Pettersson and Esmer 2006). One example of such a religious minority group in contemporary Sweden is the Christian neo-charismatic congregation Word of Life; the reflections of some of its Uppsala-based adherents form a focus of this chapter.

Family and Values in Sweden and the Word of Life Church

The material for this chapter was collected as part of a larger study into family life and values in contemporary Sweden (*Family and Values in Sweden*), performed within the *Impact of Religion* program at Uppsala University. Against the background of the overarching picture that WVS gives of value developments in the world in general and with focus on Sweden in particular, the project has aimed to gain a deeper understanding of Sweden as "most different" and the country where values connected to religion, tradition, and family are most clearly rejected.

This has been done through an interview study with parents of small children in Uppsala recruited from open day care centers, both those run by the Church of Sweden and those run by the local authority. Semi-structured interviews were held with 15 individuals, both men and women. The interviews took as their starting point a number of questions asked in the WVS questionnaire. Interviewees were asked first how they would answer the WVS question and then to elaborate on the reasons behind the answer given. In this way we know a bit, not only about the values of the interviewees, but also about how they think about these values themselves. The interviews have then been transcribed and analyzed using text-based content analysis.

The four individuals who are the focus of this chapter are more or less active in the Word of Life Church (Livets Ord) in Uppsala, which is a Swedish charismatic free church with roots in the Word of Faith movement in the United States. The Church was formed in 1983 in Uppsala and is currently active in three locations in Sweden and internationally, and it claims to have around 3,000 members affiliated with the mother church in Uppsala. The Word of Faith movement is a Charismatic Christian movement which emphasizes the activity of the Holy Spirit in the present. This is combined with evangelical theologies, an emphasis on the literal interpretation and authority of the Bible, adult baptism, and the importance of apostolic leadership. The movement is, however, a loose conglomeration of congregations and denominations, and there is considerable variety within the movement. The movement has, for example, been strongly connected with theologies of Healing and Prosperity, although these teachings have been toned down by the Word of Life Church in Sweden in recent years.

This congregation represents a small religiously active Christian minority in Sweden. Still, these parents chose to attend one of the Church of Sweden preschools, which was located close to the Word of Life center in Uppsala. This may in itself say something of how these parents need to negotiate their relation to the religious majority.

Four Voices from a Religiously Active Minority

This chapter focuses on a detailed reading of these four interviews with three women (Emma, Anna, and Sara) and one man (Tom) who are active in Word of Life.[1] The three women Emma, Anna, and Sara, are all what could be described as core members of the Word of Life Church. They regularly attend Sunday services and other family events, Bible study groups, etc., and clearly self-identify as members. Tom, however is less committed to Word of Life as an organization. He attends services and activities at Word of Life as well as in other Christian congregations and describes himself as seeking for a context which preaches the Christian message in a manner that suits him and his own interpretation of the Bible. Tom was also keen to participate in the interview study as a means of presenting his right-wing political views, which he strongly feels to be ignored and marginalized by the mainstream media and academia in Sweden. Potentially important for understanding his responses to interview questions are both his identity as a religious "seeker" and his sense of being marginalized by majority culture, on political as well as religious grounds. Tom is the father of a son under 5 and shares the childcare with his partner—a division of care not uncommon in Sweden, but less common among members of Word of Life. Emma, Anna, and Sara, all mothers of small children, are responsible for the vast majority of the childcare in their respective families and have taken career breaks to take care of their children full-time until these children start school. This is a contrast to the majority of Swedish families, whose children attend nursery from the age of 1–2 years old.[2] For all of these four individuals, family is often referred to as the nuclear family, and they all live in heterosexual relationships with a partner who is the mother or father of their child(ren) and were themselves born and raised in Sweden to parents also from Sweden. For Anna, however, her own story, both in terms of relationships and religious background, is more complex than those of the others. Anna is a little older than the other three parents, who are all in their late twenties. In addition to the young daughter she is currently at home caring for, she has an adult daughter from a previous relationship (and is a grandmother to her daughter's child, who the same age as her youngest) as well as being a "bonus parent" to her husband's son from his previous marriage. She had a Christian upbringing, but converted to Islam for a period as a young adult before returning to Christianity a number of years ago. In responding to questions from the WVS on traditional family values, Anna points to her own life story as a reason why she herself believes it is important not to judge others for the life choices that they make.

In the section that follows, we have chosen a number of thematic headings under which to present strategies identified in the interviews. These were identified during the analysis of the interview material but are also clearly influenced by themes in the

WVS questions which were used to structure the interviews. The starting point of the interviews is a series of questions, not for the most part directly asking about religious belief, but rather asking about values, attitudes, and behaviors in relation to these. The interviews yielded reflections by the interviewees on their values both in relation to their own faith and in relation to mainstream secular society. In turn, these reflections on values and norms reveal the extent to which the interviewees criticize the "religious other" of the secular or attempt to identify similarities between their own position and that of a perceived majority.

Swedish Values and the Norm of Individual Autonomy

In Ingelhart and Welzel's terms, the individuals interviewed here embraced traditional family values for themselves, but these values were nonetheless filtered through an acceptance of individual autonomy as a "given" or sacred value which is not questioned (2010). In response to questions about homosexuality, for example, to which we will return in greater detail later, the values expressed are seen on the one hand as self-evident and correct in a black-and-white sense. In Tom's words, "It is said in plain terms in the Bible what is applicable." On the other hand, however, it is taken as given that if others choose a different path, this is not necessarily wrong: "But according to myself, I do not judge them" (Tom).

Traditions and Religious Upbringing for the Children

In a country where a majority still belong to the Church of Sweden but far fewer identify as religious, and where this belonging is marked in particular by participation in rituals in the Church in connection with rites of passage and with festivals connected to the Church year, it would be expected that even the non-religious would place emphasis on celebrating the festivals of Christmas and Easter. For our interviewees, these festivals and traditions connected to them are celebrated and valued, but really as an opportunity to meet up and spend time with the family (in a broader sense). Emphasis is on opportunities to spend time together rather than the traditions themselves being important, and they would choose celebrating with family over the opportunity to decide exactly what is done where if necessary. Emma comments that it is having time to be together rather than the content of the traditions (what is done, where, etc.) that is important. "Tradition for me that is, of course it is the festivals that steer it, but it is still having time to be with the family." She does go on to say that because they are Christian, there is more focus on what the Christian festivals mean, why they are celebrating, etc., but that although they tend to do the same things every year, it is not that it has to be the same each time that is the important thing. Anna too, when talking about traditions, responds along the same lines—here she comments that traditions can be good, but "you want to take what is good and leave the rest…. You choose what is good." Here again, we see an emphasis in the responses not on doing what is dictated by church and tradition, but in choosing the elements of traditions that suit them. Like Beaman's respondents, our interviewees choose a pragmatic path. They choose to celebrate festivals in such a way that they feel that they can do justice to their own religious beliefs, but that also does not create conflict in relation to friends and relatives who are not actively religious.

Tradition also appears in the interviews not just in relation to festivals but also when the respondents talk about what aspects of their own upbringing they wish to pass on to their own children. Anna talked about her Free Church upbringing when her Dad would read the children's bible and say a short prayer with her and her siblings before bed. This, she says, is a "very nice and cosy tradition to have." When asked if this is something she would like to take with her to her own children she replied: "Yes, I think it is nice to transfer this to the children. As long as they want to of course." Similarly, for her, whether her 11-year-old attends church or not with the family is voluntary: "He can choose, I don't think you should force children, to come with you. Rather when they want to themselves, but still try to make it into something nice we do together as a family." This is similar to Sara's attitude—when asked about what personal qualities children should be encouraged to learn, she says "the most important is that the children believe," but then continues: "We don't force it on them… because it is one's own decision. But I think it is still important, that they have the possibility to choose." Here our interviewees place emphasis on what they value highly (having earlier in the interview also responded that religion is of particular importance in their lives), but also indicate an adherence to a hierarchy of values. Previous research into basic values has, for example, revealed the constructions of hierarchies of values by individuals as a way of structuring and negotiating value conflicts (Hofstede 2001). In this case, the arguably "sacred value" in Sweden of individual autonomy receives precedence, even above passing on their faith tradition to their children.

When talking about the importance of having respect for others in society (even if you do not share their views), Emma goes on to apply this to her own family: "Even in our own little family. I have to have respect for both Oscar and Ellen, despite the fact that they are small, they are still individuals. And then it can be hard because you want them to do things in a certain way and so on, but they also have to have the opportunity." One way of interpreting this response could be, as suggested above, to see this as part of a hierarchy of values, where individual autonomy is placed higher than religious faith by our respondents. A significant amount of research into basic values has, for example, identified noteworthy similarities in basic values across cultures, but also differences in the priorities placed on specific values (Hofstede 2001; Schwartz and Bardi 2001). This explanation is, however, difficult to understand here, given the interviewees' own profession of their religious faith as the most important element in their lives. Here, Connolly's concept of "agnostic respect" as used by Beaman is therefore perhaps a useful concept in attempting to understand these apparently contradictory stances, as such respect necessitates an abandonment of total truth claims (Beaman 2014: 98).

Individual Autonomy and Traditional Family Values

The importance placed on individual freedom and respect for others, including values that differ significantly from one's own, appears most clearly when the interviewees are asked their opinions on a whole range of issues and whether they can be justified. These were also all issues connected to "traditional family values" where a conservative and negative response would be expected from members of a conservative Christian community. Members of one such congregation, from which the four informants who form the basis of this chapter come, could be expected to fall within the category which Linda Woodhead identifies in the UK as the "moral minority" (2013). This group is in Woodhead's definition a small percentage of the population who hold a non-liberal position on issues such as abortion, same-sex marriage, and euthanasia in opposition to that of the vast majority of the population. In the UK study, self-identification as a Baptist or Muslim is, along with being male and voting conservative, a predictor of this narrow view of the family (2013). This can be well illustrated from our material with a focus on the issue of homosexuality. The World Values Survey includes a question in which the interviewees are asked whether they think homosexuality can be justified or not. For most of our interviewees in the broader study, the obvious answer was a surprised yes. Some were even provoked by the idea that same-sex relations somehow would be in need of justification.

Not so with our informants from The Word of Life congregation, who embrace quite traditional family values in general. In a more general discussion of marriage, for example, and not in response to a particular question, Emma particularly mentions that her husband became the head of the family when they married, which is not a common attitude in Sweden and something which she also herself feels that she has to comment on. In responding to the specific question about homosexuality, our respondents' manner of answering indicates an assumption that religious conviction is unusual and may be hard to accept or interpret even for the interviewer. For example, Anna responds, when asked if homosexuality could be justified:

> First I have to say that I never want to judge anyone… and that you distinguish between thing and person is important to me too . . . I can never justify homosexuality. But I don't judge anyone who lives like that. Because I have talked to many homosexuals and I notice that they are very sensitive so to say for… I can say that we belong to Word of Life and it is very often misunderstood how we think. We absolutely have nothing against homosexuals. The condition, so to speak, we are against, however. Because the Bible says so too.

She also comments that "there is a difference in how people live and how you yourself think that you should live… like homosexuality. I can never justify that. But I don't judge anyone who lives like that." Emma responds similarly: "I would say that it cannot be justified at all. Then I have friends who are homosexuals and I respect them, absolutely, but I do not agree at all." Sara says:

> That is the kind of question you do not wish to answer. But I do believe in the Bible and there it says that it is not ok, but I would, that is I, it is hard to say because I have nothing against them. I can like them and socialize with them and love them, but I can never stand by their life choices.

Here, our interviewees obviously navigated between attitudes typical of modern Swedes and attitudes clearly connected to their religious commitment. Any elaboration on the extent to which their responses reflect their deeper convictions or not would be pure speculation, but it is interesting to note that their responses are in many ways self-contradictory. It is quite clear that despite a deep personal conviction, related to their faith, they know that their views are "unusual" in contemporary Sweden and they thus seem to be at pains in their answers to paint themselves as empathetic and rational people. Their way of answering indicates an assumption that religious conviction is not common and that the interviewer, as a representative of "mainstream Sweden" and therefore presumably not actively religious, is a "secular believer" and may not understand where they are coming from. They also seem to assume that the interviewer will hold mainstream values broadly in line with those indicated by the WVS survey as the norm in Sweden, that is, broad acceptance of homosexuality, gender equality, and individual autonomy in general.

Having to decide on a scale between "never" and "always" regarding the justifiability of homosexuality, Sara says never, but exclaims that she feels awful doing so. Tom does not seem to have the same emotional trouble with declaring his standpoint on homosexuality as the three women. Like the others, however, he argues on many levels in trying to combine his trust in the Bible with his respect for individual choice, which seems much more in line with the typical secular Swedish belief system. We have divided his statement into sections in order to illustrate the various, and in part contradictory, standpoints. Tom starts positively, maybe in an effort to satisfy the interviewer: "People may live as they wish. Absolutely. So it may always be justified." Then he states his personal standpoint, according to faith: "Not according to the Bible, not according to Christian faith, that is not possible. It is said in plain terms in the Bible what is applicable and there homosexuality is a sin, straight off." But then again, what he thinks himself is a bit ambiguous: "But according to myself, I do not judge them... I do not see them as of less worth." He then ends his argument by blaming society: "I do however [searching for words] despise society's efforts to impose homosexuality on me." He exemplifies by talking about homosexuals appearing in children's programs and that homosexuality is idealized as cool. He is particularly opposed to the Pride parade, where he imagines men dancing on flatbed trucks in scanty underwear. *That can never be justified*, he says:

> People may be like that and I have nothing against it... if only I am allowed to be me, so to say. And my son is allowed to be who he is... if he becomes homosexual, then he is of no less worth... and I would still love him as much, but I don't want to have it in my face each and every day that it is so cool to be gay.

Interpreting his statements, it appears that they are not so much about homosexuality as about being "othered" by a dominant secular majority. "It is very often misunderstood how we think," as Anna said; and "if only I am allowed to be me," as Tom said. They seem to long for, in other words, not necessarily a religious society, but an "open strategy" on the part of "secular people" in Sweden who they come into contact with.

Personal Faith

Despite feeling misunderstood and othered by the "religious others" of mainstream Swedish society, there are times when the interviewees embrace their own religious identity, seeing it as a resource which they have when engaging with people of other beliefs and values. For Sara, for example, her personal faith means that she feels it is maybe easier for her to defend her beliefs about what is morally right or wrong than it is for those without faith. At the same time, she indicates that she is aware that this position may well be incomprehensible for those without faith:

> I believe in the Bible. And my values follow that too, in cases like this because it is there in black and white on these things. It says that, it is hard to understand if you aren't a believer, but yes I have of course, everyone has the law in their hearts. That is, you know what is right and wrong, so somewhere I believe that most maybe anyway know and feel… but then I know it because I have it black on white because I believe in God. So I can say that I stand behind it… but I understand that it isn't as easy for everyone else.

Here Sara turns what could be perceived as a potential point for conflict between her and "secular people" who she comes into contact with into a strength which she has. She does not, however, argue that she has the moral high ground, but rather seeks to find similarity between herself and others in arguing that all people have a moral compass. The fact that it isn't as easy for those without faith as it is for those with faith to follow that moral compass is then for her a way of explaining why her own position can sometimes be so far from that of many others in Swedish society.

Strategies for Engagement

Analysis of these interviews with our small number of actively religious conservative Christians in Sweden today suggests that they assume that they will be met by a hostile and secularist or at least restrictionist strategy, both by individuals with whom they converse and by social structures as they make everyday life choices for themselves and their children grounded in their faith perspective. The interviewees indicate in various ways in their responses that they realize that placing an importance on religious belief is not a common position in Sweden today and therefore might not be easily understood by "secular people" in mainstream society.

Furthermore, the interviews reveal that for these individuals, religion is to a large extent an individual matter. Our four interviewees say that for them, religion has a significant impact on family life and on how they raise their children, but still highlight the importance of individual life choices, both for others they come into contact with and for their children, rather than the supremacy of their own beliefs and religion. Also, even though these individuals are active members of a (fairly tight-knit) religious community, religion is attributed weak authority in matters of family values as compared to the individual's interpretation of the Bible based on personal faith.

Deep religious conviction and rational scientific attitudes are not seen as contradictory. While embracing traditional family values for themselves, these individuals can otherwise be seen to be representative of the Swedish mainstream as described by the WVS in attributing significant priority to individual autonomy, even in questions where issues of firmly held values are concerned.

This ability to balance apparently contradictory beliefs is intriguing, but perhaps not surprising. As noted above, earlier research has shown how individuals construct hierarchies of values when negotiating value conflicts. Meanwhile, other lines of inquiry have also revealed the role personal interpretation can play in negotiating value conflicts, where one and the same "basic value" can be called upon by proponents of opposite viewpoints in support of their arguments. As Linda Woodhead has shown at the level of public debate, for example, individual freedom has been called upon as the foundational value both by those who argue that Muslim women should be free to wear a headscarf in public spaces and those who oppose it (2009). In the conversations with our four interviewees above, however, what is striking is not any attempt on their part to argue for a particular moral standpoint or to present their own convictions as the only valid approach, but rather an attempt to carve out a space for their convictions in what is assumed to be a hostile environment. Their approach in these interviews in all four cases, although to varying degrees, is to refrain from passing judgment on issues on which they also clearly express deeply held beliefs. Thus, they refrain from active criticism of "secular people," i.e., the non-religious majority (as they see it). Yet in their interactions with their secular surroundings and attempts to integrate their moral values with living a life within mainstream Swedish institutions, they seek at the same time to find ways to present their own position in a manner which may be understood by those from the secular mainstream. They apply, in other words, an "open strategy" of critique in the hopes that this "openness" will be reciprocated.

Elements of this approach are reminiscent of strategies adopted by religious college students in the US, who research has revealed can pack away religious and spiritual identities in an "identity lockbox" during their college years: "This lockbox protects religious identities, along with political, racial, gender, and civic identities, from tampering that might affect their holders' future entry into the American cultural mainstream" (Clydesdale 2007: 2). The American cultural mainstream however, unlike the Swedish, could be equally hostile to the non-religious as to the extremes of religiosity, and interestingly in this context, Christel Manning's research has revealed how in the American context the actively non-religious sometimes choose to raise their children including elements of religion, such as Sunday school, as a way of ensuring their children have the tools with which to negotiate mainstream culture (2015: 107–8).

While we are not arguing that our interviewees have put away their religious identities for a time in a lockbox, their answers indicate a caution in entering into discussions on topics they assume to be sensitive with those outside their own faith community. Further research is needed to explore these issues in detail and with a larger number of individuals, but our conversations with these respondents indicate a tendency to reserve discussion of potentially contentious moral issues to within the "safe spaces" of their own religious community, where, for example, a reliance on the authority of the Bible in ethical issues does not need to be explained or justified.

In the context of this study, such a retreat would indicate an absence of interaction at least, if not necessarily a criticism of the religious other. In the lives of our interviewees, however, while there is clearly some avoidance of discussing sensitive issues such as homosexuality with those outside of the faith community, it is clearly not the case that they avoid interaction with mainstream culture. Rather, they were recruited for interviews when attending a Church of Sweden playgroup with their children. In this respect, their behavior rather mirrors that identified by Manning as practiced by non-religious parents in a US context. However, it is also clear from their responses that they do not expect their arguments for critique of mainstream culture to be understood: while they responded to questions relating to traditional family values in an interview setting, they were reluctant at times to do so, indicating that they expected to be misunderstood or not understood. As Sara said in response to a question about her views on homosexuality, "that is the sort of question you don't wish to answer." In this respect, the caution expressed by our interviewees both in voicing their own beliefs and values and in discussing the choices made by others can be seen as an example of what Beaman terms agnostic respect. They do voice their opinions, but with an acknowledgement that other perspectives can be held and are valid and are worthy of respect, in a strategy which resembles the "open strategy" Stenmark calls for. In discussing their parenting choices too, our informants place themselves within the mainstream by focusing on the challenges of raising children in Sweden today; in doing so, they illustrate their narratives with examples that both emphasize the similarities between themselves and parents of no faith and at the same time highlight the differences.

Conclusions

Lori Beaman has titled the article quoted in the beginning "From tolerance to deep equality" (2014). The ideal of tolerance seems to be what our four interviewees struggle with. They wish to be tolerant. But they do not always feel tolerated. They are stuck in the conflict.

They share the dominant discourse in Sweden about the right of the individual to choose their lifestyle. However, they do not feel that their choices, as a religious minority, are immediately respected by the allegedly liberal, secular majority. Still, they try. They negotiate, both within themselves and in relation to gay friends, other parents, and an interviewer whom they expect to have other views than themselves. In this respect, they therefore seek to move beyond tolerance, which does not require an attempt either to understand or to be constructively critical, in order to develop ways of coexisting with those around them without needing to suppress or abandon their own beliefs. They appear at the very least to aspire to a "deep equality" process in that they go beyond tolerance, which implies an allowance of others' differences and displays agnostic respect.

This volume has sought to identify examples of constructive criticism, that is to say, critiques which seek not just to debunk other worldviews but to reform, improve, or modify. Our interviewees from the Word of Life Church do just that in what they say and in what they tell us about how they live their lives. They do not go out of their way to debate issues of theological or value difference with those of other faiths or none, and neither do they actively attempt to modify the Swedish culture to fit their Christian worldview or to change the ways others live. Rather, they seek to create space within the society for themselves and their families which is both thoroughly Swedish and completely in line with their religious beliefs. In other words, the research underpinning this chapter raises the question of whether "Swedishness," defined as mainstream values, is fundamentally in tension with active religiosity. Against this background, a significant question for those wishing to facilitate constructive criticism of religion in a Swedish context is a consideration of what constructive criticism of mainstream secularity might look like.

14

Postscript:
Toward Constructive Criticism of Religion

Mia Lövheim and Mikael Stenmark

The aim of this volume has been to introduce a new approach to research about how secular democratic societies should accommodate differences in lifestyles and motivations based on a broader range of religious and secular worldviews. In the introduction, we argue that previous research, along with political debates and media reports, in Europe and North America have tended to focus on religion as a problem for the functioning of a democratic society. This approach entails an implicit critique against at least some forms of religion as incompatible with the principles of contemporary democratic society. Furthermore, much of the critique of religion expressed in current as well as longstanding debates has tended to increase hostility and conflict between people of different religious and secular worldviews rather than encourage mutual revision of beliefs, values, and patterns of behavior.

By focusing on the concept of *constructive criticism of religion*, this volume represents a step toward scholarly engagement in discussions of how the current situation can be developed toward more fruitful interaction and critique across diverse religious and secular commitments. Constructive criticism of religion represents an attempt to suggest forms of public debate in which people encounter and engage one another in critical but respectful and non-hostile ways. The task we propose scholars to undertake is to explore the conditions for civil disagreement and fair critique among individuals and groups with different and conflicting convictions about what constitutes a good life and about religion's role in that venture.

The chapters in the volume bring together philosophical and theological analyses of arguments in critique of religion within Islam, atheism, and Christianity with sociological, legal, and education-oriented analyses of how social institutions such as courts, schools, politics, and the media shape communication and interaction between individuals and groups with different backgrounds, resources, and motivations. The aim of the book, furthermore, has been to move beyond an analysis of differences between various forms of critique of religion and how these are shaped by institutional contexts toward a discussion of when and how constructive and successful forms of criticism emerge in debates and dialogue between people who embrace different worldviews.

Postscript: Toward Constructive Criticism of Religion

A key feature of this discussion has been to investigate resources for criticism expressed within particular religious frameworks, and when and how these are taken into account in criticism of religious as well as secularist values, beliefs, and arguments. In order to assess when and how constructive criticism emerges in the contexts we study—by which we mean criticism which is successful in revising beliefs, values, or behavior that hinder enhanced understanding and transformative learning—we proposed a focus on six interrelated aspects:

a) Whether the actors offering the critique—as individuals, groups, or institutions—are situated inside or outside of the religion whose beliefs, values, or practices become the target of criticism
b) The form of critique in terms of reasons or arguments used by the critics, and the goal of the critical engagement as positive or negative, reformistic, revolutionary, or debunking
c) How the actors receiving the critique understand and respond to the criticism, and what arguments that have epistemic and moral authority within their worldview
d) The implicit and explicit values and norms that enable, limit, and structure patterns of speech and social interaction within the institutional context in which the critique is expressed
e) The interplay between the critics and the receivers of the critique in terms of possibilities to offer criticism and respond to it, and how these are structured by dominant discourses and access to resources and influence in a particular society
f) The impact in terms of various outcomes of the critique: is the criticism leading to increased hostility and polarization or to mutual acknowledgment, self-criticism, enhanced understanding, and transformative learning?

Our aim has been neither more nor less than to *suggest* ways in which an inquiry into various forms of critique of religion can be undertaken and the kind of results it could generate. In this final chapter, we will discuss how the proposed model of six related aspects for exploring constructive criticism of religious and secular worldviews has been nuanced and improved through the inquiries entailed by each chapter in the volume.

First, when representatives of a national state, individual citizens, or groups within civil society criticize the (religious) worldview of another group of citizens, they base their critique on reasons or arguments of a particular sort and have an aim or a purpose in mind in doing so. This critical engagement takes place in a certain social context, which enables, limits, and structures the argumentation and interaction between critics and the criticized party or the "critique receivers." The outcome could be that the individual or group who becomes the target of criticism is offended by the critique, ignores the critique, is not granted a public space to respond to it, or rejects or accepts it based on the same kind of reasons offered by the critics or based on a different kind of reasons. However, the outcome of the critical engagement could also be that the perspective of the ones offering the critique is transformed so that they in the process gain a deeper understanding of the target group's worldview and realize that the criticism was (more or less) misguided, unjustified, or insufficient. If so, complementary learning processes may be the outcome of a civil disagreement or a fair debate. Whether these processes require, like Habermas (2006) suggests, translation of religious reason-giving and argument into secular or rather public reason-giving or argument, or merely require mutual recognition and empathetic imagination on behalf of the (secular) critics, needs to be further explored. It is worth pointing out, however, that the "restrictionist" critical engagement strategy which Stenmark identifies assumes this, whereas the "open" strategy does not.

Second, we proposed that the likelihood that the target of the criticism accepting the critique in such a way as to change something in their worldview will increase if the kinds of reasons appealed to by the critics—or at least some of the reasons—can be grounded in or located within the framework of the criticized party's own worldview rather than being externally grounded in, say, science or political ideologies. If this is correct, we would expect that such forms of immanent or internal criticism are more effective than external forms of criticism. This idea becomes clear in the chapter by Mohammad Fazlhashemi, where he stresses that religious traditions have always brought forward many critics within their own ranks and demonstrates that Islam is not an exception to this rule. This form of immanent critique is given from an insider's point of view, by someone who self-identifies, in this case, as a Muslim. Nevertheless, as Ulf Zackariasson's analysis of immanent feminist critique toward Islam shows, although these feminists self-identify with the religion they criticize, they emphasize their identities as scholars and their commitments to scholarly standards and values at the same time. This dialectic movement of offering an immanent criticism both as an insider in some respects and as an outsider in other respects shows that the categories of "insiders" and "outsiders" with regard to the religion whose beliefs, values, or practices become the target of criticism (aspect "a" above) should not be conceived of as comprising a simple either-or alternative. This is also an important outcome of Effie Fokas' analysis of the complexities regarding insider and outsider positions with regard to Greek Orthodox theologians' response to the current case processed by the European Court of Human Rights, regarding implications of transformations in the religious education program.

Third, even if the critique of religion is external, meaning that the grounds or the standards used in the critique are not derived from the worldview shared by the criticized party, the aim of the criticism (aspect "b" above) matters for whether the criticism could be perceived as constructive. This is something Stephen LeDrew highlights in his discussion of different forms of secular criticism of religion. The aim of the forms of anthropological or humanistic atheism (in contrast to those of scientific atheism) is not to directly target religious belief and individual believers. Their criticism is instead directed toward the social structure that gives religion its power. It is a secular criticism of religion that emphasizes positive social changes, rather than hostile attacks against those who profess religious beliefs of any kind. Such criticism also offers religious groups the possibility to reform their own religious outlook, and thus meet the secular critics halfway, by addressing issues of unequal social relations and oppression within their religious community and practice.

Moreover, Charles Taliaferro in his chapter draws our attention to the fact that critical engagement is not by necessity a two-party relationship between, on the one hand, the critics and, on the other, the criticized party or the critique receivers. Other individuals could also enter the debate, and they could do it on behalf of the target of the critique. He argues that the Good Samaritan virtue could and should be a part of an adequate philosophy of criticism. It is possible, perhaps even a virtue, to intervene to protect a vulnerable group of religious people as an outsider, in order to defend someone whom one thinks has been unfairly or cruelly critiqued by others. Hence, the "critique responders" do not have to be those who are the target of the criticism; it could just as well be an outsider. This argument is, again, illustrated by Effie Fokas' case study, which includes different positions and degrees of insiderness. As she shows, the Greek Helsinki Monitor and the Grassrootsmobilise researchers seem to be considered by the theologians defending the revised religious education program as "insiders" with regard to criticism. This position is here due to the fact that these interveners are based in Greece and thus are perceived by the theologians as having "insider insight" about the Greek context in contrast to the "outsider" of the European Court.

The chapters in the second part of the present volume have enabled a deeper knowledge regarding a fourth point, namely, how implicit and explicit values and norms that enable and structure patterns of speech and social interaction within particular institutional contexts shape the kind of critique against religion that is expressed (aspect "d" above). The chapters by Effie Fokas and Pia Karlsson Minganti explore the legal system as a growing space for religious criticism and dialogue. The detailed analysis of the processing of court cases in the European Court of Human Rights and in the Administrative Court in Stockholm brings out how critique of religion is informed by formal legal regulations regarding citizens' rights and democratic values, but also by other kinds of values that more or less implicitly come to the fore in the interpretations of these rights and democratic values by various actors in the process. Karlsson Minganti analyzes the arguments used by the Swedish Agency for Youth and Civil Society through the lens of the three strategies of critique—secularist, restrictive, and open—set out by Stenmark in chapter 1. Her findings show that an open strategy, in which the expression of a variety of religious worldviews is permitted, is disenabled for constructive dialogue when the target of criticism—here Sweden's Young Muslims (SUM)—are positioned as an essentialist and separatist form of Islam that is harmful to democracy and societal cohesion in Sweden.

The analysis undertaken in these chapters thus reveals how different strategies for critique of religion are enabled and restricted through the actions of various parties in these court cases, in terms of what arguments and resources they bring to the table. These chapters also reveal the significance of *interactions* between different parties in these cases, such as religious groups and governmental bodies but also news media, think tanks, and researchers such as the Grassrootsmobilise team. Negotiations between these actors shape the kinds of critique that are expressed in these cases, for example in terms of inviting dialogue with all or certain forms of religion, and the conditions for this dialogue to take place. Furthermore, these chapters illustrate how *timing* shapes critique of religion: for example, the history of a court case in terms of previous decisions and appeals structures the content of arguments as well as who can express what critique, and how the critique is received. Thus, these chapters contribute to an analysis of the current trend of increasing judicialization of religion, in exemplifying how courts may become sites where antagonism is expressed and communication is drawn to a close or how they, by principle of safeguarding a fair trial, may work against secularist and restrictive strategies.

The issue of implicit and explicit values informing what kind of critique is expressed in particular societal contexts is further addressed in Lori Beaman and Solange Lefebvre's chapter on public commissions on religious diversity. They analyze how the format of public commissions, used by several governments in Europe and Canada, works as a strategy to structure criticism of religion in highly polarized debates within these societies. Their significant contribution to the model proposed by this book is to shed light on how sociocultural and historical drivers, along with particular mediatized events, contextualize religious critique within these commissions. As they show in their chapter, these drivers structure the kind of critique that is expressed by "external critics" but also what aspects of critique within religious institutions, here the Catholic Church, are taken into account in the commissions' critique of religion. This becomes evident in how religion in the commission reports is mainly addressed through certain themes: a growing anxiety about the erosion of gender equality highlighted by Muslim women's head coverings, and the connection of the majority religious tradition (Catholicism) with national culture and heritage. Although the mandate of these commissions was to address diversity with the aim of enabling coexistence in pluralistic societies, the critique expressed in the reports seemed to favor a secularist or restrictive strategy rather than an open strategy which included arguments from critical voices within religious institutions. Thus, Beaman and Lefebvre's analysis contributes to a refining of the model by showing how the form of external critique of religion, as well as the concept of internal or immanent criticism of religion, needs to be nuanced through a closer analysis of the entanglement of what is perceived as religious convictions and the given cultural and social context.

The importance of analyzing constructive criticism of religion with a sensitivity to religion as a *constituted and contested* concept is also salient in Per-Erik Nilsson's chapter. His analysis highlights how the meaning of religion, as well as the possibility of constructive critique of religion, is constituted in the interaction between various actors with different and sometimes opposing interests. In Nilsson's chapter as well as in the analyses by Karlsson Minganti and Beaman and Lefebvre, religious beliefs, identities, and practices are always discussed in alignment with contested categories of race, ethnicity, and national identity which draw on historical as well as contemporary political tensions within Europe and North America as well as in a broader global perspective.

The chapters analyzing critical debates about the influence of religion in general and Islam in particular in the Swedish public sphere offer insights into a fifth point for refining the model above. This pertains to aspect "e" regarding the interplay between the critics and the receivers of the critique in terms of possibilities to offer criticism and respond to it, and how these are structured by dominant discourses in a particular society. As pointed out by Johan von Essen, the fact that religion in contemporary Sweden as well as in other parts of Europe is becoming more of a public and conflictual societal phenomenon may open possibilities for productive criticism, which can revitalize and refine religious convictions and contribute to reasonable and communicative relations between groups with diverging worldviews. Von Essen's and Linnea Jensdotter and Mia Lövheim's chapters analyze whether the mediatized public sphere can work as a context for citizens to interact across diverse commitments and develop a productive criticism of religion, without the interference of state, political, or commercial interests. Their analyses of debates in Swedish media regarding confessional independent schools and the acting out of religious convictions among politicians both address a core value in a dominant secularist discourse in Swedish society: the strict separation of religion from the state and from politics (Lövheim 2017). Both von Essen's and Jensdotter and Lövheim's analyses show how opinion articles (editorials and debate articles) in the daily press structure the content of the criticism that is offered, as well as the interplay between various actors in these debates. Von Essen shows how the format of debate articles as a means to influence the political agenda disenabled the possibility for the expression of commitments and arguments regarding the role of religion in a democratic society. Furthermore, the participants in the debate acted from a position of political interest rather than as actors in civil society, thus using the debate articles as a means to influence the political or the legal system. These factors led to a debate dominated by secularist critique rather than an attempt develop a constructive criticism of religion.

Jensdotter and Lövheim shed additional light on the implications of how the media saturation of highly modernized societies shape spaces as well as conditions for public debate by comparing debates in the form analyzed by von Essen, editorials and debate articles, with debates in social media, which in theory can allow for a larger plurality of voices than conventional forms of mediated public spheres. Jensdotter and Lövheim find, in unison with von Essen's analysis, that critique of religion in the editorials was solely expressed by actors that have an established position in mass media and focus on secular political values and premises rather than religious beliefs. The Facebook debates represent a democratization of the public discussions, in terms of the range of participants, opinions, and experiences expressed, including participants that argue from a religious worldview. However, these debates also include more frequent practices of accusations and antagonistic portrayals of the other, which can further polarization and hostility rather than mutual respect. In sum, Jensdotter and Lövheim argue that examples of constructive criticism of religion can be found in these debates when actors move from generalizing statements to more nuanced ways of discussing how religious commitments can be expressed in political debates as well as in public discussions in general. Thus, on the one hand, these chapters show how secularist discourses on religion strongly influence critique of religion as expressed in mediated public discussions. On the other hand, they offer valuable insight into the contextual conditions, in terms of values, norms, and patterns of social interaction, that may enable such debates to become public spaces which allow for interactions across diverse commitments and a constructive critique of religion. In focusing on the range of actors that take part in these debates, they also show the importance of analyzing access to public spaces for debating religion in a society, as well as how these actors are positioned in relation to structures of power in a particular society.

Finally, we turn to the last aspect of the model proposed in this volume, the outcomes of critique of religion in terms of increased hostility and polarization or mutual acknowledgment, self-criticism, enhanced understanding, and transformative learning. Most chapters in Parts Two and Three of the present volume are skeptical regarding the possibility for constructive criticism to take place in the contexts that they study. In terms of outcome of the critique, Karlsson Minganti, Nilsson, and von Essen find that more of the criticism leads to increased hostility and polarization between actors than to mutual acknowledgment and enhanced understanding. In particular, these chapters show how secularist or restrictive strategies based in narrow or essentialist understanding of religion limit openness for understanding internal religious criticism and variations in the arguments and actions of deeply devoted religious believers. This is a foundation for immanent criticism and thus for constructive criticism of religion to be accomplished. Thus, these chapters underline the need for critical self-reflection on the part of public institutions in secular democratic societies with regard to if and how their legal, media, and political institutions can accommodate citizens who base their convictions about what constitutes a good life and a just society on religious convictions.

A few of the chapters highlight attempts and openings for mutual acknowledgment, enhanced understanding, and transformative learning. Malin Löfstedt and Anders Sjöborg find in their chapter that although the task of being a Religious Education teacher in a secularized and religiously plural society is challenging, the teachers they interview are able to develop didactic strategies that increase their pupils' ability to reflect on and communicate about religion and to reflect critically on their own values and worldviews. They conclude that this kind of critical religious literacy, based on communicative and self-reflective abilities, is likely to contribute to a constructive criticism of religion. Meanwhile, Linnea Jensdotter and Mia Lövheim argue that while social media such as Facebook polarize debates on the role of religion in Swedish politics, they also allow a broader spectrum of voices to be heard; among these there are examples of mutual acknowledgement, a deeper understanding of others' arguments, and perhaps reconsideration of entrenched secularist positions. Lastly, the deeply devoted religious parents interviewed by Martha Middlemiss Lé Mon and Ninna Edgardh show in practice ways of handling the tension between choices they make based on their religious commitments and the attitudes of the allegedly liberal, secular majority in the Swedish society. As they write, these parents in their reasoning and everyday life seek to develop ways of coexisting with those around them without needing to suppress or abandon their own beliefs. This involves an aspiration toward constructive criticism in an allowance of others' differences at the same time as they ask for an acknowledgement that their own perspectives can be held, are valid, and are worthy of respect. Across these chapters, willingness to examine different arguments and to be self-reflective concerning one's own motivations, along with access to spaces where mutual disclosure and respect are encouraged, seem to be crucial in order to enable a transformative learning process and thus constructive criticism of religion.

Challenges for Future Research

Most chapters in this volume have explored aspects which concern the form of the critique, the beliefs, values, and norms shaping critique within particular institutional contexts, and how possibilities to offer criticism and respond to it are structured by dominant discourses in these contexts. The volume thus also shows where challenges for future research are primarily located. This concerns, firstly, research on how the actors receiving the critique understand and respond to the criticism (aspect "c" in the model above). This is something we need to know much more about. One example concerns how the target groups for the feminist immanent critique of Islam analyzed by both Fazlhashemi and Zackariasson respond to these challenges. Another example concerns whether the response from religious people is different depending on if the critique is formulated from representatives of New Atheism or from the more constructive anthropological atheistic critique that LeDrew discusses in his chapter on secular criticism of religion. To obtain this kind of knowledge is especially challenging when it comes to response to criticism by those who are marginalized and perhaps stigmatized by the surrounding society in which they live. How could researchers gain the trust necessary to be able to obtain such information from the people involved in such situations? In pursuing further research on how actors receive critique toward their worldview commitments, the experiences from the Grassrootsmobilise research team shared in Effie Fokas' chapter offer valuable insights. However, as she points out in the end of her chapter, these experiences also raise new questions concerning the final aspect of the model regarding the possible outcomes of the critique.

As presented above, some chapters in this volume suggest ways in which further research can be undertaken concerning the aspect of impact in terms of when critique can be constructive and lead to processes of mutual acknowledgment, self-criticism, enhanced understanding, and transformative learning. Is it possible, for instance, to develop educational settings in which critical engagement strategies are tested and further developed? Can the classroom function as a social space in which such "experiments" can take place? Can philosophers identify and develop intellectual norms of conduct that, if respected and followed, could promote a "debate climate" in which it is likely that mutual acknowledgment, self-criticism, enhanced understanding, and transformative learning would flourish?

Trust, as is highlighted by both Karlsson Minganti and Zackariasson, seems to be of utmost importance to obtain a constructive critical dialogue between two disputing parties. In a climate of distrust between the state and some youth organizations, as described in Karlsson Minganti's chapter, there is no obvious site for dialogue. If one cannot trust a someone offering critique to be knowledgeable enough, concerned about one's well-being, and respectful of one's intellectual and moral integrity, why take this critique seriously? As shown in Fokas' chapter, the potential for misinterpretation of critique is heightened when critique comes in a form that is less familiar to or perceived as aggressive by those receiving the critique. This insight points to the need to further explore the relation between the means of critique against certain worldviews and the impact of the critique, in terms of its potential to be constructive. The role of trust as well as divergences in understanding arguments and aims in critical engagement between disputing parties needs to be further studied both theoretically and empirically.

Middlemiss Lé Mon and Ninna Edgardh raise in their chapter a significant question for those wishing to facilitate constructive criticism of religion, especially in strongly secularized countries like Sweden: what might constructive criticism of mainstream secularity look like? One way of addressing this question is to enlarge the scope of the kinds of criticism that become the object of study. Although the model proposed in the introduction in theory can be used for critique of religious as well as secular worldviews, most chapters in this volume have focused on critique of religious worldviews. Further development of the model of analyzing constructive criticism in terms of including constructive criticism of secular worldviews can contribute to challenging a simplistic perception of some actors in contemporary debates about religion as "neutrals" (non-committed people or religious nones) and others as "partisans" (religious believers). A more fruitful starting point for further research would be to acknowledge that some people advocate a religious worldview and others a secular worldview, and both of these outlooks can be subject to criticism. We can then explore what life-orienting beliefs that secular worldviews like naturalism and secular humanism contain or what the differences are between, for example, the seven types of atheism that John Gray (2018) identifies. An important task would then be to critically analyze how these philosophical conceptions of different non-religious worldviews can (possibly) be correlated to the beliefs and values of people who self-identify as secular in modern liberal democratic societies. In other words, we need to understand more clearly the "immanent construals of human flourishing" (Taylor 2007: 9) that people who are searching for secular alternatives to traditional religions try to develop, and include their commitments and outlooks in our discussion of constructive criticism.

In the introduction to this volume, we argue that research concerning more productive ways of critically engaging with differences in worldview commitments requires an interdisciplinary approach. Working with this volume has shown that researchers studying constructive criticism of religion also have to be prepared to practice the principles of constructive criticism in their interaction—meaning to cross over entrenched disciplinary boundaries and engage in mutual acknowledgment and self-criticism in order to enable enhanced understanding and transformative learning. The book has revealed issues and points of agreement as well as of tension between various disciplinary perspectives. We therefore end on the same note, by encouraging further interdisciplinary engagement in the discussion initiated in this volume.

Notes

Chapter 1

1 In this chapter, I will focus on critique of religion, whereas critique of worldviews is a broader category, including criticism of both religious and secular worldviews.
2 See also the introductory chapter (p. 3).
3 "Being scientistic just means treating science as our exclusive guide to reality, to nature—both our own nature and everything else's" (Rosenberg 2011: 8).
4 I have defended this idea in Stenmark (2006) in respect to the issue of whether or not religious people should be exclusivists.

Chapter 3

1 See, for instance, Per-Erik Nilsson's chapter in this volume.
2 One important difference between Stout and Sabia is that Stout's main opponent is the universalist who thinks that critique should rely on standards that all reasonable human beings would endorse, whereas Sabia already takes for granted that critique should have an immanent character: the important task is to determine which forms of immanent critique are most promising and interesting.
3 Cf. Mikael Stenmark's chapter in this volume.

Chapter 4

1 "Men have authority over women on account of the qualities with which God has caused the one of them to excel over the other and for what they spend of their property; therefore the righteous women are obedient, guarding the unseen that which God has guarded; and as to those whose perverseness you fear, admonish them, then avoid them in bed, then beat them; and if they obey you, then seek not a way against them; Verily, God is Ever-High, Ever-Great" (Quran, 4:34).
2 "Among His signs is that He created you from dust, and from that you have become human beings scattered all around." (Quran, 30:20); "[God] began the creation of human from clay. Then He made His offspring from the extract of base fluid. Then gave the human proper shape and breathed into the human His spirit." (Quran, 32:7–9).

Chapter 5

1 Cited by Andrew Harvey (1996: 185).
2 As may be witnessed in the widely praised, magisterial *Christianity: The First Three Thousand Years* by Diarmaid MacCulloch, among other sources.

3   There is a scathing portrait of such petty self-concern in academic life in "Creativity, Vanity and Narcissism" by Matthew Kieran in *Creativity and Philosophy* (Gaut and Kieran 2017), chapter 5.
4   The stress on the love of the good in this chapter is part of the Cambridge or, really, Christian Platonism I defend in *The Golden Cord: A Short Book on the Secular and the Sacred* (2012).
5   As in *The Book of Common Prayer*, currently in use by the Episcopal Church in the United States.
6   See Zagzebski (2012).
7   See Stendahl, "Three Rules of Religious Understanding."
8   See *The Blackwell Companion to Natural Theology*.

Chapter 6

1   This text is based on data generated in the European Research Council-funded Grassrootsmobilise research programme (ERC GA no. 338463, 2014–2019), of which the author was Principal Investigator. As with all output of this research program and in line with both Hellenic National Data Protection Authority guidelines and ERC research ethics, all data is strictly anonymized. I would like to thank the two theologians who contributed to this research and offered their invaluable feedback on this chapter; I also thank the volume's editors for their dedicated work on this text.
2   The ECtHR is an institution of the Council of Europe (CoE), established to defend the European Convention on Human Rights (ECHR). The CoE has 47 member states, all of which are necessarily signatories of the ECHR. Though the ECtHR is not a European Union institution, the EU does require that all of its member states be signatories of the ECHR, and therefore the Court also has jurisdiction over all EU member states. So too the Court of Justice of the European Union, which tends to all aspects of EU law and is not strictly a human rights court; its active engagement with religion-related claims is relatively recent. On this see Fokas 2016.
3   It should be noted that in the Court's first 33 years (1959–1992), cases related to the right to religious freedom were dealt with exclusively by the European Commission of Human Rights and not by the Court. Until the introduction of Protocol 11 in 1998, a two-tiered system was in place, with the Commission filtering which cases would reach the Court; Protocol 11 abolished that Commission, and allowed for direct access of individual applicants to the Court.
4   This section presents material general to the Grassrootsmobilise research results and not specific to the topic at hand; accordingly, it draws heavily on the already published Fokas 2018.
5   By "involved in," I mean somehow engaged in the development of the new RE curriculum (theologians opposed to RE reform are "involved" in a different sense to that which I take here).
6   This section relies heavily on the work of Dr. Margarita Markoviti, the postdoctoral researcher for the Greek case study in Grassrootsmobilise.
7   According to one respondent theologian, however, "while this law is still in place, the new Greek RE program is not inspired by this principle as it has overcome the traditional strong connection between religion and nation." Written communication June 22, 2019.

8   The great legal significance of what exactly entails "more" or "less" in such issues lies beyond the scope of this chapter, though it is central to the ECtHR case law on RE.
9   "Kairos" means "time" in Greek; the group's stated belief is that "it is time for the reform of religious education in Greece" (See the "declaration" page of the Kairos website, http://www.kairosnet.gr/about-us/declaration).
10 The latter two are mother and daughter, whereas Papageorgiou and his child share the same surname.
11 EU Directive 95/46/EU, later replaced by the currently-in-effect Regulation (EU) 2016/679.
12 This practice was the subject of another case before the Greek Council of State, which ruled in June 2019 that it must be brought to an end.
13 This part of the chapter is based on my personal experience of the topic, through my drafting on behalf of the Grassrootsmobilise research team an intervention in the case of *Papageorgiou and Others v. Greece* and through my and the research team's engagements with relevant social actors, particularly in our local-level dissemination of our research on RE and in our planning and carrying out of a workshop on the *Papageorgiou* case. Much of this section is based on my own assessments of perspectives and approaches of the social actors in question; I take full responsibility for any potential misinterpretations.
14 Written communication, June 20, 2019.
15 Grassrootsmobilise Third Party Intervention in the case of *Papageorgiou and Others v. Greece*, July 13, 2018; on file with author.
16 Surely the intervention led to far broader disappointment in some circles, but the focus here is on the former category of actors, not least because some of that disappointment was expressed directly to Grassrootsmobilise members, and also became part of the discussion in a workshop hosted by the Grassrootsmobilise project on RE and the *Papageorgiou* case, involving both theologians either directly or indirectly involved in the Greek RE reform process and representatives of the GHM (the human rights association which issued one of the other two interventions in *Papageorgiou*), the legal counsel of Papageorgiou and his co-claimants, other Greek social and legal actors with experience of the topic, and finally two external-to-Greece scholars on RE. That workshop took place on the premises of the Hellenic Foundation for European and Foreign Policy (ELIAMEP), host institution to the Grassrootsmobilise research program, on March 30, 2019. For more information, see http://grassrootsmobilise.eu/grassrootsmobilise-workshop-on-religion-and-education-in-the-ecthr-context-papageorgiou-v-greece-and-beyond.
17 The ways in which the *Folgero* case leaves open questions (and questions highly relevant to the *Papageorgiou* case) are beyond the scope of this chapter, but see Brems 2012 on problems around the ECtHR's legal reasoning, and Sullivan 2005 and DeGirolami 2013 on difficulties at the intersection between law and religion.

Chapter 7

1   I would like to thank Mosa Sayed, Associate Professor of Private International Law at Uppsala University, for insightful comments during the conception and writing of this chapter.

2 At the same time the nationalistic youth association YoungSwedes was denied governmental funding due to failure to meet the democracy criterion, and several more organizations were denied funding for other reasons, such as the Young Left of Sweden for insufficient accounting and Booster for not carrying out any activities.
3 Swedish Code of Statutes (in Swedish: Svensk författningssamling, SFS).
4 In this chapter, translations from Swedish into English have been made by the author.
5 It should be underscored that some of the authors present this view on SUM as a fact, while others report on opinions and expressions from different actors.

Chapter 8

1 The two authors collaborated on three research projects on which this text draws: the *Religion and Diversity Project*; *Secularization, Laïcité and Religious Identities in the Quebec Context*; *Cultural and Religious Diversity in Four National Contexts: A Comparative Study of the Identity Dynamic and Regulation of Religion (Quebec, France, Belgium, Britain)*.
2 We are referring to how public debates were reported and disseminated through mass and social media. See the chapters in this volume by Linnea Jensdotter and Mia Lövheim.
3 See also the chapter by Stephen LeDrew in this volume.
4 Some of the recommendations of the commissions were also clearly inspired by a critical posture toward religion—not only toward majoritarian religion, but also toward minority religions.
5 This paragraph is taken from Lefebvre and Beaman (2013).
6 For a critical analysis of religion as culture, see Beaman (2012).

Chapter 9

1 Mattias Gardell (2015) touches upon the subject matter in a Swedish context by bringing up how conspirational anti-Jewish and anti-Muslim have come to merge within the national socialist *Svenska motståndsrörelsen* (The Swedish Resistance Movement) during the last decade. On the issue in a European setting, see James Renton and Ben Giley (2017).
2 Carlqvist left the DFS and *Svegot* in July 2018 for, at the time of writing, unknown reasons.
3 The access to DFS's material on *Svegot* requires membership. For the sake of this article, I paid for a one-month membership on the portal. All the material is in Swedish and the translations are my own.
4 For analysis of forerunners to *Svegot*, see Niklas Bernsand (2013), Dan Lindquist (2010), and Mathias Wåg (2010).
5 They are Sweden's third largest party with 62 MPs out of 349 in Parliament and with 17.6% of the popular vote in the 2018 elections.
6 I see "radical nationalism" as a useful category, since it avoids the problematic classifications of "far right" or "extreme right." It is also an emic category for certain Swedish radical nationalist groups (Lundström and Lundström 2011).

7   Other distinctions can be made between cultural nationalists, race revolutionaries, and identitarians (cf. Teitelbaum 2017: 4).
8   On similar strategies used by radical nationalists in Europe, see Nilsson (2019).
9   Steve Bannon, the American alt-right icon and former chief strategist in the Trump Administration, has for example been on a European tour to rally radical nationalist and populist parties with a nonprofit organization called the Movement, which has been theorizing how to turn negative identity markers, such as "racist," into rallying emblems (Nougayrède 2018).
10 Arthur Kemp is a former intelligence officer in the South African apartheid government and former high-ranking member of the British ethno-nationalist party British National Party (BNP). Quote from original version (Kemp 2008: 1225).
11 At the time of writing, research on the topic is sparse. There are, however, several journalistic accounts (e.g., Henley 2018).
12 The state-financed foundation is called *Samefonden* (the Sami Foundation). For further information see Sametinget's website: https://www.sametinget.se/65187.
13 The relation to Jews and Israel has been ambiguous in European radical nationalist milieus. At the beginning of the twenty-first century, acclaiming a pro-Israeli stance became a tactic for radical nationalists tainted by their fascist and Nazi roots to show that anti-Semitism was a thing of the past. The state of Israel and Jews' right to a state was defended in an ethno-pluralist logic. However, Jews were still seen as a problematic group within a particular national community (cf. Kahmann 2017).

Chapter 10

1   *Teaching Religion in Late Modern Sweden—Professionalism on the Borders between Public and Private (TRILS)* is a research project funded by the Swedish Research Council (VR). The project lasted from 2014 to 2019. A survey was distributed among a nationally representative sample of teachers of RE, and classroom observations and interviews were conducted among 22 of these teachers.
2   The depictions of Muhammad in question are those created by Lars Vilks, a quite controversial Swedish artist. One of his most provocative planned exhibitions was one about dogs in art. Three of the drawings in the exhibitions represented the prophet Muhammad with the body of a dog. When this became known to a wider audience, vivid discussions and protests started, and his exhibition was cancelled.

Chapter 11

1   For the distribution of articles among the newspapers, see Appendix.
2   Protocol 1, Art. 2 of the European Convention of Human Rights indicates that "in the exercise of any functions which it assumes in relation to education and to teaching, the State shall respect the right of parents to ensure such education and teaching in conformity with their own religious and philosophical convictions."

Chapter 12

1. All quotes from newspaper articles and Facebook comments in Swedish have been translated to English by the authors. As far as possible, we have strived to follow the style and vocabulary of the original quote.
2. The search period was April 14 to May 15, 2016. The editorials are collected from the Media Archive Retriever through the following search words: Kaplan, Khan, islam, islam*, muslim*, religi*, Miljöpartiet, MP, handskak*, hälsning. All references are included, also published Tweets, citations, etc.
3. Of the 19 editorials, 4 were published in *Aftonbladet*, 10 in *Dagens Nyheter*, 3 in *Expressen*, and 1 in *Svenska Dagbladet*.
4. The Green Party's feminist standpoint is clearly stated in the Party Program: "The Swedish Green Party is a feminist party and has been so from the start" (Miljöpartiet 2013: 10). Since 2018, the party has been part of a coalition that self-identifies as "the first feminist government in the world" (Government Offices of Sweden 2018).
5. These are the same news outlets as for the editorials, with the addition of the public service television broadcaster *SVT Nyheter*.
6. Three of ten social media users are "following" a news editor (Hedman 2016). A growing number of Swedish Internet users read news via social media, with Facebook as the most important social media channel for the larger audience.
7. The sample contains comments mentioning hand* and/or häls*. The comments are collected from 26 comment threads during the period between April 14 and May 15, 2016. This means that comments discussing the handshaking without explicitly writing out any of these search words are not included in the material. However, the limitation makes possible a deeper analysis and shows a good cross-section of the debate. The sample is a minor part of a larger material about "The Green Party Crisis."
8. Should have shaken hands (995), must not shake hands (236).

Chapter 13

1. The names given here are not the interviewees' own names, but have been allocated by the authors. Quotations from the interviews in this text have been translated from Swedish by the authors.
2. In Sweden, 84% of children aged 1–5 and 95% of those aged 4–5 were registered at a nursery school in 2017. https://skl.se/skolakulturfritid/forskolagrundochgymnasieskola/forskolafritidshem/forskola/faktaforskola.3292.html.

Bibliography

Introduction

Abdel-Fadil, M., and H. Årsheim (2019), "Introduction: Media and Religious Controversy," in Special Issue: *Media and Religious Controversy. Journal of Religion, Media and Digital Culture*, 8(1): 1–10.

Asad, T. (2003), *Formations of the Secular: Christianity, Islam, Modernity*, Stanford: Stanford University Press.

Asad, T., W. Brown, J. Butler, and S. Mahmood (2013), *Is Critique Secular?* New York: Fordham University of Press.

Bäckström, A., D. Grace, N. Edgardh, and P. Pettersson (2011), *Welfare and Religion in 21st Century Europe: Volume 2, Gendered, Religious and Social Change*, Farnham: Ashgate.

Beckford, J. A. (2003), *Social Theory and Religion*, Cambridge: Cambridge University Press.

Beckford, J. A. (2012), "SSSR Presidential Address: Public Religions and the Postsecular: Critical Reflections," *Journal for the Scientific Study of Religion*, 51(1): 1–19.

Beckford, J. A. (2011), "Re-thinking Religious Pluralism," in G. Giordan and E. Pace (eds.), *Religious Pluralism: Framing Religious Diversity in the Contemporary World*, 15–29, London: Springer.

Berger, P., and T. Luckmann (1966), *The Social Construction of Reality*, London: Penguin.

Brubaker, R. (2017), "Between Nationalism and Civilizationism: The European Populist Moment in Comparative Perspective," *Ethnic and Racial Studies*, 40(8): 1191–226.

Butler, J., J. Habermas, C. Taylor, and C. West (2011), *The Power of Religion in the Public Sphere*, New York: Columbia University Press.

Calhoun, C., M. Juergensmeyer, and J. VanAntwerpen, eds. (2011), *Rethinking Secularism*, New York: Oxford University Press.

Casanova, J. (2011), "The Secular, Secularizations, Secularism," in C. Calhoun, M. Juergensmeyer, and J. VanAntwerpen (eds.), *Rethinking Secularism*, 54–75, Oxford, New York: Oxford University Press.

Cornille, C. ed. (2013), *The Wiley-Blackwell Companion to Inter-Religious Dialogue*, London: Wiley-Blackwell.

Davie, G. (2015), *Religion in Britain: A Persistent Paradox*, Chichester: Wiley Blackwell.

Dawson, A. ed. (2016), *The Politics and Practice of Religious Diversity: National Contexts, Global Issues*, London, New York: Routledge.

Drees, W. B. (2010), *Religion and Science in Context: A Guide to the Debates*, London: Routledge.

Engelstad, F., H. Larsen, J. Rogstad, and K. Steen-Johnsen (2017), "Introduction: The Public Sphere in Change. Institutional Perspectives on Neo-corporatist Society," in F. Engelstad, H. Larsen, J. Rogstad, and K. Steen-Johnsen (eds.), *Institutional Change in the Public Sphere: Views on the Nordic Model*, 1–21, Warsaw: De Gruyter Open.

Fergusson, D. (2009), *Faith and Its Critics: A Conversation*, Oxford, New York: Oxford University Press.

Ferrari, S., and S. Pastorelli, eds. (2012), *Religion in Public Spaces: A European Perspective*, Farnham: Ashgate.

Furseth, I., ed. (2018), *Religious Complexity in the Public Sphere: Comparing Nordic Countries*, Basingstoke: Palgrave Macmillan.

Ganssle, G. E. (2009), *A Reasonable God: Engaging the New Face of Atheism*, Waco: Baylor University Press.

Giordan, G., and E. Pace, eds. (2011), *Religious Pluralism: Framing Religious Diversity in the Contemporary World*, London: Springer.

Gray, J. (2018), *Seven Types of Atheism*, London: Allen Lane.

Habermas, J. (2006), "Religion in the Public Sphere," *European Journal of Philosophy*, 14: 1–25.

Habermas, J. (2008), "Notes on Post-Secular Society," *New Perspectives Quarterly*, 25(4): 17–29.

Hitchens, C. (2006), *God Is Not Great*, London: Random House.

Hjarvard, S. (2014), "From Mediation to Mediatization: The Institutionalization of New Media," in A. Hepp and F. Krotz (eds.), *Mediatized Worlds*, 123–39. New York: Palgrave/Macmillan.

Hjelm, T. (2014a), *Social Constructionisms*, Basingstoke: Palgrave Macmillan.

Hjelm, T. (2014b), "Understanding the New Visibility of Religion: Religion as Problem and Utility," *Journal of Religion in Europe*, 7(3–4): 203–22.

Hjelm, T. (2015), "Is God Back? Reconsidering the New Visibility of Religion," in T. Hjelm (ed.), *Is God Back? Reconsidering the New Visibility of Religion*, 1–16, London: Bloomsbury.

Khalil, M. H. (2018), *Jihad, Radicalism and the New Atheism*, Cambridge: Cambridge University Press.

Kitcher, P. (2008), "Science, Religion and Democracy," *Episteme: A Journal of Social Epistemology*, 5: 5–18.

Kitcher, P. (2014), *Life after Faith: The Case for Secular Humanism*, New Haven: Yale University Press.

La Borde, C. (2017), *Liberalism's Religion*, Cambridge, MA: Harvard University Press.

Larson, E. J., and M. Ruse (2017), *On Faith and Science*, New Haven: Yale University Press.

Lefebvre, S., and P. Brodeur, eds. (2017), *Public Commissions on Cultural and Religious Diversity: Analysis, Reception and Challenges*, London: Routledge.

Levine, G., ed. (2011), *The Joy of Secularism*, Princeton: Princeton University Press.

Lind, A., M. Lövheim, and U. Zackariasson, eds. (2016), *Reconsidering Religion, Law, and Democracy: New Challenges for Society and Research*, Lund: Nordic Academic Press.

Lövheim, M., and L. I. Lied (2018), "Approaching Contested Religion," in K. Lundby (ed.), *Contesting Religion: The Media Dynamics of Cultural Conflicts in Scandinavia Berlin*, 65–80, Boston: De Gruyter.

Lundby, K. ed. (2018), *Contesting Religion: The Media Dynamics of Cultural Conflicts in Scandinavia*, Berlin, Boston: DeGruyter.

Lundby, K., and P. Repstad (2018), "Scandinavia: Traits, Trends and Tensions," in K. Lundby (ed.), *Contesting Religion: The Media Dynamics of Cultural Conflicts in Scandinavia*, 13–31, Berlin, Boston: DeGruyter.

Mendieta, E., and J. VanAntwerpen, eds. (2011), *The Power of Religion in the Public Sphere*, New York: Columbia University Press.

Nagel, T. (2010), *Secular Philosophy and the Religious Temperament*, Oxford: Oxford University Press.

Nussbaum, M. C. (2012), *The New Religious Intolerance*, London: The Belknap Press of Harvard University Press.

Pigliucci, M. (2013), "New Atheism and the Scientistic Turn in the Atheism Movement," *Midwest Studies in Philosophy*, 37: 142–53.

Plantinga, A. (2011), *Where the Conflict Really Lies: Science, Religion and Naturalism*, Oxford: Oxford University Press.

Shah, P., M. Foblets, and M. Rohe, eds. (2014), *Family, Religion and Law: Cultural Encounters in Europe*, Farnham: Ashgate.

Stout, J. (2004), *Democracy and Tradition*, Princeton: Princeton University Press.

Weller, P. (2016), "Balancing within Three Dimensions: Christianity, Secularity and Religious Plurality in Social Policy and Theology," *Studies in Interreligious Dialogue*, 26(2): 130–46.

Chapter 1

Akhtar, S. (2008), *The Quran and the Secular Mind: A Philosophy of Islam*, London: Routledge.

Audi, R. (2011), *Rationality and Religious Commitment*, Oxford: Oxford University Press.

Dawkins, R. (2006), *The God Delusion*, Boston: Houghton Mifflin Company.

Geaves, R. (2010), *Islam Today*, London: Continuum.

Habermas, J. (2006), "Religion in the Public Sphere," *European Journal of Philosophy*, 14(1): 1–25.

Hitchens, C. (2007), *God Is Not Great: How Religion Poisons Everything*, Toronto: Emblem.

Kimball, C. (2002), *When Religion Becomes Evil*, San Francisco: HarperSanFrancisco.

Kitcher, P. (2011), "Challenges for Secularism," in G. Levine (ed.), *The Joy of Secularism*, 24–56, Princeton: Princeton University Press.

Nagel, T. (2010), *Secular Philosophy and the Religious Temperament*, Oxford: Oxford University Press.

Pigliucci, M. (2013), "New Atheism and the Scientistic Turn in the Atheism Movement," *Midwest Studies in Philosophy*, 37(1): 142–53.

Rorty, R. (2007), "Anticlericalism and Atheism," in S. Zabala (ed.), *The Future of Religion*, 29–42, New York: Columbia University Press.

Rosenberg, A. (2011), *The Atheist's Guide to Reality*, London: W. W. Norton.

Stenmark, M. (2006), "Exclusivism, Tolerance and Interreligious Dialogue," *Studies in Interreligious Dialogue*, 16(1): 100–14.

Stout, J. (2004), *Democracy and Tradition*, Princeton: Princeton University Press.

Taliaferro, C. (2009), *Philosophy of Religion*, Oxford: OneWorld.

Taylor, C. (2007), *A Secular Age*, Cambridge, MA: The Belknap Press.

Taylor, C. (2011), "Why We Need a Radical Redefinition of Secularism," in J. Butler, J. Habermas, C. Taylor, and C. West (eds.), *The Power of Religion in the Public Sphere*, 34–59, New York: Columbia University Press.

Thiessen, J., and S. Wilkins-Laflamme (2017), "Becoming a Religious None: Irreligious Socialization and Disaffiliation," *Journal for the Scientific Study of Religion*, 56(1): 64–82.

Weinberg, S. (2006), "Closing Statements of Presentation at the Conference: 'Beyond Belief: Science, Religion and Survival,'" Salk Institute, La Jolla, November 5–7.

Chapter 2

Beckford, J. A. (1989), *Religion and Advanced Industrial Society*, London: Unwin Hyman.
Berman, D. (1988), *A History of Atheism in Britain: From Hobbes to Russell*, London: Croom Helm.
Bruce, S. (2011), *Secularization: In Defence of an Unfashionable Theory*, Oxford: Oxford University Press.
Buckley, M. J. (2004), *Denying and Disclosing God: The Ambiguous Progress of Modern Atheism*, New Haven: Yale University Press.
Casanova, J. (1994), *Public Religions in the Modern World*, Chicago: University of Chicago Press.
Chadwick, O. (1975), *The Secularization of the European Mind in the 19th Century*, Cambridge: Cambridge University Press.
Dawkins, R. (2006), *The God Delusion*, Boston: Houghton Mifflin.
Dennett, D. (2006), *Breaking the Spell: Religion as a Natural Phenomenon*, New York: Penguin Books.
Eagleton, T. (2007), *Reason, Faith and Revolution: Reflections on the God Debate*, New Haven: Yale University Press.
Feuerbach, L. (1841), *The Essence of Christianity*, New York: Harper and Row.
Harris, S. (2004), *The End of Faith: Religion, Terror, and the Future of Reason*, New York: W. W. Norton & Company.
Hitchens, C. (1995), *The Missionary Position: Mother Theresa in Theory and Practice*, London: Verso.
Hitchens, C. (2007), *God Is Not Great: How Religion Poisons Everything*, Toronto: Emblem.
Hyman, G. (2007), "Atheism in Modern History," in M. Martin (ed.), *The Cambridge Companion to Atheism*, 27–46, Cambridge: Cambridge University Press.
LeDrew, S. (2015), *The Evolution of Atheism: The Politics of a Modern Movement*, New York: Oxford University Press.
Marx, K. (1845), "Concerning Feuerbach," in J. Raines (ed.), *Marx on Religion*, 182–84, Philadelphia: Temple University Press.
Norris, P., and Inglehart, R. (2004), *Sacred and Secular: Religion and Politics Worldwide*, Cambridge: Cambridge University Press.
Simmons, J. S. (2017), "Atheism Plus What? Social Justice and Lifestyle Politics among Edmonton Atheists," *Canadian Journal of Sociology*, 42(4): 425–46.

Chapter 3

Adler, R. (1998), *Engendering Judaism: An Inclusive Theology and Ethics*, Philadelphia and Jerusalem: The Jewish Publication Society.
Barlas, A. (2002), *"Believing Women" in Islam: Unreading Patriarchal Interpretations of the Quran*, Austin: University of Texas Press.
Brandom, R. (1994), *Making It Explicit: Reasoning, Representing and Discursive Commitment*, Cambridge: Cambridge University Press.
Gergen, K. J. (2014), "From Mirroring to World-Making: Research as Future Forming," *Journal for the Theory of Social Behavior*, 45(3): 287–310.

Green, J. (2004), "Critique, Contextualism and Consensus," *Journal of Philosophy of Education*, 38(3): 511–25.

Hartman, T. (2005), "Restorative Feminism and Religious Tradition," *Common Knowledge*, 11(1): 89–104.

Hauerwas, S. (2010), *Christian Existence Today: Essays on Church, World, and Living in Between*, Eugene, OR: Wipf and Stock.

Jantzen, G. (1996), *Power, Gender and Christian Mysticism*, Cambridge: Cambridge University Press.

Kripke, S. (1980), *Naming and Necessity*, Oxford: Blackwell.

Kwok, P. (2005), *Postcolonial Imagination & Feminist Theology*, London: SCM Press.

LeDrew, S. (2015), *The Evolution of Atheism: The Politics of a Modern Movement*, Oxford: Oxford University Press.

McKenna, M. F. (2015), "Renewing Intellectual Discourse by Means of a New Philosophy of Knowledge for Nonnatural Sciences: Implications for the Role of Religion in the Research University," *Religion and Education*, 41(1): 2–16.

Moore, H. (2012), "From the 'Gotcha!' To Immanent Critique," *PhiloSOPHIA*, 2(1): 87–91.

Putnam, H. (1975), *Mind, Language, and Reality: Philosophical Papers Volume 2*, Cambridge: Cambridge University Press.

Sabia, D. (2010), "Defending Immanent Critique," *Political Theory*, 38(5): 684–711.

Särkelä, A. (2017), "Immanent Critique as Self-Transformative Practice: Hegel, Dewey, and Contemporary Critical Theory," *The Journal of Speculative Philosophy*, 31(2): 218–30.

Stout, J. (1989), *Ethics after Babel: The Languages of Morals and Their Discontents*, Cambridge: James Clarke.

Stout, J. (2004), *Democracy and Tradition*, New Forum Books, Princeton, NJ: Princeton University Press.

Zagzebski, L. (2017), *Exemplarist Moral Theory*, Oxford: Oxford University Press.

Chapter 4

Ali, K. (2006), *Sexual Ethics & Islam: Feminist Reflections on Qur'an, Hadith, and Jurisprudence*, Oxford: One World.

Arkoun, M. (2006), *The Unthought in Contemporary Islamic Thought*, London: Saqi Books.

Bano, M., and H. E. Kalmbach, eds. (2012), *Women, Leadership and Mosques: Changes in Contemporary Muslim Authority*, Leiden, Boston: Brill.

Fazlhashemi, M., and R. Ambjörnsson (2017), *Visdomens hus: Muslimska idévärldar 600–2000 (The House of Wisdom: The Muslim World of Ideas 600–2000)*, Stockholm: Natur & Kultur.

al-Jabri, M. A. (2011), *Formation of Arab Reason: Text, Tradition and the Construction of Modernity in the Arab World*, New York: I. B. Tauris.

Mernissi, F. (1991), *The Veil and the Male Elite: A Feminist Interpretation of Women's Rights in Islam*, Reading, MA: Addison-Wesley.

Mojtahed Shabestari, M. (2004), *Ta'ammulati dar qera't-e ensani az din (Reflections on a Human Reading of Religion)*, Teheran: Tarh-e nô.

an-Naim, Abdullahi, A. (1990), *Toward an Islamic Reformation: Civil Liberties, Human Rights and International Law*, Syracuse: Syracuse University Press.

Sachedina, A. (2009), *Islam and the Challenges of Human Rights*, Oxford and New York: Oxford University Press.
Soroush, A. (1997), *Mudara va mudiriyyat (Tolerance and Administration)*, Teheran: Serat.
Soroush, A. (1999), *Serathaye mustaqim (Straight Ways)*, 3d ed., Teheran: Serat.

Chapter 5

Augustine of Hippo (1961), *Confessions of Saint Augustine*, trans. R. S. Pine-Coffin, New York: Penguin Books.
Camus, A. See https://www.christianforums.com/blogs/the-unbeliever-and-christians-albert-camus-1948.56232, accessed May 15, 2019.
Craig, W. L., and J. P. Moreland (2009), *The Blackwell Companion to Natural Theology*, Oxford: Wiley Blackwell.
Havvey, A. (1996), *The Essential Mystics*, San Francisco: Harpers, 1996.
Kieran, M. (2017), "Creativity, Vanity and Narcissism," in B. Gaut and M. Kieran (eds.), *Creativity and Philosophy*, chapter 5, London: Routledge.
MacCulloch, D. (2011), *Christianity: The First Three Thousand Years*, New York: Penguin Books.
Moser, P. (2019), "Christian Philosophy and Christ Crucified: Fragmentary Theory in Scandalous Power," in J. A. Simmons (ed.), *Christian Philosophy*, chapter 13, Oxford: Oxford University Press.
Nagel, T. (2004), *Concealment and Exposure*, Oxford: Oxford University Press.
Nietzsche, F. (1968), *The Genealogy of Morals*, trans. W. Kaufman, New York: Viking.
Scheler, M. (1961), *Ressentiment*, trans. W. W. Holdheim, New York: Knopf Doubleday.
Stendahl, K. "Three Rules of Religious Understanding." https://ancienthebrewpoetry.typepad.com/ancient_hebrew:poetry/2010/05/krister-stendahls-three-rules-of-religious-understanding.html, accessed May 9, 2019.
Taliaferro, C. (2012), *The Golden Cord: A Short Book on the Secular and the Sacred*, Notre Dame: University of Notre Dame Press.
Zagzebski, L. (2012), *Epistemic Authority: A Theory of Trust, Authority, and Autonomy of Belief*, Oxford: Oxford University Press.

Chapter 6

Brems, E., ed. (2012), *Diversity and European Human Rights: Rewriting Judgments of the ECHR*, Cambridge: Cambridge University Press.
Bürli, N. (2017), *Third-Party Interventions before the European Court of Human Rights*, Antwerp: Intersentia.
DeGirolami, M. (2013), *The Tragedy of Religious Freedom*, Cambridge, MA: Harvard University Press.
Durham, W. C., and D. Kirkham (2012), "Introduction," in W. C. Durham, R. Torfs, D. Kirkham, and C. Scott (eds.), *Islam, Europe, and Emerging Legal Issues*, 1–18, Farnham, Burlington VT: Ashgate.
Eydne, Laura Van den (2013), "An Empirical Look at the Amicus Curiae Practice of Human Rights NGOs before the European Court of Human Rights," *Netherlands Quarterly of Human Rights*, 31(3): 271–313.

Foblets, M., K. Alidadi, J. S. Nielsen, and Z. Yanasmayan, eds. (2014), *Belief, Law and Politics: What Future for a Secular Europe?*, Farnham: Ashgate.

Fokas, E. (2015), "Directions in Religious Pluralism in Europe: Mobilizations in the Shadow of European Court of Human Rights Religious Freedom Jurisprudence," *Oxford Journal of Law and Religion*, 4(1): 54–74.

Fokas, E. (2016), "Comparative Susceptibility and Differential Effects on the Two European Courts: A Study of Grasstops Mobilizations around Religion," *Oxford Journal of Law and Religion*, 5: 541–74.

Fokas, E. (2018), "The Legal Status of Religious Minorities: Exploring the Impact of the European Court of Human Rights," *Social Compass*, 65(1): 25–42.

Fokas, E. (2019), "Introduction: Religion and Education in the Shadow of the European Court of Human Rights," *Politics and Religion* 12 (Supp. 1): S1–S8.

Fokas, E., and J. T. Richardson (2017), "The European Court of Human Rights and Minority Religions: Messages Generated and Messages Received," *Religion State and Society*, 45(3–4): 166–73.

Fokas, E., and J. T. Richardson (2018), *The European Court of Human Rights and Minority Religions: Messages Generated and Messages Received*, co-edited with James T. Richardson, London: Taylor and Francis.

Galanter, M. (1983), "The Radiating Effects of Courts," in K. O. Boyum and L. M. Mathe (eds.), *Empirical Theories about Courts*, 117–42, New York: Longman.

Keller, H., and A. S. Sweet, eds. (2008), *A Europe of Rights: The Impact of the ECHR on National Legal Systems*, Oxford: Oxford University Press.

Koenig, M. (2012), "Governance of Religious Diversity at the ECHR," in J. Bolden and W. Kymlincka (eds.), *International Approaches to the Governance of Ethnic Diversity*, 51–78, Oxford: Oxford University Press.

Liu, H. (2011), "The Meaning of Religious Symbols after the Grand Chamber Judgement in *Lautsi v. Italy*," *Religion and Human Rights*, 6: 253–57.

Mancini, S. (2010), "The Crucifix Rage: Supranational Constitutionalism Bumps against the Counter-Majoritarian Difficulty," *European Constitutional Law Review*, 6(1): 6–27.

Markoviti, M. (2018), "Greece: Report on Religious Education," Report published in the Grassrootsmobilise Research Program, available online: http://grassrootsmobilise.eu/wp-content/uploads/2018/04/RE-Report-2.pdf.

Markoviti, M. (2019), "In-between the Constitution and the European Court of Human Rights: Mobilizations around Religion and Education in Greece," *Politics and Religion*, 12(S1): S31–54.

Mayrl, D. (2018), "The Judicialization of Religious Freedom: An Institutionalist Approach," *Journal for the Scientific Study of Religion*, 57(3): 514–30.

McCann, M. (1992), "Reform Litigation on Trial," *Law and Social Inquiry*, 17(4): 715–43.

Moravcsik, A. (2000), "The Origins of Human Rights Regimes: Democratic Delegation in Postwar Europe," *International Organization*, 54(2): 217–52.

Ringelheim, J. (2012), "Rights, Religion and the Public Sphere: The European Court of Human Rights in Search of a Theory?," in L. Zucca and C. Ungureanu (eds.), *Law, State and Religion in the New Europe: Debates and Dilemmas*, 283–306, Cambridge: Cambridge University Press.

Ronchi, P. (2011), "Crucifixes, Margin of Appreciation and Consensus: The Grand Chamber Ruling in *Lautsi v. Italy*," *Ecclesiastical Law Society*, 13: 287–97.

Sullivan, W. (2005), *The Impossibility of Religious Freedom*, Princeton: Princeton University Press.

Temperman, J., J. Gunn, and M. Evans (2019), *The European Court of Human Rights and the Freedom of Religion or Belief: The 25 Years since* Kokkinakis, Leiden: Brill Nijhoff.
"Violations by Article and by State 1959–2018," European Court of Human Rights. Available online: https://www.echr.coe.int/Documents/Stats_violation_1959_2018_ENG.pdf.

Chapter 7

Ackfeldt, A., et al. (2017), "Undermålig forskning i svensk myndighetsrapport," *Religionsvetenskapliga Kommentarer*, March 2. Available online: http://religionsvetenskapligakommentarer.blogspot.com/2017/03/debatt-undermalig-forskning-i-svensk.html, accessed June 19, 2019.

Administrative Court [Förvaltningsrätten i Stockholm] (2017), "Dom," case number 192/17, November 14.

Amir-Moazami, S. (2011), "Dialogue as a Governmental Technique: Managing Gendered Islam in Germany," *Feminist Review*, 98: 9–27.

Amnå, E. (2012), "How Is Civic Engagement Developed over Time? Emerging Answers from a Multidisciplinary Field," *Youth & Society*, 35: 611–27.

Berglund, J. (2012). "Islam som resurs?," in M. Lövheim and J. Bromander (eds.), *Religion som resurs? Existentiella frågor och värderingar i unga svenskars liv*, 263–86, Skellefteå: Artos.

Beydoun, K. (2018), "Acting Muslim," *Harvard Civil Rights-Civil Liberties Law Review (CR-CL)*, 53: 1–64.

Brubaker, R. (2012), "Categories of Analysis and Categories of Practice: A Note on the Study of Muslims in European Countries of Immigration," *Ethnic and Racial Studies*, 13(1): 1–8.

Carlbom, A. (2018), "Islamic Activism in a Multicultural Context: Ideological Continuity or Change?" Swedish Civil Contingencies Agency and Malmö University. Available online: https://www.msb.se/siteassets/dokument/publikationer/english-publications/islamic-activism-in-a-multicultural-context-ideological-continuity-or-change.pdf, accessed June 19, 2019.

Cesari, J. (2018), "Securitization of Islam and Religious Freedom," Religious Freedom Institute, September 11. Available online: https://www.religiousfreedominstitute.org/cornerstone/securitization-of-islam-and-religious-freedom, accessed June 19, 2019.

Coglievina, S. (2013), "Italy," in J. S. Nielsen (ed.), *Yearbook of Muslims in Europe: Volume 5*, 351–68, Leiden: Brill.

Dahlstedt, M., and C. Foultier (2018), "Förändringens agenter: Om skola, prevention och fostran till trygghet," *Platskamp*, special issue of *Arkiv Tidskrift för Samhällsanalys*, 9: 159–81.

De Vivo, L. (2017), "Timbro-tidning pressar myndighet om statsbidrag: 'Utsätts för smutskastning,'" ETC, March 29. Available online: https://www.etc.se/inrikes/timbro-tidning-pressar-myndighet-om-statsbidrag-utsatts-smutskastning?sida=1, accessed June 19, 2019.

Enkvist, V., and P.-E. Nilsson (2016), "The Hidden Return of Religion," in A.-S. Lind, M. Lövheim, and U. Zackariasson (eds.), *Reconsidering Religion, Law and Democracy: New Challenges for Society and Research*, 93–108, Lund: Nordic Academic Press.

Eriksson, T. (2014), "Jag utmanar starka krafter," *Dagens Samhälle*, October 30. https://www.dagenssamhalle.se/nyhet/jag-utmanar-starka-krafter-11659, accessed June 19, 2019.

EU (2009), "Renewed Framework for European Cooperation in the Youth Field (2010–2018)." https://eur-lex.europa.eu/legal-content/EN/TXT/?uri=CELEX%3A32009G1219%2801%29, accessed September 5, 2019.

Foblets, M.-C., K. Alidadi, J. Nielsen, and Z. Yanasmayan, eds. (2014), *Belief, Law and Politics: What Future for a Secular Europe?* Farnham: Ashgate.

Frisina, A. (2010), "Young Muslims of Italy: Islam in the Everyday Life," in G. Giordan (ed.), *Youth and Religion*, 329–51, Leiden: Brill.

Gahnertz, L. (2010), "Vi accepterar människorna: Men inte beteendet," *Sveriges Radio: Kaliber*, June 6. Available online: https://sverigesradio.se/sida/artikel.aspx?programid=1316&artikel=3750914, accessed June 19, 2019.

Gudmundsson, P. (2016), "Muslimska Brödraskapet ett udda val av kyrka," *Svenska Dagbladet*, August 9. Available online: http://www.svd.se/muslimska-brodraskapet-ett-udda-val-av-kyrkan, accessed June 19, 2019.

Gutmann, A. (2003), *Identity in Democracy*, Princeton: Princeton University Press.

Hafez, F. (2017), "Muslim Civil Society under Attack: The European Foundation for Democracy's Role in Defaming and Delegitimizing Muslim Civil Society," in J. L. Esposito and D. Iner (eds.), *Islamophobia and Radicalization: Breeding Intolerance and Violence*, 117–38, Washington DC: Palgrave MacMillan.

Iner, D. (2017), "Introduction: Relationships Between Islamophobia and Radicalization," in J. L Esposito and D. Iner (eds.), *Islamophobia and Radicalization: Breeding Intolerance and Violence*, 117–38, Washington DC: Palgrave MacMillan.

Karan, O. (2008), "State Management of Immigrant Organization in Sweden," in W. Pojmann (ed.), *Migration and Activism in Europe since 1945*, 175–92, Basingstoke: Palgrave Macmillan.

Karlsson Minganti, P. (2007), *Muslima. Islamisk väckelse och unga kvinnors förhandlingar om genus i det samtida Sverige*, Diss. Stockholm: Carlsson.

Karlsson Minganti, P. (2012), "Challenging from Within: Youth Associations and Female Leadership in Swedish Mosques," in M. Bano and H. Kalmbach (eds.), *Women, Leadership and Mosques: Changes in Contemporary Islamic Authority*, 371–91, Leiden: Brill.

Karlsson Minganti, P. (2016), "Introducing 'Fourth Space': Young Muslims Negotiating Marriage in Europe," *Ethnologia Europaea*, Special Issue, *Muslim Intimacies: Families, Individuals and Late Modern Dilemmas*, L. Stark (ed.), Copenhagen: Museum Tusculanum Press, 46(1): 40–57.

Karlsson Minganti, P. (2017), "Religion as a Resource or as a Source of Exclusion? The Case of Muslims Women's Shelters," in L. Molokotos-Liederman (ed.), with A. Bäckström and G. Davie, *Religion and Welfare in Europe: Gendered and Minority Perspectives*, 207–33, Bristol: Policy Press.

Kronqvist, P. (2015), "Även här är muslimer offer för fanatiker," *Expressen*, January 12. Available online: https://www.expressen.se/ledare/patrik-kronqvist/aven-har-ar-muslimer-offer-for-fanatikerna, accessed June 19, 2019.

Lundberg, J. (2016), "Så hamnade miljöpartiet sida vid sida med islamister," *Göteborgs-Posten*, April 20. Available online: http://www.gp.se/debatt/s%C3%A5-hamnade-milj%C3%B6partiet-sida-vid-sida-med-islamister-1.274997, accessed June 19, 2019.

Micheletti, M. (1995), *Civil Society and State Relations in Sweden*, Aldershot: Avebury.

MUCF [Swedish Agency for Youth and Civil Society] (2010), "Meddelande till styrelsen för Sveriges Unga Muslimer," July 2, Diarienummer 20-1005/10.

MUCF [Swedish Agency for Youth and Civil Society] (2016), "Beslut om bidrag för barn- och ungdomsorganisationer," December 16, Diarienummer 1439/16.

MUCF [Swedish Agency for Youth and Civil Society] (2017), *Att verka demokratiskt: Redovisning av hur MUCF granskar och följer upp demokrativillkoren för statsbidrag*. Available online: https://www.mucf.se/publikationer/att-verka-demokratiskt, accessed June 19, 2019.

MUCF [Swedish Agency for Youth and Civil Society] (2018a), "Youth Policy." Available online: https://eng.mucf.se/youth-policy, accessed June 19, 2019.

MUCF [Swedish Agency for Youth and Civil Society] (2018b). https://eng.mucf.se/grants, accessed June 19, 2019.

MUCF [Swedish Agency for Youth and Civil Society] (2018c), "Beslut," April 11, Diarienummer 1439/16; 0987/15.

MUCF [Swedish Agency for Youth and Civil Society] (2018d), *Crack the Code! A Guide on How Public Stakeholders and Civil Society Can Work Together to Prevent Violent Extremism*. Available online: https://www.mucf.se/publikationer/crack-code, accessed June 19, 2019.

Musa, R. (2014), "Rashid Musa (Sveriges Unga Muslimer): Vi är alltid skyldiga tills motsatsen bevisats," *Dagens Arena*, September 24. Available online: http://www.dagensarena.se/opinion/rashid-musa-sveriges-unga-muslimer-vi-ar-alltid-skyldiga-tills-motsatsen-bevisas, accessed June 19, 2019.

Norell, M., A. Carlbom, and P. Durrani (2017a), "Muslimska brödraskapet i Sverige," Myndigheten för samhällsskydd och beredskap (MSB). Diarienummer 2017–1287.

Norell, M., A. Carlbom, and P. Durrani (2017b), "The Muslim Brotherhood in Sweden," commissioned by the Swedish Civil Contingencies Agency (MSB) and published by Clarion Project. Available online: https://clarionproject.org/wp-content/uploads/2017/06/Muslim-Brotherhood-Sweden-Magnus-Norrell.pdf, accessed June 19, 2019.

Nyberg, L. (2017), "Slut med skattepengar till illasinnade intressen," *Göteborgs-Posten*, March 23. Available online: http://www.gp.se/debatt/slut-med-skattepengar-till-illasinnade-intressen-1.4206060, accessed June 19, 2019.

Nyhagen, L. (2019), "Mosques as Gendered Spaces: The Complexity of Women's Compliance with, and Resistance to, Dominant Gender Norms, and the Importance of Male Allies," *Religions*, 10(5): 231.

O'Toole, T., and R. Gale (2010), "Contemporary Grammars of Political Action among Ethnic Minority Young Activists," *Ethnic and Racial Studies*, 33(1): 126–43.

Phoenix, A. (2000), "Identity Politics," in C. Kamrarae and D. Spender (eds.), *Routledge International Encyclopedia of Women: Global Women's Issues and Knowledge: Volume 3*, 1097–99, New York, London: Routledge.

Puar, J. K. (2007), *Terrorist Assemblages: Homonationalism in Queer Times*, Durham: Duke University Press.

Putnam, R. D. (2000), *Bowling Alone: The Collapse and Revival of American Community*, New York: Simon & Schuster.

Sandelin, M. (2017), "Organisationen Sveriges Unga Muslimer: Ideologi och koppling till antidemokratiska miljöer," Myndigheten för ungdoms- och civilsamhällesfrågor, MUCF. Available online: http://www.mucf.se/sites/default/files/rapport_organisationen_sveriges_unga_muslimer_-_ideologi_och_koppling_till_antidemokratiska_miljoer.pdf, accessed June 19, 2019.

Schmidt, G. (2017), "The Good Citizen and the Good Muslim: The Nexus of Disciplining the Self and Engaging the Public," *MIM Working Papers Series* 17(6). Malmö: Malmö University.

Silow Kallenberg, K. (2016). *Gränsland: Svensk ungdomsvård mellan vård och straff*. Diss. Huddinge: Södertörns högskola.

Sörberg, A.-M. (2017), *Homonationalism*, Stockholm: Leopard.
SOU [Swedish Government Official Reports] (2016), *Palett för ett stärkt civilsamhälle: Betänkande*. Available online: https://www.regeringen.se/492b2d/contentassets/907 a5e554a23428f9aef3c2d7221a2de/palett-for-ett-starkt-civilsamhalle-sou-2016_13.pdf, accessed June 19, 2019.
SOU [Swedish Government Official Reports] (2018), *Statens stöd till trossamfund i ett mångreligiöst Sverige*. Available online: http://www.regeringen.se/rattsdokument/staten s-offentliga-utredningar/2018/03/sou-201818, accessed June 19, 2019.
SUM [Sweden's Young Muslims] (2010), "Meddelande gällande Abdullah Hakim Quick." Available online: http://www.ungamuslimer.se/index.php?option=com_content&view =article&id=263:meddelande-gaellande-abdullah-hakim-quick-&catid=1:latest-n ews&Itemid=53, accessed December 27, 2011.
SUM [Sweden's Young Muslims] (2016), "Ansökan från Sveriges Unga Muslimer: Organisations- bidrag för barn- och ungdomsorganisationer 2017," MUCF Diarienummer 1439/16.
SUM [Sweden's Young Muslims] (2017), "Överklagande till förvaltningsrätten i Stockholm," December 29, case number 192–17.
SUM [Sweden's Young Muslims] (2018), "Om [About]," Available online: https://www.fac ebook.com/pg/ungamuslimer/about/?ref=page_internal, accessed June 19, 2019.
Van Den Brink, N. (2016), "Trött på avstånd," *Fokus*, June 14. Available online: http://www .fokus.se/2016/06/trott-pa-avstand, accessed June 19, 2019.
Van Der Meer, T., and E. van Ingen (2009), "Schools of Democracy? Disentangling the Relationship between Civic Participation and Political Action in 17 European Countries," *European Journal of Political Research*, 48: 281–308.
Wendahl, P. (2010), "Dra tillbaka bidragen till Sveriges Unga Muslimer," *Newsmill*, March 13. Available online: https://web.archive.org/web/20100327135938/http://www.newsmi ll.se/artikel/2010/03/13/dra-tillbaka-bidragen-till-sveriges-unga-muslimer-0, accessed June 19, 2019.
Zetterman, J. (2010), "Ungdomsstyrelsen: Lätt beslut att låta religiösa ungdomsförbund ha kvar statsbidrag," *Dagen*, July 6. Available online: http://www.dagen.se/ungdomssty relsen-latt-beslut-att-lata-religiosa-ungdomsforbund-ha-kvar-statsbidrag-1.149492#, accessed June 19, 2019.

Chapter 8

Alexander, H. (2019), "Canadian Prime Minister Confirms Saudi Teen Rahaf al-Qunun to Be Granted Asylum," *The Telegraph*, January 11. Available online: https://www.telegrap h.co.uk/news/2019/01/11/saudi-woman-fled-family-granted-asylum-canada-thail and-airport, accessed May 28, 2019.
Ammerman, N. T. (2013), "Spiritual but Not Religious? Beyond Binary Choices in the Study of Religion," *Journal for the Scientific Study of Religion*, 52(2): 258–78.
Aron, R. (1955), *L'opium des intellectuels*, Paris: Calmann-Lévy.
Baum, G. (1999), "The Impact of Marxist Ideas on Christian Theology," in G. Baum (ed.), *The Twentieth Century. A Theological Overview*, 173–85, New York: Orbis Books.
Beaman, L. G. (2012), "Battles over Symbols: The 'Religion' of the Minority versus the 'Culture' of the Majority," *Journal of Law and Religion*, 28(1): 67–104.
Beaman, L. G. (2016), "Living Together v. Living Well Together: A Normative Examination of the SAS Case," *Social Inclusion*, 4(2): 3–13.

Beaman, L. G. (2017), *Deep Equality in an Era of Religious Diversity*, New York: Oxford University Press.

Béraud, C., and P. Portier (2015), *Métamorphoses catholiques. Acteurs, enjeux et mobilisations depuis le mariage pour tous*, Paris: Editions de la MSH.

Birt, J. (2006), "Good Imam, Bad Imam: Civic Religion and National Integration in Britain post-9/11," *The Muslim World*, 96(4): 687–705.

Blofield, M. (2006), *The Politics of Moral Sin: Abortion and Divorce in Spain, Chile and Argentina*, New York: Routledge.

Boffey, D. (2018), "Belgium Takes Big Step towards Decriminalising Abortion," *The Guardian*, May 2. Available online: https://www.theguardian.com/world/2018/may/02/belgium-to-debate-removal-of-abortion-from-penal-code, accessed May 28, 2019.

Bouchard, G., and C. Taylor (2008), *Building the Future: A Time for Reconciliation*, Quebec City: Gouvernement du Québec.

Brown, C. G. (2017), "The Necessity of Atheism: Making Sense of Secularisation," *Journal of Religious History*, 41(4): 439–56.

Burns, T. (1981), "Spain Passes Divorce Law After 40-Year Ban," *The Washington Post*, June 24. Available online: https://www.washingtonpost.com/archive/politics/1981/06/24/spain-passes-divorce-law-after-40-year-ban/50da980c-feb7-4350-a487-1c3654ffdc41/?noredirect=on&utm_term=.357901c8e5bc, accessed May 28, 2019.

CBC News (2019), "Muslim Head Scarf a Symbol of Oppression, Insists Quebec's Minister for Status of Women," *CBC News*, February 6. Available online: https://www.cbc.ca/news/canada/montreal/isabelle-charest-hijab-muslim-1.5007889, accessed May 28, 2019.

Clarke, B., and S. Macdonald (2017), *Leaving Christianity: Changing Allegiances in Canada since 1945*, Montreal: McGill-Queen's University Press.

Conseil Famille et Société (2012), Conférence des évêques de France, *Élargir le mariage aux personnes de même sexe ? Ouvrons le débat!* Online note.

Cragun, R. T., B. Kosmin, A. Keysar, J. Hammer, and M. Nielson (2012), "On the Receiving End: Discrimination toward the Non-Religious in the United States," *Journal of Contemporary Religion*, 27(1): 105–27.

Curran, C. E., and R. A. McCormick, eds. (1982), *The Magisterium and Morality*, New York: Paulist Press.

Curran, C. E., and R. A. McCormick (1988), *Dissent in the Church*, New York: Paulist Press.

Daly, M. (1973), *Beyond God the Father*, Boston: Beacon Press.

Daly, M. (1985), *The Church and the Second Sex*, Boston: Beacon Press.

Dawkins, R. (2006), *The God Delusion*, London: Bantam Press.

Deseret News (2018), "The American Family Survey, 2018 Summary Report: Identities, Opportunities and Challenges," Available online: https://www.deseretnews.com/media/misc/pdf/afs/2018-AFS-Final-Report.pdf, accessed May 28, 2019.

Dot-Pouillard, N. (2007), "Les recompositions politiques du mouvement féministe français au regard du *hijab*," *SociologieS*, October 31. Available online: http://journals.openedition.org/sociologies/246, accessed May 28, 2019.

The Economist (2018), "Francis on the Ropes: Clerical Sexual-Abuse Scandals Strengthen the Pope's Conservative Critics," November 8. Available online: https://www.economist.com/international/2018/11/08/clerical-sexual-abuse-scandals-strengthen-the-popes-conservative-critics, accessed April 15, 2019.

Edgell, P., D. Hartmann, E. Stewart, and J. Gerteis (2016), "Atheists and Other Cultural Outsiders: Moral Boundaries and the Non-Religious in the United States," *Social Forces*, 95(2): 607–38.

Foblets, M., and C. Kulakowski (2010), *Les Assises de l'Interculturalité*, Brussels: Ministère de l'Emploi et de l'Égalité des Chances. Available online: http://www.cbai.be/resource/docsenstock/services_aux_asbl/Assise_de_linterculturalite.pdf, accessed May 25, 2019.

Freud, S. (1955), *The Future of an Illusion*, New York: Liveright.

Gendron, L., P. S. S. (2018), "'The State Has a Legitimate Interest in Protecting the Unborn': Statement on the 30th Anniversary of the Morgentaler Decision," *Canadian Conference of Catholic Bishops*, January 27, 2018. Available online: http://www.cccb.ca/site/eng/media-room/statements-a-letters/4873-the-state-has-a-legitimate-interest-in-protecting-the-unborn-statement-on-the-30th-anniversary-of-the-morgentaler-decision, accessed May 28, 2019.

Guénif-Souilamas, N., and E. Macé (2005), *Les féministes et le garçon arabe*, Paris: Édition de l'Aube.

Harpigny, G. (2009), "Quelles influences exercent entre elles religions et sociétés?," Conference presented November 25, 2009. Accessed on the diocese website in April 2012 (our translation) but not available online anymore.

Herinckx, C. (2018), "Dépénalisation totale de l'avortement: Les évêques prennent position," *CathoBel*, June 15. Available online: https://www.cathobel.be/2018/06/15/depenalisation-totale-de-lavortement-les-eveques-prennent-position, accessed May 28, 2019.

Hitchens, C. (2007), *God Is Not Great: How Religion Poisons Everything*, New York: Twelve.

Juergensmeyer, M. (2017), *Terror in the Mind of God: The Global Rise of Religious Violence*, Oakland: University of California Press.

Keenan, M. (2012), *Child Sexual Abuse and the Catholic Church: Gender, Power, and Organizational Culture*, Oxford: Oxford University Press.

Lefebvre, S. (2014), "Les Églises et les débats sur la diversité ethno-religieuse," in K. Demasure, A. Join-Lambert, and G. Monet (eds.), *Vivre ensemble: Un défi pratique pour la théologie*, 21–32. Brussels: Novalis/Lumen vitae.

Lefebvre, S. (2016), "Secularism, Secularization, Public Theology, and Practical Theology," in C. Wolfteich and A. Dillen (eds.), *Catholic Approaches in Practical Theology: International and Interdisciplinary Perspectives*, 207–24, Paris, Bristol: Peeters Leuven.

Lefebvre, S., and L. G. Beaman (2013), "Protecting Gender Relations: The Bouchard-Taylor Commission and the Equality of Women," *Canadian Journal for Social Research*, 2(1): 95–104.

Lefebvre, S., and P. Brodeur, eds. (2017), *Public Commissions on Cultural and Religious Diversity: Analysis, Reception and Challenges*, London: Routledge.

Lefebvre, S., and G. St-Laurent G, eds. (2018), *Dix ans plus tard : La commission Bouchard-Taylor, succès ou échec?*, Montreal: Québec Amérique.

Lefebvre, S., K. J. Leyva, K. Giomny, H. Ruiz, and M. Vanasse-Pelletier (2017), "The Commissions: Caught between Media Simplifications and Political Interests," in S. Lefebvre and P. Brodeur (eds.), *Public Commissions on Cultural and Religious Diversity: Analysis, Reception and Challenges*, 143–66, London: Routledge.

Lipka, M., and D. McClendon (2017), "Why People with No Religion Are Projected to Decline as a Share of the World's Population," *Pew Research Center*, April 7. Available online: https://www.pewresearch.org/fact-tank/2017/04/07/why-people-with-no-religion-are-projected-to-decline-as-a-share-of-the-worlds-population, accessed May 28, 2019.

Lustiger, M. (2003), Cardinal-Archevêque de Paris, Stasi Commission Hearing, 23 September 2003. Accessed on the diocese website in July 2012 (our translation) but not available online anymore.

Mamdani, M. (2004), *Good Muslim, Bad Muslim: America, The Cold War, and the Roots of Terror*, New York: Three Leaves Press.

Marks, L. (2017), *Infidels and the Damn Churches: Irreligion and Religion in Settler British Columbia*, Vancouver: UBC Press.

Marx, K. (1844), "A Contribution to the Critique of Hegel's Philosophy of Right." Available online: https://www.marxists.org/archive/marx/works/1843/critique-hpr/intro.htm, accessed May 28, 2019.

Meunier, E., and J. Warren (2002), *Sortir de la « grande noirceur » : L'horizon personnaliste de la Révolution tranquille*, Sillery: Septentrion.

Molligan, S. (2010), *Confronting the Challenge: Poverty, Gender and HIV in South Africa*, Oxford: P. Lang.

Nagra, B. (2011), "'Our Faith Was Also Hijacked by Those People': Reclaiming Muslim Identity in Canada in a Post-9/11 Era," *Journal of Ethnic and Migration Studies*, 37(3): 425–41.

Nemo, S. Z. (2018), "Liberation Theology: Why Pope Francis Failed to Deal with Pedophile Priests," *Communities Digital News*, August 28. Available online: https://www.commdiginews.com/politics-2/liberation-theology-pope-francis-pedophile-priests-105470, accessed May 28, 2019.

Nietzsche, F. (1982), "The Antichrist," in W. Kaufmann (ed.), *The Portable Nietzsche*, 565–656, New York: Penguin Group.

Pew Research Center (2018), "The Age Gap in Religion Around the World," *Pew Research Center*, June 13. Available online: https://www.pewforum.org/wp-content/uploads/sites/7/2018/06/ReligiousCommitment-FULL-WEB.pdf, accessed May 28, 2019.

Pew-Templeton (2015a), "America's Changing Religious Landscape," *Pew Research Center*, May 12. Available online: https://www.pewforum.org/2015/05/12/americas-changing-religious-landscape, accessed May 28, 2019.

Pew-Templeton (2015b), "Global Religious Futures Project: Belgium," *Pew Research Center*. Available online: http://www.globalreligiousfutures.org/countries/belgium#/?affiliations_religion_id=0&affiliations_year=2010&region_name=All%20Countries&restrictions_year=2016, accessed May 28, 2019.

Pew-Templeton (2015c), "Global Religious Futures Project. Sweden," *Pew Research Center*. Available online: http://www.globalreligiousfutures.org/countries/sweden#/?affiliations_religion_id=0&affiliations_year=2010&region_name=All%20Countries&restrictions_year=2015, accessed May 28, 2019.

Pope Francis (2013), *Apostolic Exhortation Evangelii Gaudium*. Available online: http://w2.vatican.va/content/francesco/en/apost_exhortations/documents/papa-francesco_esortazione-ap_20131124_evangelii-gaudium.html.

Pope Francis (2016), *Amoris Lætitia*. Available online: https://w2.vatican.va/content/dam/francesco/pdf/apost_exhortations/documents/papa-francesco_esortazione-ap_20160319_amoris-laetitia_en.pdf.

Quack, J., and C. Schuh, eds. (2017), *Religious Indifference: New Perspectives from Studies on Secularization and Nonreligion*, Cham: Springer.

Ratzinger, J. Cardinal (1986), "Congregation for the Doctrine of the Faith: Letter to Father Charles Curran," *Vatican*, July 15. Available online: http://www.vatican.va/roman_curia/congregations/cfaith/documents/rc_con_cfaith_doc_19860725_carlo-curran_en.html, accessed May 28, 2019.

Rayside, D., and C. Wilcox, eds. (2011), *Faith, Politics and Sexual Diversity in Canada and the United States*, Vancouver: University of British Columbia Press.

Razack, S. (2004), "Imperilled Muslim Women, Dangerous Muslim Men and Civilised Europeans: Legal and Social Responses to Forced Marriages," *Feminist Legal Studies*, 12(2): 129–74.
Razack, S. (2008), *Casting Out: The Eviction of Muslims from Western Law and Politics*, Toronto: University of Toronto Press.
Ricœur, P. (1965), *De l'interprétation: Essai sur Freud*, Paris: Seuil.
Ross, S. (2001), "Féminisme et théologie," *Raisons Politiques*, 4(4): 133–46.
Schermer, T. (2017), *Sex, God, and the Conservative Church: Erasing Shame from Sexual Intimacy*, New York: Routledge.
Schüssler Fiorenza, E. (1984), *Bread Not Stone: The Challenge of Feminist Biblical Interpretation*, Boston: Beacon Press.
Schüssler Fiorenza, E., M. Collins, and M. Lefébure (1985), *Women, Invisible in Theology and Church*, Edinburgh: T. & T. Clark.
Scott-Bauman, A. (2009), *Ricœur and the Hermeneutics of Suspicion*, London: Continuum.
Selby, J., A. Barras, and L. G. Beaman (2018), *Beyond Accommodation: Everyday Narratives of Muslim Canadians*, Vancouver: UBC Press.
Shazad, F. (2014), "The Discourse of Fear: Effects of the War on Terror on Canadian University Students," *American Review of Canadian Studies*, 44(4): 467–82.
Simard, J. (1998), "La philosophie française des XIXe et XXe siècles," in R. Kilbansky and J. Boulad-Ayoub (eds.), *La pensée philosophique d'expression française au Canada: Le rayonnement du Québec*, 45–118, Quebec City: Les presses de l'Université Laval.
Stasi, B. (2003), *Commission de réflexion sur l'application du principe de laïcité dans la République: Rapport au président de la République*, Paris: La Documentation Française.
Statistics Canada (2011), "Religion (108), Immigrant Status and Period of Immigration (11), Age Groups (10) and Sex (3) for the Population in Private Households of Canada, Provinces, Territories, Census Metropolitan Areas and Census Agglomerations, 2011 National Household Survey," Statistics Canada. Available online: https://www12.statcan.gc.ca/nhs-enm/2011/dp-pd/dt-td/Rp-eng.cfm?LANG=E&APATH=3&DETAIL=0&DIM=0&FL=A&FREE=0&GC=0&GID=0&GK=0&GRP=1&PID=105399&PRID=0&PTYPE=105277&S=0&SHOWALL=0&SUB=0&Temporal=2013&THEME=95&VID=0&VNAMEE=&VNAMEF, accessed May 28, 2019.
Thistlethwaite, S. (2014), "In the Eyes of Patriarchal Religion, All Women Are Secular: Gender in Religion and Secularism," in J. Berlinerblau, S. Fainberg, and A. Nou (eds.), *Secularism on the Edge: Rethinking Church-State Relations in the United States, France and Israel*, 191–98, New York: Palgrave MacMillan.
WIN-Gallup International (2012), *Global Index of Religion and Atheism*, Zurich: Gallup International.
Woodhead, L. (2016), "The Rise of 'No Religion' in Britain: The Emergence of a New Cultural Majority," *Journal of the British Academy*, 4: 245–61.
Zuckerman, P. (2012), *Faith No More: Why People Reject Religion*, Oxford: Oxford University Press.

Chapter 9

Aday, S., H. Farrell, M. Lynch, J. Sides, J. Kelly, and E. Zuckerman, eds. (2010), *Blogs and Bullets: New Media in Contentious Politics*, Washington DC: United States Institute of Peace.

Asad, T. (2009), "Free Speech, Blasphemy, and Secular Criticism," in T. Asad, W. Brown, J. Butler, and S. Mahmood (eds.), *Is Critique Secular*, 20–63, Berkeley, Los Angeles, London: University of California Press.

Asprem, E. (2011), "The Birth of Counterjihadist Terrorism: Reflections on Some Unspoken Dimensions," *The Pomegranate*, 13(1): 17–32.

Bartlett, J., J. Birdwell, and M. Littler, eds. (2011), *The New Face of Digital Populism*, London: Demos.

Bauman, Z. (1997), *Postmodernity and Its Discontents*, New York: New York University Press.

Berggren, L. (2014a), *Blodets renhet: En historisk studie av svensk antisemitism*, Malmö: Arx förlag.

Berggren, L. (2014b), "Intellectual Fascism: Per Engdahl and the Formation of 'New-Swedish Socialism,'" *Fascism*, 3: 69–92.

Bernsand, N. (2013), "Friend or Foe? Contemporary Debates on Islam and Muslim Immigrants among Swedish Identitarians," in T. Hoffman and G. Larsson (eds.), *Muslims and the New Information and Communication Technologies*, 163–89, New York, London: Springer.

Bjørgo, T. (1997), *Racist and Right-Wing Violence in Scandinavia: Patterns, Perpetrators, and Responses*, Oslo: Tane Aschhoug.

Björkqvist, B. (2017a), "Var profeten Muhammed ingen muslim?," *Svegot*, January 20. Available online: https://www.svegot.se/2017/01/20/var-profeten-muhammed-ingen-muslim, accessed July 1, 2018.

Björkqvist, B. (2017b), "Vad är rasism?," *Svegot*, February 9. Available online: https://www.svegot.se/2017/02/09/vad-ar-rasism, accessed July 1, 2018.

Björkqvist, B. (2017c), "Invandringen är mer än kostnader och brott," *Svegot*, February 20. Available online: https://www.svegot.se/2017/02/20/invandringen-ar-mer-kostnader-och-brott, accessed July 1, 2018.

Björkqvist, B. (2018), "Låt oss svenskar föra vår egen talan," *Svegot*, April 15: Available online: https://www.svegot.se/2018/04/15/lat-oss-svenskar-fora-var-egen-talan, accessed July 1, 2018.

Brown, W. (2009), "Introduction," in T. Asad, W. Brown, J. Butler, and S. Mahmood (eds.), *Is Critique Secular? Blasphemy, Injury, and Free Speech*, 7–19, Berkeley, Los Angeles, London: University of California Press.

Brubaker, R. (2017), "Why Populism?," *Theory and Society*, 46(5): 357–85.

Camus, R. (2012), *Le grand remplacement*, Plieux: Chez l'auteur.

Carlqvist, I. (2018a), *Från Sverige till Absurdistan*, Helsingborg: Logik Förlag.

Carlqvist, I. (2018b), "Egohumanisternas lilla Twitterstorm," *Svegot*, March 1. Available online: https://www.svegot.se/2018/03/01/egohumanisternas-lilla-twitterstorm, accessed July 1, 2018.

Carlqvist, I. (2018c), "Ann Heberlein kommer ut som etnonationalist," *Svegot*, March 14. Available online: https://svegot.se/2018/03/14/ann-heberlein-kommer-ut-som-etnonationalist, accessed July 1, 2018.

Carlqvist, I. (2018d), "Minoriteterna gaddar sig samman mot svenskarna," *Svegot*, March 17. Available online: https://www.svegot.se/2018/03/17/minoriteterna-gaddar-sig-samman-mot-svenskarna, accessed July 1, 2018.

Carlqvist, I. (2018e), "Nyhetssvepet med Ingrid & Conrad: KD åker ur, fejkundersökning och den eviga islamofobin," *Radio Svegot*, April 17. Availble online: https://www.svegot.se/2018/04/17/kd-aker-ur-fejkundersokning-och-den-eviga-islamofobin-nyhetssvepet-180417, accessed July 1, 2018.

Carlqvist, I. (2018f), "Grattis till oss alla: Tusen prenumeranter på Svegot Plus!," *Svegot*, May 29. Available online: https://www.svegot.se/2018/05/29/grattis-till-oss-alla-tusen-prenumeranter-pa-svegot-plus, accessed July 1, 2018.

Carlqvist, I. (2018g), "Niklas Orrenius: En lättlurad svenne eller en islamist i vardande?" *Svegot*, June 8. Available online: https://svegot.se/2018/06/08/niklas-orrenius-en-lattlurad-svenne-eller-en-islamist-i-vardande, accessed February 10, 2019.

Carlqvist, I., and D. Frändelöv (2017), "Nyhetssvepet: 2018 är segrarnas år, muslimer fruktar helvetet och Robinson är död," *Radio Svegot*, November 16. Available online: https://www.motgift.nu/2017/11/16/ar-sanningen-olaglig-sverige-nyhetskollen-26, accessed July 1, 2018.

Carr, M. (2006), "You Are Now Entering Eurabia," *Race & Class*, 48(1): 1–22.

Carr, M. (2017), *Blood and Faith: The Purging of Muslim Spain, 1492–614*, London: Hurst.

Cohn, N. (2005), *Warrant for Genocide: The Myth of the Jewish World Conspiracy and the Protocols of the Elders of Zion*, London: Serif.

Deland, M. (1997), "The Cultural Racism of Sweden," *Race and Class*, 39(1): 51–60.

Det Fria Sverige (2017), "Det Fria Sverige: Föreningen och visonen," October 27.

Ekman, M. (2016), "The Dark Side of Online Activism: Swedish Right-Wing Extremist Video Activism on Youtube," *MedieKultur*, 56: 79–99.

Engesser, S., N. Ernst, F. Esser, and F. Büchel (2017), "Populism and Social Media: How Politicians Spread a Fragmented Ideology," *Information, Communication & Society*, 20(8): 1109–26.

Eriksson, D. (2014), "Den svenska nationalstaten är död," *Motgift*, June 19. Available online: https://www.motgift.nu/2014/06/19/den-svenska-nationalstaten-ar-dod, accessed July 1, 2018.

Eriksson, D. (2017), "Sverige har två val: Men bara ett om hon vill överleva," *Svegot*, October 20. Available online: https://svegot.se/2017/10/20/sverige-har-tva-val-men-bara-ett-om-hon-vill-overleva, accessed July 1, 2018.

Eriksson, D. (2018a), "Den här Dan: Dina skattepengar går till islamiseringen av Sverige," *Motgift*, February 7. Available online: https://www.motgift.nu/2018/02/07/dina-skattepengar-gar-till-islamiseringen-av-sverige-den-har-dan-18, accessed July 1, 2018.

Eriksson, D. (2018b), "Den här Dan: Islamisering—sanning eller myt," *Motgift*, February 13. Available online: https://www.youtube.com/watch?v=XVdR9wmCT6Q, accessed July 1, 2018.

Eriksson, D. (2018c), "Den här Dan: Politiskt våld: En realitet vi måste förhålla oss till," *Radio Svegot*, February 28. Available online: https://svegot.se/2018/02/22/politiskt-vald-en-realitet-vi-maste-forhalla-oss-till-den-har-dan-27, accessed July 1, 2018.

Eriksson, D. (2018d), "Den demografiska verkligheten," *Radio Svegot*, March 21. Available online: https://www.svegot.se/2018/03/21/den-demografiska-verkligheten-den-har-dan-43, accessed July 1, 2018.

Eriksson, D. (2018e), "Den här Dan: Islam i Sverige och vårt ansvar som svenskar," *Radio Svegot*, May 4. Available online: www.svegot.se/2018/05/04/islam-i-sverige-och-vart-ansvar-som-svenskar, accessed July 1, 2018.

Eriksson, D., M. Söderman, and B. Björkqvist (2017), "Nyhetskollen: Är sanningen olaglig i Sverige," *Motgift*, November 16. Available online: https://www.motgift.nu/2017/11/16/ar-sanningen-olaglig-sverige-nyhetskollen-26, accessed July 1, 2018.

Fekete, L. (2018), *Europe's Fault Lines: Racism and Rise of the Right*, London: Verso.

Fitzgerald, T., T. Stack, and N. Goldenberg, eds. (2015), *Religion as a Category of Government and Sovereignty*, Leiden: Brill.

Friberg, D. (2015), *Högern kommer tillbaka*, Göteborg: Arktos Förlag.

Gardell, M. (2010), *Islamofobi*, Stockholm: Leopard Förlag.
Gardell, M. (2015), *Raskrigaren*, Stockholm: Leopard Förlag.
Hawley, G. (2017), *Making Sense of the Alt-Right*, New York: Columbia University Press.
Henley, J. (2018), "George Soros: Financier, Philanthropist: and Hate Figure for the Far Right," *The Guardian*, February 8. Available online: https://www.theguardian.com/business/2018/feb/08/george-soros-demonised-by-populists-nationalists-and-right-wing-press, accessed July 1, 2019.
Kahmann, B. (2017), "'The Most Ardent Pro-Israel Party': Pro-Israel Attitudes and Anti-antisemitism among Populist Radical-Right Parties in Europe," *Patterns of Prejudice*, 51(5): 396–411.
Kavada, A. (2015), "Creating the Collective: Social Media, the Occupy Movement and Its Constitution as a Collective Actor," *Information, Communication & Society*, 18(8): 872–86.
Kemp, A. (2008), *Jihad: Islam's 1,300 Year War on Western Civilization*, Burlington, IA: Ostara Publications.
Krämer, B. (2017), "Populist Online Practices: The Function of the Internet in Right-Wing Populism," *Information, Communication & Society*, 9(20): 1293–309.
Kundnani, A. (2008), "Islamism and the Roots of Liberal Rage," *Race & Class*, 50: 40–68.
Larsson, G. (2012), "The Fear of Small Numbers: Eurabia Literature and Censuses on Religious Belonging," *Journal of Muslims in Europe*, 1: 142–65.
Lindquist, D. (2010), "Mellan myt och verklighet," in M. Deland, F. Hertzberg, and T. Hvitfeldt (eds.), *Det vita fältet*, 127–54, Stockholm: Swedish Science Press.
Lööw, H. (2015), *Nazismen i Sverige*, Stockholm: Ordfront förlag.
Lööw, H. (2016), "I gränslandet: Symbiosen mellan det organiserade och oorganiserade," in M. Gardell, H. Lööw, and M. Dahlberg-Grundberg (eds.), *Den ensamme terroristen: Om Lone Wolves, näthat och brinnande flyktingförläggningar*, 21–86, Stockholm: Ordfont.
Lundström, M., and T. Lundström (2011), "Hundra år av radikal nationalism," *Arkiv Tidskrift för samhällsanalys*, 1: 39–66.
Meer, N. (2013), "Racialization and Religion: Race, Culture and Difference in the Study of Antisemitism and Islamophobia," *Ethnic and Racial Studies*, 36(3): 385–98.
Motgift (2016), "Samarbeten mellan vita nationalister och muslimer," *YouTube*, December 20. Available online: https://www.youtube.com/watch?v=DlAZGIiG31Y, accessed July 1, 2018.
Murji, K., and J. Solomos, eds. (2005), *Racialization: Studies in Theory and Practice*, Oxford: Oxford University Press.
Nilsson, P. (2019), *French Populism and Discourses on Secularism*, London, New York: Bloomsbury.
Nougayrède, N. (2018), "Steve Bannon Is on a Far-Right Mission to Radicalise Europe," *The Guardian*, January 6. Available online: https://www.theguardian.com/commentisfree/2018/jun/06/steve-bannon-far-right-radicalise-europe-trump, accessed July 1, 2018.
Pink, S., H. Horst, J. Postill, L. Hjorth, T. Lewis, and J. Tacchi, eds. (2016), *Digital Ethnography: Principles and Practices*, London: Sage.
Renton, J., and B. Giley, eds. (2017), *Antisemitism and Islamophobia in Europe*, London: Palgrave Macmillan.
Rydgren, J., and S. van der Meiden (2018), "The Radical Right and the End of Swedish Exceptionalism," *European Political Science*, May 2: 1–17.
Söderman, M. (2014), "Vithetsnormen: Islam är en expansiv religion," *Motgift*, September 30. Available online: https://www.youtube.com/watch?v=MJJ05kiS-cw, accessed July 1, 2018.

Söderman, M. (2016), "Gomorron med Magnus: Muslimer går samman för att för att ställa krav i Sverige," *Motgift*, November 15. Available online: https://www.youtube.com/watch?v=NPbtckRpgqU, accessed July 1, 2018.

Söderman, M. (2018a), "Kväll med Svegot: Varför konverterar så många svenskar till Islam," *Radio Svegot*, May 9. Available online: https://www.svegot.se/2018/05/09/varfor-konverterar-svenskar-till-islam-kvall-med-svegot-27, accessed July 1, 2018.

Söderman, M. (2018b), "Med 100 år av svensk opposition i ryggsäcken," *Svegot*, March 5. Available online: https://svegot.se/2018/03/05/med-100-ar-av-svensk-opposition-i-ryggsacken, accessed July 1, 2018.

Söderman, M. (2018c), "Kväll med Svegot: Hur ska återvandringen gå till?," *Radio Svegot*, June 14. Available online: https://svegot.se/2018/06/14/kms-51-hur-ska-atervandringen-ga-till, accessed July 1, 2018.

Teitelbaum, B. (2017), *Lions of the North: Sounds of the New Nordic Radical Nationalism*, Oxford: Oxford University Press.

Torfing, J. (2005), "Discourse Theory: Achievements, Arguments, and Challenges," in D. Howarth and J. Torfing (eds.), *Discourse Theory in European Politics Identity: Policy and Governance*, 1–32, Hampshire, New York: Palgrave Macmillan.

Tuten, T. L., and M. R. Solomon (2014), Social Media Marketing, London: Sage.

Wåg, M. (2010), "Nationell kulturkamp: Från vit maktmusik till metapolitik," in M. Deland, F. Hertzberg, and T. Hvitfeldt (eds.), *Det vita fältet*, 97–126, Stockholm: Swedish Science Press.

Weaver, S. (2013), "A Rhetorical Discourse Analysis of Online Anti-Muslim and Anti-Semitic Jokes," *Ethnic and Racial Studies*, 36(3): 483–99.

Wieder, R. (2013), "En kartläggning av det högerextrema nätverket på internet: Strukturella mönster 2006–2011," *Tidskrift för samhällsanalys*, 2: 101–37.

Wodak, R. (2018), "The Radical Right and Antisemitism," in Jens Rydgren (ed.), *The Oxford Handbook of the Radical Right*, 61–85, London: Oxford University Press.

Zúquete, J. P. (2019), *The Identitarians: The Movement against Globalism and Islam in Europe*, Notre Dame: University of Notre Dame Press.

Zia-Ebrahimi, R. (2018), "When the Elders of Zion Relocated to Eurabia: Conspiratorial Racialization in Antisemitism and Islamophobia," *Patterns of Prejudice*, 52(4): 314–37.

Chapter 10

Brömssen, K. (2012), "Religious Literacy: Är det ett användbart begrepp inom religionsdidaktisk-/pedagogisk forskning?," in B. Afset, K. Hatlebrekke, and K. H. Valen (eds.), *Kunnskap til hva? Om religion i skolen*, 117–43, Trondheim: Akademika Forlag.

Church of Sweden (2018). Svenska kyrkan i siffror. https://www.svenskakyrkan.se/statistik

Davie, G. (2015), "Foreword," in A. Dinham and M. Francis (eds.), *Religious Literacy in Policy and Practice*, vii–xi, Bristol: Policy Press.

Dinham, A., and M. Francis (2015), *Religious Literacy in Policy and Practice*, Bristol: Policy Press.

Furseth, I. (2018), "Secularization, Deprivatization, or Religious Complexity?," in I. Furseth (ed.), *Religious Complexity in the Public Sphere: Comparing Nordic Countries*, 291–312, Cham: Springer International Publishing.

Goldburg, P. (2010), "Developing Pedagogies for Inter-religious Teaching and Learning," in K. Engebretson, M. De Souza, G. Durka, and L. Gearon (eds.), *International Handbook of Inter-religious Education*, 341–60, Dordrecht: Springer.

Hammer, A., and Å. J. Schanke (2018), "'Why Can't You Just Eat Pork?' Teachers' Perspectives on Criticism of Religion in Norwegian Religious Education," *Journal of Religious Education*, 66: 151–64, doi:10.1007/s40839-018-0063-y

Hjelm, T. (2014), "Understanding the New Visibility of Religion: Religion as Problem and Utility," *Journal of Religion in Europe*, 7(3–4): 203, doi:10.1163/18748929-00704002

Kittelmann Flensner, K. (2015), *Religious Education in Contemporary Pluralistic Sweden*, Gothenburg: University of Gothenburg.

Klingenberg, M., and A. Sjöborg (2015), "Religion i ungas vardagsliv," in M. Lövheim and M. Nordin (eds.), *Sociologiska perspektiv på religion i Sverige*, 69–89, Malmö: Gleerups.

Löfstedt, M., and A. Sjöborg (2018), "Addressing Existential Issues through the Eyes of Swedish Religious Education Teachers," in G. Skeie, K. Sporre, and J. Ristiniemi (eds.), *Challenging Life: Existential Questions as a Resource for Education*, 83–100, Münster: Waxmann Verlag.

Lövheim, M., J. Lindberg, P. K. Botvar, H. K. Christensen, K. Niemelä, and A. Bäckström (2018), "Religion on the Political Agenda," in I. Furseth (ed.), *Religious Complexity in the Public Sphere: Comparing Nordic Countries*, 137–91, Cham: Springer International Publishing.

Lundby, K., and P. Repstad (2018), "Scandinavia: Traits, Trends and Tensions," in K. Lundby (ed.), *Contesting Religion: The Media Dynamics of Cultural Conflicts in Scandinavia*, 13–31, Berlin, Boston: DeGruyter.

Lundby, K., H. R. Christensen, A. K. Gresaker, M. Lövheim, K. Niemelä, S. Sjö, and Á. S Daníelsson (2018), "Religion and the Media: Continuity, Complexity, and Mediatization," in I. Furseth (ed.), *Religious Complexity in the Public Sphere: Comparing Nordic Countries*, 193–249, Cham: Springer International Publishing.

Moore, D. L. (2007), *Overcoming Religious Illiteracy: A Cultural Studies Approach to the Study of Religion in Secondary Education*, New York, London: Palgrave Macmillan Ltd.

Moore, D. L. (2015), "Diminishing Religious Literacy: Methodological Assumptions and Analytical Frameworks for Promoting the Public Understanding of Religion," in A. Dinham and M. Francis (eds.), *Religious Literacy in Policy and Practice*, 27–38, Bristol: Policy Press.

National Agency for Education (2011), The Swedish National School Agency, Official website. Steering documents. Retrieved April 18, 2011, from http://www.skolverket.se/sb/d/493.

Prothero, S. (2007), *Religious Literacy: What Every American Needs to Know—and Doesn't*, New York: Harper One.

Schreiner, P. (2013), "Religious Education in the European Context," *Hungarian Educational Research Journal*, 3(H.4): 5–15, doi: 10.14413/herj.2013.04.02.

Sjöborg, A. (2012), "Centralt eller perifert? Ungas kontakter med religion i vardagen," in M. Lövheim and J. Bromander (eds.), *Religion som resurs? Existentiella frågor och värderingar i unga svenskars liv*, 107–29, Skellefteå: Artos.

Toft, A., and M. Broberg (2018), "Perspectives: Mediatized Religious Education," in K. Lundby (ed.), *Contesting Religion: The Media Dynamics of Cultural Conflicts in Scandinavia*, 225–42, Boston, Berlin: DeGruyter.

Wright, A. (2003), "The Contours of Critical Religious Education: Knowledge, Wisdom, Truth," *British Journal of Religious Education*, 25(4): 279–91.

Chapter 11

Alexander, J. (1998), "Introduction. Civil Society I, II, III: Constructing an Empirical Concept from Normative Controversies and Historical Transformations," in J. Alexander (ed.), *Real Civil Societies: Dilemmas of Institutionalization*, 1–19, London: SAGE.

Alexander, J. (2006), *The Civil Sphere*, Oxford, New York: Oxford University Press.

Avci, G., M. Nilsson, and C. Elving (2017), "Liberala kvinnor: Stäng de religiösa friskolorna," *Svenska Dagbladet*, March 17.

Axner, M. (2013), *Public Religions in Swedish Media: A Study of Religious Actors on Three Newspapers Debate Pages 2001–2011*, diss., Uppsala: Uppsala University.

Bengtsson, J., P. Carlsson, D. Färm, R. Hammarstrand, et al. (2017a), "Dags för S att säga nej till religiösa friskolor," *Dagens Nyheter*, March 24.

Bengtsson, J., P. Carlsson, D. Färm, R. Hammarstrand, et al. (2017b), "Dags för S att säga nej till religiösa friskolor," *Dagens Nyheter*, March 25.

Benhabib, S. (1992), "Models of Public Space: Hannah Arendt, the Liberal Tradition, and Jürgen Habermas," in C. Calhoun (ed.), *Habermas and the Public Sphere*, 73–99, Cambridge, MA: The MIT Press.

Benhabib, S. (2000), *The Reluctant Modernism of Hannah Arendt*, Lanham: Rowman & Littlefield.

Burell, O. (2017), "Elever ska inte sorteras utifrån religion," *Svenska Dagbladet*, April 27.

Burén, R. (2017), "Att inte be med sina barn är också att påverka dem," *Svenska Dagbladet*, May 7.

Calhoun, C. (2008), "Secularism, Citizenship, and the Public Sphere," *Hedgehog Review*, 10(3): 7–21.

Calhoun, C. (2011), "Civil Society and the Public Sphere," in M. Edwards (ed.), *The Oxford Handbook of Civil Society*, Oxford Handbooks in Politics and International Relations, 267–80, New York: Oxford University Press.

Douib, R., and M. Westergård (2017), "Svensk inställning till religion en ytterkantsåsikt," *Dagens Nyheter*, March 30.

Dryzek, J. (1990), *Discursive Democracy*, Cambridge: Cambridge University Press.

Ericson, E., U. Gustafsson, P. Lindenfors, and C. Sturmark (2017a), "Politiker, förbjud de religiösa friskolorna," *Aftonbladet*, April 12.

Ericson, E., U. Gustafsson, P. Lindenfors, and C. Sturmark (2017b), "Era argument ekar av USA:s kristna höger," *Aftonbladet*, April 25.

Esping-Andersen, G. (1990), *The Three Worlds of Welfare Capitalism*, Cambridge: Polity Press.

Evers, A., and J. von Essen (2019), "Volunteering and Civic Action: Boundaries Blurring, Boundaries Redrawn," *Voluntas: International Journal of Voluntary and Nonprofit Organizations*, 30(1): 1–14.

Ferree, M., W. Gamson, J. Gerhards, and D. Rucht (2002), "Four Models of the Public Sphere in Modern Democracies," *Theory and Society*, 31(3): 289–324.

Garnham, N. (1992), "The Media and the Public Sphere," in C. Calhoun (ed.), *Habermas and the Public Sphere*, 359–77, Cambridge, MA: The MIT Press.

Göndör, E. (2017), *Religionskollision: Minoritet, majoritet och toleransens gränser*, Stockholm: Timbro Förlag.

Habermas, J. (1962/1984), *Borgerlig offentlighet: Kategorierna "privat" och "offentligt" i det moderna samhället*. Lund: Arkiv förlag.

Habermas, J. (1992), "Further Reflections on the Public Sphere," in C. Calhoun (ed.), *Habermas and the Public Sphere*, 421–62, Cambridge, MA: MIT Press.

Hegel, F. (1820/1991), *Elements of the Philosophy of Right*, Cambridge: Cambridge University Press.

Hohendahl, P. (1992), "The Public Sphere: Models and Boundaries," in C. Calhoun (ed.), *Habermas and the Public Sphere*, 99–109, Cambridge, MA: The MIT Press.

Köhrsen, J. (2012), "How Religious Is the Public Sphere? A Critical Stance on the Debate about Religion and Post-secularity," *Acta Sociologica*, 55(3): 273–88.

Laborde, C. (2017), *Liberalism's Religion*, Cambridge, MA: Harvard University Press.

Lundgren Aslla, A. (2017a), "Religiösa friskolor: En fristad i hatsamhället," *Svenska Dagbladet*, April 5.

Lundgren Aslla, A. (2017b), "Det behövs fler religiösa friskolor i Sverige," *Altinget*, August 17.

Lundgren Aslla, A. (2017c), "Skolan måste utvecklas bortom förtyckande normer," *Altinget*, August 24.

McCarthy, T. (1992), "Practical Discourse: On the Relation of Morality to Politics," in C. Calhoun (ed.), *Habermas and the Public Sphere*, 51–73, Cambridge, MA: The MIT Press.

Meyer, B., and A. Moors (2006), "Introduction," in B. Meyer and A. Moors (eds.), *Religion, Media and the Public Sphere*, 1–26, Bloomington: Indiana University Press.

Mouffe, C. (2006), "Religion, Liberal Democracy, and Citizenship," in H. De Vries and L. Sullivan (eds.), *Political Theologies: Public Religions in a Secular World*, 318–26, New York: Fordham University Press.

Moyn, S. (2015), *Christian Human Rights*, Philadelphia: University of Pennsylvania Press.

Nyberg, B., M. Westergård, S. Magnusson, and R. Douid (2017), "Absurt att S vill stänga religiösa skolor," *Dagen*, April 11.

Olofsgård, J., and A. Ekström (2017), "Religiösa skolor är en tillgång: Inte ett hot," *Svenska Dagbladet*, March 21.

Ouis, P. (2009), "'Den verkliga kulturkonflikten'? Islamisk sexualmoral i liberala Sverige," *Socialvetenskaplig Tidskrift*, 16(3–4): 350–68.

Quarsebo, J. (2013), "Konfessionella friskolor, religion och toleransens gränser," in L. Trägårdh, P. Selle, L. Skov Henriksen, and H. Hallin (eds.), *Civilsamhälle klämt mellan stat och kapital: Välfärd, mångfald, framtid*, 160–76, Stockholm: SNS Förlag.

Ricœur, P. (1992), *Oneself as Another*, Chicago: University of Chicago Press.

Salamon, L., and H. Anheier (1998), "Social Origins of Civil Society: Explaining the Nonprofit Sector Cross-Nationality," *Voluntas: International Journal of Voluntary and Nonprofit Organizations*, 9(3): 213–48.

SCB (2015), *Befolkningsstatistik i sammandrag 1960–2015*, Stockholm: Statistiska Centralbyrån.

Selander, M. (2017), "Det finns inga ideologiskt neutrala skolor," *Dagen*, April 14.

Sigurdson, O. (2000), *Den lyckliga filosofin: etik och politik hos Hägerström, Tingsten, makarna Myrdal och Hedenius*, Eslöv: B. Östlings bokförlag Symposion

Sigurdson, O. (2009), *Det postsekulära tillståndet: Religion, modernitet, politik*, Munkedal: Glänta Produktion.

Tännsjö, T. (2013), "Yttrandefrihet i trängt läge," *Kurage* 8. Stockholm.

Tracy, D. (1987), *Plurality and Ambiguity: Hermeneutics, Religion, Hope*, Chicago: University of Chicago Press.

von Essen, J. (2012), "Vilse i civilsamhället," in J. von Essen and G. Sundgren (eds.), *En Mosaik av mening: Om studieförbund och civilsamhälle*, 21–43, Göteborg: Daidalos.

Walzer, M. (1997), *On Toleration*, New Haven: Yale University Press.

Westergård, M., and R. Douib (2017), "Fördomsfull beskrivning av kristna skolor," *Svenska Dagbladet*, March 20.

Chapter 12

Abdel-Fadil, M. (2018), "Nationalizing Christianity and Hijacking Religion on Facebook," in K. Lundby (eds.), *Contesting Religion: The Media Dynamics of Cultural Conflicts in Scandinavia*, 97–116, Berlin, Boston: De Gruyter.

Andersson, U., and L. Weibull (2018), "Polariserat medieförtroende," in U. Andersson, A. Carlander, E. Lindgren, and M. Oskarson (eds.), *Sprickor i fasaden: SOM-undersökningen 2017*, 71–92, Göteborg: SOM-institutet.

Beckford, J. (1989), *Religion and Advanced Industrial Society*, London: Unwin Hyman.

Benhabib, S. (1992), "Models of Public Space: Hannah Arendt, the Liberal Tradition, and Jürgen Habermas," in C. J. Calhoun (ed.), *Habermas and the Public Sphere*, 73–98, Cambridge, MA: MIT Press.

Benhabib, S. (2002), *The Claims of Culture: Equality and Diversity in the Global Era*, Princeton: Princeton University Press.

Chadwick, A. (2017), *The Hybrid Media System: Politics and Power*, 2nd ed., New York: Oxford University Press.

Cottle, S. (2006), *Mediatized Conflict: Developments in Media and Conflict Studies*, Maidenhead: Open University Press.

Dagens Nyheter (2016), "I stället för ett uteblivet handslag borde diskussionen ha handlat om…" *Dagens Nyheter*, April 21. Available online: https://www.facebook.com/dn.se/posts/10153491802321680

Demker, M. (2018), "Oförändrat motstånd mot flyktingmottagning men stärkt hotbild kring religion och svensk kultur," in U. Andersson, A. Carlander, E. Lindgren, and M. Oskarson (eds.), *Sprickor i fasaden: SOM-undersökningen 2017*, 393–405, Göteborg: SOM-institutet.

Downey, J., and N. Fenton (2003), "New Media, Counter Publicity and the Public Sphere," *New Media & Society*, 5(2): 185–202.

Evolvi, G. (2017), "#Islamexit: Inter-Group Antagonism on Twitter," *Information, Communication & Society*, 22(3): 386–401.

Expressen (2016), "MP-politikern Yasri Khan föreslogs ta plats i MP:s partistyrelse…," *Expressen*, April 21. Available online: https://www.facebook.com/expressen/posts/10153712944080345.

Government Offices of Sweden (2018), "A Feminist Government." Available online: http://www.government.se/government-policy/a-feminist-government.

Habermas, J. (1992), "Further Reflections on the Public Sphere," in C. J. Calhoun (ed.), *Habermas and the Public Sphere*, 421–61, Cambridge, MA: MIT Press.

Habermas, J. (2006), "Religion in the Public Sphere," *European Journal of Philosophy*, 14(1): 1–25.

Hedman, U. (2016), "Primära nyhetspubliker i sociala medier," in J. Ohlsson, H. Oscarsson, and M. Solevid (eds.), *Ekvilibrium: SOM-undersökningen 2015*, 361–75, Göteborg: SOM-institutet.

Helmerson, E. (2016), "Handtag, famntag, klapp eller kyss," Dagens Nyheter, April 21: 5.

Hepp, A., S. Hjarvard, and K. Lundby (2010), "Mediatization—Empirical Perspectives: An Introduction to a Special Issue," *Communications*, 35: 223–28.

Hjarvard, S., and K. Lundby (2018), "Understanding Media Dynamics," in K. Lundby (ed.), *Contesting Religion: The Media Dynamics of Cultural Conflicts in Scandinavia*, 51–64, Berlin, Boston: De Gruyter.

Hjarvard, S., M. Mortensen, and M. Fugl Eskjær (2015), "Three Dynamics of Mediatized Conflicts," in M. Fugl Eskjær, S. Hjarvard, and M. Mortensen (eds.), *The Dynamics of Mediatized Conflicts*, 1–27, New York: Peter Lang.

Hjelm, T. (2014), "Understanding the New Visibility of Religion: Religion as Problem and Utility," *Journal of Religion in Europe*, 7(3–4): 203–22.

Hutchens, M. J., V. J. Cicchirillo, and J. D. Hmielowski (2015), "How Could You Think That?!?!: Understanding Intentions to Engage in Political Flaming," *New Media & Society*, 17(8): 1201–19.

Lifvendahl, T. (2016), "Ett handslag kan betyda så mycket," Svenska Dagbladet, April 23: 4.

Lindberg, A. (2016), "Håller nationalism på att bli väster?," Aftonbladet, May 2: 2.

Lövheim, M. (2017), "Religion, Mediatization, and 'Complementary Learning Processes' in Swedish Editorials," *Journal of Religion in Europe*, 10(4): 366–83.

Lövheim, M., and A. Linderman (2015), "Media, Religion and Modernity: Editorials and Religion in Swedish Daily Press," in T. Hjelm (ed.), *Is God Back? Reconsidering the New Visibility of Religion*, 32–45, London: Bloomsbury.

Madon, S. (2016), "Röstfiske bakom MP:s magplask," Expressen, April 23: 2.

Miljöpartiet de gröna (2013), "Party Programme." Available online: https://www.mp.se/sites/default/files/ mp_partiprogram_english.pdf.

Mouffe, C. (2013), *Agonistics: Thinking the World Politically*, London: Verso.

Nord, L. (2001), *Vår tids ledare: En studie av den svenska dagspressens politiska opinionsbildning*, diss., Stockholm: University of Stockholm.

Pettersson, K. (2016), "Storkrig om kultur löser ingenting: Det viktigaste börjar med skolan," Aftonbladet, May 1: 2.

Pollack, E. (2015), "Personalised Scandalisation: Sensationalising Trivial Conflicts?," in M. Fugl Eskjær, S. Hjarvard, and M. Mortensen (eds.), *The Dynamics of Mediatized Conflicts*, 129–54, New York: Peter Lang.

Rasmussen, T. (2008), "Panel Discussion II: Culture and Media Technology: The Internet and Differentiation in the Political Public Sphere," *Nordicom Review*, 29(2): 73–83.

SvD (2016), "Löfven: 'Man ska ta både kvinnor och män i hand,'" Svenska Dagbladet, April 21. Available online: https://www.svd.se/folj-fragestunden-med-stefan-lofven.

Svensson, J. (2014), *Sociala medier och politiskt deltagande i Sverige: Om det digitala deltagandets drivkrafter*, Stockholm: SE Stiftelsen för Internetinfrastruktur.

SVT Nyheter (2016a), "[TV]: Miljöpartiet har lovat att Haninge ska bli en vänortskommun med bland annat Kulu...," *Sveriges Television*, April 21. Available online: https://www.facebook.com/svtnyheter/posts/1251315158231355.

SVT Nyheter (2016b), "Hur går Miljöpartiet vidare efter sin mardrömsvecka?... ," *Sveriges Television*, April 24. Available online: https://www.facebook.com/svtnyheter/videos/1252185001477704.

Chapter 13

Af Burén, A. (2015), *Living Simultaneity: On Religion among Semi-Secular Swedes*, Stockholm: Södertörn Doctoral Dissertations.

Bäckström, A., N. Edgardh and P. Pettersson (2004), *Religious Change in Northern Europe: The Case of Sweden*, Stockholm: Verbum.

Beaman, L. (2014), "Deep Equality as an Alternative to Accommodation and Tolerance," *Nordic Journal of Religion and Society*, 27(2): 89–111.
Clydesdale, T. (2007), Abandoned, Pursued, or Safely Stowed? Published on: February 6, 2007 http://religion.ssrc.org/reforum/Clydesdale.pdf.
Connolly, W. (2005), *Pluralism*, Durham: Duke University Press.
Davie, G. (2000), *Religion in Modern Europe: A Memory Mutates*, Oxford: Oxford University Press.
Edgardh, N. (2018), "Where We Belong: Family as an Overlooked Interspace in the Passing On of Christian Tradition in Twenty-First Century Sweden," in J. Ideström and T. Stangeland Kaufman (eds.), *What Really Matters: Scandinavian Perspectives on Ethnography*, 138–56, Eugene: Pickwick Publications.
Hofstede, G. (2001), *Culture's Consequences: Comparing Values, Behaviors, Institutions and Organizations across Nations*, 2nd ed., Newbury Park, CA: Sage.
Ingelhart, R. and C. Welzel (2015), Cultural Map—WVS wave 6 (2010-2014). Available online: www.worldvaluessurvey.org/WVSContents, accessed September 26, 2019.
Jonsson, P. (2018), "Tro och tillhörighet under förändring: En fråga om organisation," in *Nyckeln till Svenska Kyrkan*, 19–36, Uppsala: Svenska kyrkan.
Manning, C. (2015), *Losing Our Religion: How Unaffiliated Parents Are Raising Their Children*, New York, London: New York University Press.
Pettersson, T. (2009), "Religion och samhällspraktik: En jämförande analys av det sekulariserade Sverige," *Socialvetenskaplig tidskrift*, 16(3–4): 233–64.
Pettersson, T., and Y. Esmer (2006), *Vilka är annorlunda? Om invandrares möte med svensk kultur*, Norrköping: Integrationsverket.
Schwartz, S., and A. Bardi (2001), "Value Hierarchies across Cultures: Taking a Similarities Perspective," *Journal of Cross Cultural Psychology*, 32: 268–90.
Welzel, C., and R. Inglehart (2010), "Values, Agency, and Well-Being: A Human Development Model," *Social Indicators Research*, 97: 43–63.
Woodhead, L. (2009), "The Muslim Veil Controversy and European Values," *Swedish Missiological Themes*, 97(1): 89–105.
Woodhead, L. (2013), "Note from across the Pond: Church-State Separation Isn't for Everyone." *Religion Dispatches*. Available online: http://religiondispatches.org/note-from-across-the-pond-church-state-separation-isnt-for-everyone, accessed January 8, 2019.
Woodhead, L. (2014), "Religious Other or Religious Inferior," *IIC Quarterly*, 40(3–4): 1–14.

Chapter 14

Gray, J. (2018), *Seven Types of Atheism*, London: Allen Lane.
Habermas, J. (2006), "Religion in the Public Sphere," *European Journal of Philosophy*, 14: 1–25.
Lövheim, M. (2017), "Religion, Mediatization, and 'Complementary Learning Processes' in Swedish Editorials," *Journal of Religion in Europe*, 10(4): 366–83.
Taylor, C. (2007), *A Secular Age*, Cambridge, MA: The Belknap Press.

Index

Note: page numbers followed by "n" refer to notes.

academic feminism, as immanent critique   44
accommodation   8–9, 118
  cultural   42
  reasonable   118
  religious   42
Adler, R.   11, 55
  immanent critique   45, 52–4
Aftonbladet   155, 168–70
agnostic respect   9, 178
agonism   167, 173, 174
Akthar, S.   24
Alexander, J.   155
Ali, K.   62–3
Alternativ för Sverige (AFS, Alternative for Sweden)   127
American Academy of Religion   139
American Christian Right   43
Amir-Moazami, S.   107
an-Naim, A. A.   61, 69–70
antagonism   37, 111, 167, 174, 194, 195
anthropoemic logic   126–7
anticlerical criticism   58, 71
anti-essentialist ontology   128
anti-foundationalist epistemology   128
anti-Semitism   127, 129, 203 n.12
Aquinas, T.   82
Arendt, H.   162
Arkoun, M.   63–6
ars disputandi   74
Asad, T.   6, 128
atheism   7
  anthropological   10, 36–42
  humanistic   10
  New Atheism   10, 32–6
  scientific   10
Attfield, R.   80
Audi, R.   27
Augustine   74, 78
authorities   67–9

Bannon, S.   202 n.9
Barlas, A.   11
  immanent critique   45, 48–50, 55, 56
Beaman, L. G.   9, 12, 101, 109, 112, 177, 178, 194, 202 n.5, 202 n.6
Beckford, J. A.   6, 165
Belgium   118, 120, 123
  gender equality   119
Benhabib, S.   164, 166–7, 175
Berman, D.   32–3, 36
Bernsand, N.   202 n.4
Berry, W.   80
Björkqvist, B.   125, 129–32
Boko Haram   62
Bouchard-Taylor Commission   119, 120
Brandom, R.   46
bridging and bonding social capital   108
British National Party (BNP)   203 n.10
Brown, W.   128
Buckley, M. J.   37
Butler, J.   8, 82

Camus, A.   80, 115
Canada   9, 12, 112, 113, 116, 118–19, 194
Carlbom, A.   108
Carlqvist, I.   124, 125, 127, 129–32, 202 n.2
Casanova, J.   6, 7, 33, 35, 42
Catholicism   116, 194
Cesari, J.   101, 109
Chadwick, O.   40
children, traditions and religious upbringing for   182–3
Christianity, criticism and   4, 18, 22, 50–2, 73–83, 130
  golden rule   78–9
  Good Samaritan virtue   81–3, 193
  loving the good, primacy of   75–6
citizen journalism   125–7
civil society   152, 153–5

cognitive critique 33, 37, 42
common schools 158–60
communism, theory of 34
complementary learning processes 4, 167
confessional independent schools, in Sweden 151–2, 155–6, 158–63
  civil society and public sphere 153–5
  open and public character of religion 152
  public or private 157–8
  public sphere, fragility of 161–2
Connolly, W. 178
constructive criticism of religion 4, 19–20, 45, 57, 97, 190–8
  accommodation and dialogue 8–9
  in mediatized public debate 172–5
Convention on the Rights of Children 161
Cottingham, J. 82
Cottle, S. 165
Council of Europe (CoE) 200 n.2
counter-public spheres 166, 173
Court of Justice of the European Union 200 n.2
courts, as critics 87–98
critical intellectual forces 114–15
critical religious literacy 12
critique of religion 18–21. *See also individual entries*
  secular (*see* secular criticism of religion)
  in secular democratic society (*see* secular democratic society, critique of religion in)
cultural Catholicism 120–2

Daesh/ISIS 21, 62
Dagen 155
Dagens Nyheter 155, 168–70
Davie, G. 5, 179
Dawkins, R. 7, 8, 25, 32–6, 42–3, 80
de Beauvoir, S. 115
deep equality 13, 118, 177, 178
DeGirolami, M. 201 n.17
deliberative democracy 166–7
Dennett, D. 34, 35
Derrida, J. 64

Det fria Sverige (DFS) 124–5, 127–31, 133, 134, 202 n.2, 202 n.3
d'Holbach, B. 32, 33, 40, 42
dialogical imagination 51
dialogue 8–9
diasporic imagination 51
didactical strategies 146
Dimitras, P. 96
Dimitras v Greece 1, 2, and 3 96
Dot-Pouillard, N. 120
Downey, J. 164, 166, 173–4

Eagleton, T. 40
ECHR. *See* European Convention of Human Rights
ECtHR. *See* European Court of Human Rights
Edgardh, L. 13, 177, 196–8
editorials 168–70
ego-humanists 128, 129
engagement strategies 186–8
Engdahl, P. 127
Engesser, S. 126
environmental scanning 106
Erasmus, D. 74
Eriksson, D. 125, 129, 130, 132
EU. *See* European Union (EU)
Europe 1, 7, 21, 44, 190, 194
  Papageorgiou and Others v. Greece 94–5
European Commission 5
European Convention of Human Rights (ECHR) 158, 161, 200 n.2
  Art. 2 of Protocol 1 of 89, 203 n.2
European Court of Human Rights (ECtHR) 11, 121, 193, 200 n.2, 201 n.8, 201 n.17. *See also* courts, as critics
European Foundation for Democracy (EFD) 109
European Union (EU) 93, 109
  Directive 95/46/EU 201 n.11
evolutionary epistemology 67
Evolvi, G. 172
Expressen 155, 165, 168–70
extremism 117

faith bubble 13, 177
family life and values, in Sweden 180–1
Fazlhashemi, M. 11, 58, 197

Fenton, N.   164, 166, 173–4
Feuerbach, L.   33, 34, 36–9, 41–3
fideism   30
fitra   61
Flensner, K.   146
Fokas, E.   11, 87, 193, 197
Folgero case   201 n.17
Foucault, M.   64
France   118, 120, 123
Francis, Pope   116
Frändelöv, D.   125, 129, 130
Frankfurt School   46
Freud, S.   80, 114, 115

Galanter, M.   89–90, 97–8
Gardell, M.   202 n.1
gender equality   62, 117, 119–20
gender inequality   60, 72
Gergen, K.   47
al-Ghazali, A. H.   64
Giley, B.   202 n.1
Giovani Musulmani d'Italia [Young Muslims of Italy, GMI]   110–11
Goldburg, P.   140, 146
golden rule   78–9
Good Samaritan virtue   81–3, 193
Gray, J.   198
Great Replacement   128, 132
Greece
    Council of State (*Symvoulio tis Epikratias*, StE)   93
    Law on Education (1985)   92
    "New School" program   92
Greek constitution, Art. 16(2) of   91–2
Greek Council of State   201 n.12
Greek Helsinki Monitor (GHM)   94–6, 193, 201 n.16
Green, J.   55
Green Party crisis   168, 173
Griffin, N.   131
Gutmann, A.   108

Habermas, J.   4, 6, 7, 27, 155, 162, 166, 167, 192
hadith   49
Hafez, F.   109
Halakhah   53
Hammer, A.   146

handshaking controversy, in media   107, 165, 175–6
Harpigny, G.   121
Harris, S.   32, 34
Harvey, A.   199 n.1
hegemony   64
Hellenic National Data Protection Authority   200 n.1
Helmerson, E.   169
hermeneutics   48, 56, 65
hermeneutics of suspicion   114
historical feminism   120
historical imagination   51
Hitchens, C.   7, 8, 32, 34
Hjelm, T.   7
homosexuality   62, 63, 184
humanistic atheism   10
human rights   117
Huxley, T.   36
hybrid feminism   120
hybrid media space, handshaking controversy debate in   170–2

ijma'   59, 63
immanent criticism   4, 10, 11, 29. *See also* academic feminism, as immanent critique
individual autonomy
    Swedish values and norm of   182
    and traditional family values   183–5
Inglehart, R.   43
insiders   45, 47, 51, 56, 95–7, 193
institution   3–5
    structures of   4–5
internal critique, in Muslim context   58–60, 71–2
internal strategy   30–1
Irigaray, L.   115
Islam   1, 4, 7, 18, 22, 130. *See also* Quran
    internal critique of (*see* internal critique, in Muslim context)
    sexual ethics in   62–3
Islamic jurisprudence   58, 59, 62, 65, 71
Islamic theological ethics   61–3
Islamization of Europe   128, 132
Islamophobia   81, 117, 124, 127, 129
al-Jabri, M. A.   67–8

Jackson, W.   80
Jantzen, G.   56

Index

Jensdotter, L.   13, 107, 164, 195, 196
Jihad   130
Judaism   52–4, 131, 133
   self-examination in   77
judgmentalism   73–4

Kadivar, M.   69
Kallenberg, K. S.   106
Kaplan, M.   165
Kemp, A.   203 n.10
Khan, Y.   165, 166, 168–75
Kieran, M.   200 n.3
Kimball, C.   27
King, M. L.   77
Kitcher, P.   7–8, 26
Kokkinakis v. Greece   88
Kripke, S.   45
Kwok Pui-Lan   11
   immanent critique   45, 50–2, 55

laïcité   118, 119, 121, 122
Lautsi v. Italy   89, 93
LeDrew, S.   10, 32, 197
Lefebvre, S.   12, 96, 101, 109, 112, 194, 202 n.5
Lé Mon, M. M.   13, 177, 196, 197–8
Lindquist, D.   202 n.4
Linzey, A.   80
Löfstedt, M.   12, 92, 135, 196
Löfven, S.   165
Lövheim, M.   1, 13, 46, 47, 112, 164, 190, 195, 196
Lustiger, M.   122

MacCulloc, D.   199 n.2
Manning, C.   187
Markoviti, M.   200 n.6
Marx, K.   33, 34, 36, 38–43, 80, 114, 115
mediatization   164–5, 168–72
   constructive critique of religion in public date   172–5
Mernissi, F.   60–1
militant secularism   6–7
Minganti, P. K.   12, 99, 193, 194, 196, 197
Miskawayh, Ibn   64
Mojtahed Shabestari, M.   70
Moore, D.   139
moral-subjective critique   33
More, T.   79

Mouffe, C.   164, 166, 167, 173–5
Musa, R.   104, 107
Muslim Brotherhood   107, 111
Muslim heritage, complexity of   66–7
Muslimska Brödraskapet i Sverige (The Muslim Brotherhood in Sweden)   105
Myndigheten för ungdoms- och civilsamhällesfrågor (MUCF)   99–111

Nagel, T.   8, 26, 73, 74
New Atheism   10, 32–6
New Atheists   80, 81
Nietzsche, F.   41, 75, 79, 114, 115
Nilsson, P.-E.   12, 124, 194, 196, 202 n.8
non-religion, as a generator of criticism   113–14
non-restrictionists   28–30
norm-critical reading   60–1
Norris, P.   43
North America   1, 44, 190
Nussbaum, M. C.   8

Öffentlichkeit   162
open strategy   28–30, 110
Orthodox Christianity   83
outsiders   45, 47, 51, 56, 95–7, 193
Oxford Centre for Animal Ethics   80

Panhellenic Union of Theologians (PETH)   92
Papageorgiou and Others v. Greece   11, 98, 201 n.13, 201 n.15, 201 n.16
persecution, avoidance of   79
personal faith   186
Pew Research Center   113–14
philosophical or value-inclusive secularist strategy   26
Pigliucci, M.   25–6
Plantinga, A.   82
pluralistic society, religion in   22–5
political deliberation, theory of   167
political secularism   68
Popper, K.   67
populist logic   127
postcolonial imagination   51
post-secularity   6–7
power analysis   21

practical-political critique 33, 41
private character of religion 157–8
Protocol 11 200 n.3
Protocols of the Elders of Zion, The 133
public character of religion 152, 157–8
public commissions on cultural and religious diversity, critique of religion in 112, 123
   Catholic critical theologies and conservative counterpart 115–17
public space 152, 161, 162, 195
public sphere 13, 166, 174, 194–5
   civil society and 153–5
   fragility of 161–2
Putnam, H. 45
Putnam, R. 108

qiyas 67
Quebec 12, 112, 118–19, 122–3
Quebec Charter of Human Rights and Freedoms 119–20
Quick, A. H. 102–3
al-Qunun, R. M. 113
Quran 28–9, 48–50, 56, 59, 69, 199 n.1, 199 n.2. *See also* Islam
   critical reading 64, 65
   gender inequality 60

radical multiculturalism 6, 7
Radio Svegot 124
Rasmussen, T. 166, 173
religion 3–5. *See also individual entries*
   open and public character of 152
   problematic sides of 142–5
   in secular society 5–9
   and Swedish radical nationalism 129–33
   teaching, in secular context 135–6
religious diversity 5–6, 12, 147, 177, 178, 194
   critique of religion in public commissions and 112–22
religious education (RE) 196
   didactical strategies 141–2
   in Greece 91–4
   tolerance and criticism within 135–47
   working with secularistic attitudes 140–1

religious freedom 12, 88, 111, 153, 200 n.3
religious literacy 138–9
   methods and material 140
religiously active minority 181–6
religious nones 22, 198
religious others 107, 109, 110, 178–80, 186
religious pluralism 5–6, 89, 138
religious symbols 4, 88, 119–20, 122, 123
Renton, J. 202 n.1
restrictionist strategy 26–8, 107, 109–10
Ricoeur, P. 114–15
Rolston III, H. 80
Rorty, R. 27

Sabia, A. 46, 47, 54, 199 n.2
Sachedina, A. 69
Saint Augustine's Prayer Book 77
Salve Regina 39
Samefonden (the Sami Foundation) 203 n.12
Sandelin, M. 106
Särkelä, A. 46
Sartre, J.-P. 115
Schanke, Å. J. 146
Scheler, M. 75, 79–80
schism, avoidance of 79
Schleiermacher, F. 70
School Act (Sweden) 136
schools, criticism of religion in 136–8
scientific atheism 10
scientistic secularist strategy 25
secular criticism of religion 32–4
secular democratic society, critique of religion in 17–25
   internal strategy 30–1
   open strategy 28–30
   restrictionist strategy 26–8
   secularist strategy 25–6
secularistic attitudes 140–1
secularist strategy 25–6, 107, 140, 146
secularity 6–7, 67–9
secular people 8, 10, 23, 26–7, 178, 185–7
secular society, religion in 5–9, 22–5
secular state 9, 22, 171
Sharia law 58, 59, 62, 71
   criticism against 69–70
   gender inequality 60, 72

Shiite Islam   59
Sjöborg, A.   12, 92, 135, 196
Söderman, M.   125, 129–32
Soros, G.   131–2
Soroush, A.   67–8
Stasi Report   119–21
Stendahl, K.   78–9
Stenmark, M.   1, 10, 13, 17, 46, 112, 146, 190, 199 n.4
Stout, J.   46, 47, 55, 199 n.2
Sufism   65, 67
Sullivan, W.   201 n.17
Sunnah   48, 49
Sunni Islam   59
Svegot   124–6, 128, 129, 202 n.2–4
Svenska Dagbladet   129, 155, 168–70
Svenska motståndsrörelsen (The Swedish Resistance Movement)   202 n.1
Svenskarnas parti (The Swedes' Party)   125
Sverigedemokraterna (The Sweden Democrats, SD)   126
SVT Nyheter   170, 204 n.5
Sweden
  Administrative Procedure Act, Article 17 of   105
  Discrimination Ombudsman   105
  National Council of Swedish Youth Organizations   105
  School Act   136
Sweden's Young Muslims (Sverige Unga Muslimer, SUM)   99–111, 193, 202 n.4
Swedish Agency for Youth and Civil Society   12, 99, 193
Swedish Civil Contingencies Agency (Myndigheten för Samhällsskydd och Beredskap, MSB)   105
Swedish Code of Statutes   201 n.2
Swedish National Socialism   127

Swedish Public School Regulation of 1842, general education (*Folkskolan*) in   136
Swedish radical nationalism   124–34
  and citizen journalism   125–7
  critique into context, placing   127–9
  religion and   129–33
Swedish Research Council   203 n.1

Taliaferro, C.   11, 29, 73, 193
Taylor, C.   22
Teaching Religion in Late Modern Sweden (TRILS)   140, 203 n.1
Tracy, D.   154
tradition, significance of   46–7
traditional family values   183–5
Trump, D.   80

UN Convention on the Rights of the Child   99
UN Declaration of Human Rights   62

Vilks, L.   203 n.1
vivre ensemble   118
von Essen, J.   13, 151, 195, 196

Wåg, M.   202 n.4
Weinberg, S.   25
Wendahl, P.   101
Western Europe   44
White, L.   80
Woodhead, L.   177–8, 184, 187
Word of Life Church   180, 181, 189
World Values Survey (WVS)   179–82, 186

Zackariasson, U.   10–11, 44, 192, 197
Zagzebski, L.   45, 200 n.6
Zia-Ebrahimi, R.   124

www.ingramcontent.com/pod-product-compliance
Lightning Source LLC
Chambersburg PA
CBHW052035300426
44117CB00012B/1825